Why we need more

# INNOVATION
# IN CANADA

*and what we must do to get it*

## Invenire Books

**I**NVENIRE is an Ottawa-based "idea factory" specializing in collaborative governance and stewardship. INVENIRE and its authors offer creative and practical responses to the challenges and opportunities faced by today's complex organizations.

INVENIRE BOOKS welcomes a range of contributions – from conceptual and theoretical reflections, ethnographic and case studies, and proceedings of conferences and symposia, to works of a very practical nature – that deal with problems or issues on the governance and stewardship front. INVENIRE BOOKS publishes works in French and English.

This is the sixteenth volume published by INVENIRE BOOKS.

INVENIRE also publishes a quarterly electronic journal, found at www.optimumonline.ca

Why we need more
# INNOVATION
# IN CANADA
*and what we must do to get it*

## TOM BRZUSTOWSKI

INVENIRE BOOKS
Ottawa, Canada
2012

© Invenire Books 2012

Library and Archives Canada Cataloguing in Publication

Brzustowski, T. A. (Thomas A.), 1937-
 Innovation in Canada : why we need more and what we must do to get it / by Tom Brzustowski.

Includes bibliographical references.
Issued also in electronic format.
ISBN 978-1-927465-00-4

 1. Technological innovations--Economic aspects--Canada.
2. Canada--Economic policy--21st century. I. Title.

HC120.T4B79 2012      338'.0640971      C2012-905258-2

Invenire Books would like to gratefully acknowledge the financial support for the publication of this book by the Centre on Governance, University of Ottawa.

Published by Invenire
P.O. Box 87001
Ottawa, Canada K2P 1X0
www.invenire.ca

Cover design by Sandy Lynch
Cover image by Bear66 | Dreamstime.com
Back cover photo of the author by Mélanie Provencher
Layout and design by Sandy Lynch

Printed in Canada by Marquis Imprimeur Inc.

Distributed by:
Commoners' Publishing
631 Tubman Cr.
Ottawa, Canada  K1V 8L6
Tel.: 613-523-2444
Fax: 613-260-0401
sales@commonerspublishing.com
www.commonerspublishing.com

For Louise

# TABLE OF CONTENTS

# INTRODUCTION

This book was written to contribute to solving today's prosperity problem and to building the foundation for the new ingenuity in innovation by describing how innovation in Canada occurs today.

The title, *Why we need more INNOVATION IN CANADA and what we must do to get it*, signals that the book begins by defining the imperative and ends with a call for action. In between, it provides a big-picture guide to innovation for many audiences: policy makers, regulators, investors, entrepreneurs, engineers, scientists, students, teachers, managers, scholars and creative people in any sector of the economy and any segment of society. Each of these audiences has access to its own body of much more detailed knowledge about innovation, but I believe that all can benefit from seeing where their own activities fit into the broad landscape of innovation in Canada. Of necessity, the book deals mostly with the present and with innovation to achieve quantitative change, but it should also be thought of as part of the foundation of knowledge for future innovations that will have to produce extensive qualitative change.

The book is divided into three parts: I. "Setting the stage", II. "Where we are now", and III. "What needs to be done". Parts I and II each consist of several chapters, Part III has the final chapter, and each chapter addresses some element of the thesis.

In Part I, the introductory chapter is a broad introduction to the thesis of the book and to the current state of innovation in Canada. This is the sketch on the canvas that the succeeding chapters will fill in with detail and colour. It offers an overview, a big picture that shows how the pieces fit together. Some readers may choose to read chapter 1 and then skip right over to chapter 13 for the discussion of innovation policy, and come back to the intermediate chapters later to drill down on the various issues raised in the book-end chapters.

The thesis is introduced in detail in chapter 2. The main argument is that the country urgently needs a boost in wealth creation to reverse the decline in prosperity over the last three decades. Some atlas-style data on countries with the world's largest economies are presented to illustrate Canada's position among them. There is a useful international correlation between prosperity and research excellence in science and engineering. Canada places in the top tier on both measures but, in spite of that, our prosperity continues to depend on commodity products to a great extent. In fact, our wealth from natural resources has paid for building the capacity for excellent research. Moving into the future, we will have to learn how to reverse that arrow, and rely much more on excellence in science and engineering for our prosperity, as many other countries do. Innovation driven by both competition and entrepreneurship and enabled by our competence in science and engineering will be very important. The chapter discusses the main cross-border flows between Canada and the rest of the global economy, and argues for increasing our prosperity through innovation that will lead to producing more valuable products across the economy.

Chapter 3 develops the thesis by treating innovation as a change process. It shows how difficult it is to assess the outcome and impact of change. The frequent need to use input quantities as proxies for the outcomes and impacts is an unfortunate state of affairs that might be mitigated but perhaps never eliminated. A useful construct in the public policy arena is the change process effected by a national innovation system that increases wealth creation in response to good government policy, smart regulations and effective programs. That's an appealing idea, but perhaps unrealistically tidy and optimistic. Given Canada's decentralized constitutional structure and vast territory, our reality is probably better represented by a far less neat collection of different regional innovation systems in which the senior governments (federal, provincial) are just one source of influence, along with local factors and with the rest of the world.

Chapter 4 provides some details about two key elements of the thesis: value-added, and the economic impact of innovation. A discussion of how value-added is created and how it is used connects innovation with commerce and wealth creation. This provides an opportunity to emphasize the importance of commercial exchange in the process of wealth creation. The representation of industrial innovation as invention followed by commercialization is a useful construct that has been in the literature for decades, but it is still largely missing in policy discussions where it might be very useful. The chapter includes a summary of the various ways in which expert bodies, committees, councils, etc. have defined innovation. This illustrates the variety of perspectives and interests that different groups bring to the discussion of innovation.

The chapter ends with an introduction of some of the language of innovation. It offers a consistent set of definitions of the key terms to help make the discussion more precise. It deals with 'R&D' and other related 'words that everybody knows,' starting with innovation itself and then invention. It provides definitions that draw clear distinctions between science, engineering, technology and design. It includes the definitions of research, in general, as well as the particular cases of basic, applied and project research. It also includes definitions of both entrepreneurship and creativity, and shows the relationship between them.

Chapter 5 is a short technical note on productivity and its relationship to innovation. Both the productivity of labour and multifactor productivity (MFP) are discussed and numerical examples are offered. The expression for the MFP is derived in a few lines of simple mathematics.

Part II "Where we are now" describes the activities from which we must build up the surge in innovation. It begins with a short chapter 6 that introduces the cost and other business aspects of industrial innovation in Canada. The framework for discussion is a taxonomy that divides the innovation space into four quadrants, based on whether the innovation is design-based or research-based, and whether commercialization is done by a new venture or by an established firm. Typical financial histories of innovation projects for established firms in three sectors are illustrated. Some hard numbers for the costs of industrial innovation come from the spending on R&D which is relatively easy to quantify, but is only one input to much of industrial innovation. The chapter concludes with a snapshot of Canada's national R&D spending, and some implications of the numbers.

Chapter 7 uses models to show how innovation actually happens in industry. The discussion builds on the quad taxonomy introduced in chapter 6. It begins with the Kline-Rosenberg chain-link model for research-based innovation and Douglas Barber's innovation-commerce cycle for design-based innovation, in both cases by established firms. Two new models of design-based and research-based innovation by new ventures are also introduced. The important roles of design and of entrepreneurship in innovation receive particular attention in this chapter.

Chapter 8 describes the connections between post-secondary education and innovation in Canada. All post-secondary institutions educate highly qualified people and many are also active in research. These are most of the universities and some of the colleges, particularly the ones that are now called polytechnics. In the universities, the connections with industrial innovation arise in five predictable ways. The first three all involve students: the hiring of graduates by industry, research by graduate students on industrial problems done in partnership with industry, and new ventures that commercialize inventions coming out of basic research that generally also involves graduate students. The other two are contract research, which may or may not involve students, and faculty consulting. In the colleges, the predictable connections arise from the employment of graduates, often as R&D employees, from the involvement of students in projects of assistance to industry, and from faculty consulting. Entrepreneurship by both college and university students provides additional connections, but it is more unpredictable. Much of the discussion in this chapter is illustrated by three detailed diagrams: the position of university research in science and engineering in the national innovation system; an example of a university-industry research partnership; and an example of an innovation by a new venture that might arise out of basic university research in science and engineering. This last process has been the focus of much public policy, investment and great expectations on the part of governments and the public, because it is thought capable of producing revolutionary 'game-changing' innovations that significantly affect people's life and work. Such successes do happen, but they are not frequent. The Canadian system of support for university basic research is designed to build the foundations for long-term success by promoting research excellence and supporting the training of highly qualified people. Innovations in the short term are an incidental outcome of this system.

Chapter 9 is about innovation in services. Services are a very large and important part of the Canadian economy, now responsible for about three-quarters of both GDP and employment, but there are some measurement issues behind that number. The discussion of services seems much simplified if one thinks of them not as certain forms of economic goods to which special conditions apply, but rather as actions. In contrast, the goods of 'goods and services' are objects. Many of the differences between innovation in services and innovations in goods arise from that basic difference. If one then divides services into two components: diagnosis and execution, the distinction between knowledge-intensive services and the rest becomes clearer as well. Innovation in services in the private sector is discussed in some detail within the framework of the quad taxonomy introduced earlier. The chapter ends with a discussion of innovation in services in the public sector and in government, which are not exposed to market competition.

Interactions in innovation are the subject of chapter 10. The discussion begins with interactions among creative people and the cultural factors that influence them. It then moves on to an illustrative sample of six very different Canadian clusters: aerospace in Montreal, photonics in Ottawa, medical biotechnology in Toronto, information communications technology (ICT) in Waterloo, plant biotechnology in Saskatoon and biotechnology in BC. All six have taken decades to develop, all six can claim excellence in research, but only two are engaged in world-scale manufacturing and marketing of products incorporating their IP. Selling the new ventures and their IP seems to be more common than growing them to a competitive scale. Innovation intermediaries are also included in this chapter. While these organizations are not uniformly defined, they all fill gaps in the capabilities of innovators. Three so-called Canadian 'fourth pillar' organizations (CMC Microsystems, CANARIE and PRECARN) and three much larger international organizations (Battelle, ITRI and Fraunhofer) are compared using their own descriptions of their activities as innovation intermediaries. It quickly becomes evident that Canada does not have established large, versatile and expert institutions focused on the business of helping entrepreneurs get their ideas to market. The chapter ends with a brief discussion of partnerships as interactions in innovation and some rules for making them work, based on the author's personal experience.

Chapter 11, entitled "Innovations in innovation," deals with five ideas in innovation that are new, or at least have recently begun to be noted and discussed frequently. The five are: open innovation; innovation in business models; open source; user-driven innovation; and social innovation. They are listed as independent but, in fact, there are many interesting connections among them. For example, open innovation has led to the development of new business models in which a company's unused IP is treated as an asset. And open source can itself be thought of as a new business model. This chapter is the first place in the book where business models are discussed explicitly, but they have always worked quietly in the background of many of the specific examples of innovation discussed.

Chapter 12, "What corporate data show," focuses on the performance of many of Canada's best known firms that spend on R&D. Most of the discussion is based on the author's unique representation of publicly available data, namely the time series over 8 to 12 years of R&D spending, sales revenue, and the ratio of the two called R&D intensity for major R&D spenders – more than three dozen Canadian companies in the manufacturing and resource sectors that annually spend millions of dollars on R&D. The data show that established firms spend a small percentage of revenue on R&D and operate more or less steadily. In contrast, many new ventures spend more on R&D than their sales revenues. They are financed to do R&D and develop their first products and they experience deep and rapid change in their technical and financial circumstances. This pattern has policy implications; it suggests that government support to them must be delivered very promptly to be effective. The economic impact of these new ventures is hard to assess since, on balance, they don't generate wealth but consume it. However, they are important because they are the source of future large innovative firms.

Part III is entitled "What needs to be done." It has one chapter: chapter 13 "An Innovation Policy for Canada" that ends the book with a proposal for a national innovation project. Called the "Innovation Action Plan," it would be planned and executed under joint leadership from the highest levels of government and Canadian business. The chapter discusses ten principles of an innovation policy to support it, and nine principles of government programs to implement the policy. These proposals are made on the assumption that the federal and provincial governments will want to continue promoting and assisting innovation in Canada. They have been doing it for years for the reasons that are summed up in chapter 2, and all the countries with which we trade do the same thing for very similar reasons. The proposed points to be incorporated in public policy on innovation would make it flexible, forward-looking and evidence-based. It would recognize that innovation occurs in different ways in different circumstances, and that 'one-size-fits-all' approaches are far from optimal. It would also recognize that some assistance measures have proven more effective than others, and that program delivery is a large part of the difference. It would acknowledge that innovation has important impacts not just on the supply side, but on the demand side as well. Similarly, in the delivery of support programs, demand-side issues must be taken into account, not just supply-side considerations. Readers particularly interested in policy may decide to limit their first reading of the book to chapters 1 and 13, and return to the chapters in between as more detailed information is needed.

We must remember, of course, that these thirteen chapters offer only a thin introduction to the subject of innovation as a whole, and even to industrial innovation which takes up most of the space. Innovation is the subject of a vast literature that includes contributions from many disciplines. Moreover, there are many innovations that are not technological, and not to be found in a market, but still very important in determining people's quality of life in various ways. I shall call them collectively human innovations. They are only mentioned here and will not be pursued in this book, but each has a vast literature devoted to it, a literature that undoubtedly dwarfs the writings on industrial innovation. They may not have anything to do with economic activity at the outset, and might not be monetized in any obvious way but, in the long term, they may turn out to have a huge impact on people. They are innovations in political ideas, in religious ideas, in social institutions, in forms of governance, in laws and regulations, in the creative arts and many more.

## *Details of presentation*

Innovation is a generic term that has come into widespread use relatively recently and, as a result, discussions of innovation in the popular literature and at public meetings can sometimes be imprecise and vague. For that reason, much attention is given in this book to the precise definition of important terms. A common understanding of 'words that everybody knows' is not taken for granted. For convenience, all the defined terms are collected in a separate section on the language of innovation. Some of these definitions come from dictionaries, encyclopedias and other published works, but some are original here. Other writers have used other definitions of the same terms for their own reasons, and that's their right, provided they indicate what the reasons are. But I hope that in considering definitions, readers will not confuse vagueness with generality or flexibility. The definitions presented here are precise and succinct, but no shorter than they have to be to make the concepts clear.

In light of this concern with precision, it may seem paradoxical that large parts of this book could probably have been written without using the word 'innovation' at all. These are the parts dealing with the economic impacts of innovation. Instead of 'innovation,' I could have used the phrase 'new way that value-added is created.' Some people might have found the longer expression more satisfying, since it stayed within familiar terminology. However, I preferred to use 'innovation' throughout the book, because it is a broader concept. There are important innovations that may have an important effect on the quality of people's lives, but not involve value-added.

I must also make a comment about graphics. As an engineer, I find the use of diagrams useful as an aid to understanding. There are many diagrams in this book, many more than is usual for books that I've been reading on this subject, and some of these diagrams look quite complicated. But bear with them: they're important. It is a feature of the print medium that diagrams seem more complicated than they really are. When I present this material in PowerPoint slides, I start off with a blank screen and build up the diagram one mouse-click at a time, and audiences seem to have no trouble with that. The full diagram then serves as a reminder of that building-up process. Unfortunately, the readers of this book get to see only the final version, and only in grey tones. For that reason, I have described the diagrams in the text in considerable detail.

I have also included a short technical chapter that connects innovation with productivity. It is important to remember that productivity is only an indicator of the performance of the economy. Saying that Canada has a productivity problem really means that the country has a wealth-creation problem that is illustrated by low productivity, among other indicators. Productivity comes in two flavours: the productivity of labour which is the value produced per hour worked, and the multi-factor productivity (MFP) which is a measure of the ingenuity with which labour and capital are used to add value. The productivity of labour is intuitive and can be used to show the effect of factors such as demographics, the work week, unemployment rate, etc. In contrast, the MFP is a much more abstract concept derived from a theoretical model of the economy. However, because MFP is widely used and many readers will need to understand it, chapter 5 contains its derivation from first principles using just a few lines of elementary mathematics.

## *Acknowledgements and thanks*

This book was not written to be a contribution to the research literature on innovation, but it draws on that literature as one source of knowledge. It also draws on public data, on the business press, and on the so-called 'grey literature' of reports by task forces, expert panels, think-tanks, consultants and government agencies. The sources are always cited as completely as possible, so that readers might access them if interested. The focus is on innovation in Canada, but some comparisons with other nations are offered when there is a point to be made, and where comparable data are available.

Many of the ideas presented below were included in my speeches and presentations at various meetings and conferences over the last half-dozen years, as well as in an earlier book. They were tested at the University of Ottawa in presentations to colleagues at the Telfer School of Management, and also in the graduate course on innovation systems offered in the M.Sc. in Management program. Part of the long introductory chapter is based on an essay written as a stand-alone introduction to innovation for the students in that course as well as a variety of other audiences.

I shall conclude with a final word on my own motivation in writing this book. During the decade 1995-2005 when I served as President of the Natural Sciences and Engineering Research Council of Canada (NSERC) – the main federal agency funding Canadian university and college research in science and engineering – I gradually came to believe that the excellence of the research far outstripped our nation's ability to derive benefits for Canadians by using the new knowledge produced. "If we're so good in research in science and engineering," I asked myself, "then why is our prosperity slipping in the knowledge-based economy?" At the same time, as an outside but close observer of Canadian industry, I became convinced that industry's capacity to develop new technologies often exceeded the capacity to use them for sustainable wealth creation in the Canadian economy. "If our industrial technology and our business community are so good, why don't we have more world-leading technology companies?"

When I retired from NSERC, I was fortunate to be given the opportunity at the University of Ottawa to study these disparities and get to understand them better. As the Royal Bank of Canada Financial Group Professor in the Commercialization of Innovations at the Telfer School of Management, I have had the privilege of learning from many people in a field new to me. They included new colleagues and students, and large numbers of knowledgeable people that I listened to at the various lectures, seminars, conferences, meetings, round tables, break-out sessions and other events that I have attended across Canada, including notably the eleven annual Re$earch Money Conferences. Much of what follows is based on what I managed to learn from their collective experience and understanding. The mistakes, of course, are all my own work.

Finally, I dedicate this book to my wife, Louise, whose contribution to it has been indirect, but enormous. For almost half a century, she has given me a loving family life of much happiness and little stress, and made it possible for me to immerse myself in the many learning challenges that I have had in my career. For that, and much else, I am immensely grateful to her.

# PART I
## SETTING THE STAGE

# CHAPTER 1

## SKETCHING THE BIG PICTURE

### The thesis

Canada has a prosperity problem. As a nation, we have important needs that we can't afford to meet. Business as usual is not a solution because it got us where we are; the solution must be something new. And it must be reached in the context of growing pressures on the Canadian economy. We are already starting to feel the effects of the aging of our population, and today's tightly connected global economy produces new challenges every day.

In the longer term, we will also face relentless pressures arising in many different ways from climate change and from global population growth. Today we can only begin to guess what form some of these new pressures might take.

The inevitable conclusion is that we must change and do things differently, and keep changing as our circumstances evolve. We need to innovate – to develop new ideas and put them into practice – to solve our current problem, and we need to learn how to do that in new ways in the future to deal with whatever pressures come up.

What Canada needs today is a seismic shift of wealth creation to raise our prosperity by creating more value in new ways in all sectors of the Canadian economy.

In the wealth-producing sectors, we must find new ways of creating value – that's what innovations are – and, in that way, raise the value of goods and services produced in the Canadian economy and sold to the world. Canadian business must build up a surge of innovation in traded goods and services that will be sustained for the long term. This cannot be a blip or a cyclic phenomenon; it must be a structural shift in the Canadian economy.

The necessary innovations in goods and services must come from all possible sources: from established firms of all sizes in all sectors, and from new ventures. The innovations can be responses to new needs in today's markets, or they can be new products that create entirely new markets. They can be new uses of prior knowledge, created by new design. Or they can be new uses of new knowledge, based on inventions resulting from research done in companies, government labs, or universities and hospitals. But they must all be commercialized in a way that will increase the value added in the Canadian economy.

The impact of moving the Canadian economy up the value chain will be to increase wealth creation, grow profits and wages, generate greater tax revenues without increasing the tax rates, and create economic growth substantially greater than the "business as usual" scenario. This will show up as increasing GDP/capita and productivity, and the growing ability of Canadians individually and collectively to pay for the needed things that we can't afford today.

But innovation must go beyond the wealth-creating sectors. In the wealth-consuming sectors, we need widespread innovation to raise the effectiveness and efficiency of meeting the various growing needs of Canadians. The first priority in this effort must be to achieve sustained accessibility, affordability and high quality in both education for the young and health care for the old.

Canada's environment is an asset for the nation, important to both the wealth-creating and the wealth-consuming sectors. We must find the resources needed not only to preserve and protect it from future damage, but also to repair the damage done by previous generations.

To move to the new, higher level of wealth creation that we need and to stay there, our appetite for innovation must be insatiable. Business must create the new wealth by competing successfully on a global scale in all the areas where Canadian companies can establish an advantage. We must become the world's best in those areas, and keep working to maintain that lead. We can't afford to rest on our oars as we celebrate isolated successes; we must keep working to succeed across the board. And we must learn to do this on a scale large enough to make a difference for the nation as a whole.

Fortunately we have a good foundation to build on. Our research, technical knowledge and skill base are strong, and we have some splendid examples of entrepreneurs and innovative companies. We know what success looks like. The challenge is to replicate it many times over and in appropriate forms across the economy, and keep doing it, so that the total effort might reach a scale that will have lasting national impact. There is much to be learned to make this happen and, in Canada today, more of that learning needs to be on the social and business side of innovation than on the technical side.

A great deal has been said and written about innovation in Canada, many aspects of it have been studied, much detailed information has been published, many wise recommendations made and, as a result, many aspects of innovation are becoming well understood. But we lack the big picture – a system perspective – that makes sense of the rich variety of forms in which innovation appears in Canada, of the different actors and interactions involved, and of the essential factors that influence what happens. Life would be easier if all innovation were the same, with a recipe that could be fixed once and for all when the silver bullet was found. But it's nothing like that. Innovation is the product of a dynamic web of interacting human activity, and we must learn who does what to make it happen, and how their contributions fit together. And as we do that, we must learn how to enable it – to create the conditions under which innovation in Canada will grow and flourish and improve the lives of Canadians now and in the future. As a nation, we must find ways to make it attractive for those who already innovate to do more, and for those who have not needed to innovate to see new opportunities, change their minds, learn to innovate, and start reaping benefits for themselves and for Canada.

The thesis of this book is that we need to do all these things, and that we know how. Most importantly, we need to bring all the pieces together and act in concert.

A lot of innovation is going on in Canada, and many very capable people are engaged in it. But more is needed. It turns out that innovation is key to solving some big problems of today, and more that are coming down the road. This book is written to help increase the capacity for innovation in Canada in order to solve those problems.

Innovation is change introduced with a purpose. The thesis of this book is that more innovation will help us deal better with the problems we face. These problems have multiple dimensions, both in time and in extent, and our innovative response must match them. There is a short-term economic challenge that we know how to solve, at least in principle. But we will also face large-scale, long-term problems that will be challenging in unpredictable new ways, and we will need to learn a lot and learn fast as we try to deal with new situations whose shape we can barely begin to see today. Nevertheless, one thing seems sure: we will be better prepared for more innovating tomorrow if we understand really well how innovation occurs in Canada today.

The immediate problem is economic – the prosperity challenge. The needs of our growing and aging population have been increasing steadily for decades. Moreover, Canada is a country with high fixed costs because of our great distances and challenging climate. The result is a shortage of resources for dealing with many problems that go far beyond health care and education, ranging all the way from urgent issues of social justice, such as the intolerable living conditions on many First Nations reserves and the widespread poverty of children, through continuing sources of environmental damage such as the dumping of untreated sewage and the burning of coal in old generating stations, to traffic congestion and decaying transportation infrastructure, such as the dangerous state of some major bridges.

Relative to many nations with which we trade, Canadian prosperity has been in decline for years. For example, we were the 11th largest economy in 2005; in 2011 we were the 14th. In 1995, the ratio of our GDP per capita to the world average was 3.6; in 2011 it was 3.4. This trend will continue unless we change the way we create wealth. The value of what Canadians produce per hour of work, and the ingenuity with which we use our labour and capital – two forms of what we call our productivity – not only lag our major competitors, but also show signs of falling behind even further. If that trend continues, we will fall further behind in solving our problems, and Canadians will increasingly not be able to afford many important things that people in other industrialized countries will buy routinely. The way out of this situation is to increase the value of what the Canadian economy produces – to move the economy up the value chain and increase our productivity – and to do it with more innovation.

This change must begin with the state of our economy as it is today, and that state is a paradox. Canada has a low value-added resource economy that creates a great deal of wealth. At the same time we have the capacity to produce new high value-added goods and services, but that activity contributes far less to our wealth creation. It is mainly the wealth created in the resource sectors that has made it possible for Canada to invest in science, engineering and health research to the point that we have achieved high technical competence and are now competitive with most of the industrialized world in these areas. We have recently become very conscious of the need to connect that capability with greater prosperity, and we are learning to work towards that goal both in established firms and in new ventures. A high level of technical competence has diffused through the economy, and the design and manufacturing capabilities of Canadian industry have created some big successes. But what holds the Canadian economy back and keeps it in the state of paradox is that the scale of this activity is still very limited.

Various factors have been suggested as reasons for this state of affairs, namely a culture of risk aversion in both the private and public sectors, a shortage of risk capital, a weak venture capital industry and a shortage of growth capital, a lack of competition in protected sectors, ineffective government programs, a bias against commerce in education, broad-based complacency, a bias in favour of North-South thinking over East-West thinking, weak leadership at the top levels of the public and private sectors, the role of Canada as upstream supplier of resources to downstream value-added industry in the US and other nations, etc., etc. Indeed, in any particular case, the explanation may lie in some combination of these factors, and possibly others as well.

There have, of course, been some spectacular exceptions, but by and large Canada has not been able to grow value-added technology companies that are big enough to compete with the global giants. Our domestic market is too small to pay for developing the leading new technologies in most sectors, so success for Canadian firms requires growth in world markets. Our new ventures in the technology sectors must be "born global." In fact, we are good at creating new ventures with promising intellectual property, but too many of them grow to only a modest size and then are sold to big multinationals. A shortage of growth capital leads to many bargain-basement sales of Canadian technology start-ups long before their intellectual property has reached its full value in the market. Too often the products we sell are the new ventures and their intellectual property (IP), rather than the value-added products that incorporate that IP.

There are ways out of that paradox. First, one must see the opportunities in it. The excellence of Canadian science and engineering is an obvious opportunity. Another one that I see is Canada's unique potential for developing strength in international trade. The great diversity of our population means that many students in Canadian colleges and universities have family or community ties to just about every country in the world where Canadian producers will seek markets. Developed strategically, these relationships could produce a world trading powerhouse. A third opportunity is our social, political, legal and fiscal stability, and the general reputation of the nation. One might think of many others, but my point is that we have what it takes to resolve the paradox and meet our prosperity challenge by moving the Canadian economy up the value chain. And this must not be limited to new and emerging sectors; it must be done across all sectors, particularly the natural resource sectors, that are already successful in wealth creation on a world scale.

At this point innovation comes into the picture. There are many kinds of innovation, but four are most directly related to raising the value of what we produce. They are innovations in products, processes, marketing and business models. Organizational and institutional innovations can be very important in enabling the success of these four, and they will be referred to in later chapters as appropriate in the discussion.

Different firms will have different opportunities to innovate to meet the prosperity challenge. Some companies may make their products more valuable through updating and improvements. Others may find the opportunity to deliver and sell existing products in new markets. In some sectors, entrepreneurial companies will find opportunities for disruptive innovations that will change the direction of product evolution and allow them to leap ahead of the competition and open up new avenues for growth. In some commodity sectors, exporting firms may be able to increase the value of what they sell by some upstream processing of the raw materials they now ship to established markets. Manufacturers may be able to do something similar by moving to the production of more nearly finished goods. In still other areas, new ventures commercializing research-based innovations may create entirely new kinds of products that create a new demand and new markets. All told, we may expect to see a blend of quantitative and qualitative change as this effort unfolds across the Canadian economy.

But even if we don't know the details of what we might be able to do, we do know the dimensions of what we must achieve. Averaged out over the Canadian economy as a whole, the increase in wealth creation needs to be quite substantial. A rough estimate is that we could probably meet our short-term prosperity challenge, a deficit of some 20 to 25 percent in real gross domestic product (GDP) per capita or productivity relative to the US,[1] by increasing the annual rate of growth of the Canadian GDP by two percentage points over the "business as usual" performance, and sustaining that increase for a decade. Such a goal is a stretch – very difficult to meet at any time, and even more difficult in today's economic climate of very low GDP growth in the industrialized world. But I don't think it's impossible if it's planned and managed strategically. I believe that a strategic, concerted and sustained national thrust in innovation to restore our prosperity could succeed. I also believe that the companies contributing to it would benefit by becoming more competitive and profitable in their own operations.

This kind of challenge is great, but other smaller countries have managed to meet it and Canada can meet it too. It will take national will and leadership, with all levels of government pulling together. It will require a sustained collaboration of the private and public sectors, and a great deal of learning across them both. And it will need a public policy on innovation that

---

[1] The Expert Panel on Business Innovation. 2009. *Innovation and Business Strategy: Why Canada Falls Short*. Ottawa: Council of Canadian Academies, p. 32.

is flexible, forward-looking, patient and based on the evidence of what works and what doesn't.

But even if we succeed completely, the challenge won't end there. When we move beyond the immediate prosperity deficit and consider the longer term, the extent of necessary innovation looms even larger, and its character changes as well. In 2050, there will be another two or more billion people crowded into the world, and they will demand food, water, shelter and energy. There will be a much greater proportion of elderly people in the developed countries. And everybody will be living in a world whose overall climate will be warmer than today. At the local level, the climate may become warmer or colder, it may become more variable or more stable, but it will almost certainly be different from the one in which today's patterns of life and work had developed. Traditional forms of innovation will continue to respond to traditional economic opportunities and needs, but the pressure to innovate in new ways to adapt to the huge effects of the new demographics and the changed climate will be a matter of survival. Marginal quantitative change in what we already do will not suffice; we (meaning mainly our descendants) are going to face much more difficult qualitative change that will substantially alter our work and our lives.

In the face of these irresistible global pressures for change, we cannot expect that four decades from now Canadians will still live largely as we do today. We will adapt to the new global conditions to our advantage, or fall by the wayside. Our enormously roomy country with its great reservoirs of fresh water and energy, with a vast area of arable land, and huge storehouses of natural resources of many kinds will be under pressure to meet the needs of many more people than our own modest population and our current export markets. The required changes in many aspects of life and work in Canada will be big, and they will be qualitative rather than just quantitative. We will be concerned with doing more – perhaps much more – of what we do now, but also with using our land and our resources in new ways and on a new larger scale. Finding the opportunities for success in those circumstances will be the great long-term challenge of entrepreneurship in Canada. We will enter a time of qualitative change that will affect us in new ways and, if we want that to happen under our own control, then we'd better start to develop the required new ingenuity in innovation right now.

Here I use the word "ingenuity" in the same sense as Homer-Dixon (2007):[2] "Ingenuity... consists not only of ideas for new technologies like computers or drought-resistant crops but, more fundamentally, of ideas for better institutions and social arrangements, like efficient markets and competent governments." I agree with that and believe that five ingredients are necessary for developing that new ingenuity in innovation. They are: good education to acquire knowledge and competence; basic research to keep learning about nature and about humans in nature; imagination to foresee better ways of doing things; entrepreneurship to find and seize opportunities to do so; and leadership to mobilize the effort and keep it pointed in the right direction. I also believe that developing that ingenuity for innovation tomorrow requires having a deep understanding of how innovation happens in Canada today.

But there is more. We can be very sure about one aspect of the future problems we shall have to solve: they will not be purely technical or purely social; they will be both technical and social at the same time. That means that the new ingenuity must also include a sharpened capacity for judgment, for choice and for timely and trusted decision by Canadian society on matters where social and technical issues are intertwined. A wise man once said, "Not to decide is to decide," but I believe that we will not be able to afford either the delays of indecision or the risk of decisions by default on the issues that are coming. Tomorrow's Canadians will have to be literate in both the social and technical aspects of life in Canada, and our institutions and leaders will have to bring an understanding of both to the decision table. The public will have to trust not only that the leaders act with integrity but also that they understand both the social and technical issues in sufficient depth.

The big new problems coming down the road will generally not have unique solutions. Some innovations will be better than others – better in producing satisfactory outcomes, better in the long-term impacts on people and on the environment, better in reflecting and supporting our values. We will have to make

[2] Thomas Homer-Dixon. 2007. *The Ingenuity Gap*. New York and Toronto: Alfred A. Knopf, p. 2.

judgments, choices and decisions in some very unfamiliar and difficult territory. But we cannot allow "We've never done it that way before" to become the final word in making our choices. Competing interests that may be far apart will need to be reconciled in effective political processes that will have to be part of that new ingenuity that produces the necessary innovations. This will require a high level of trust across society. And that tells me that today's outstanding social justice issues must be resolved urgently, so that we might approach the difficult future decisions as a trusting cohesive society pulling together, not weakened by internal cracks, divisions or resentment, and free of suspicion that some may get left behind.

## What innovation is and what it is not

*Necessity may be the mother of invention,*
*but competition is the father of innovation.*

Innovation is change. It is the change achieved by developing a new idea and putting it into practice. The same word is used for the process of this kind of change and also for its result. These two elements, having the new idea and putting it into practice, are the key features of innovation of any kind.

Innovation appears in many contexts and in many forms. A few innovations prove to be revolutionary; most others change things just a little. There are product innovations, evident in the myriad of new and improved goods and services always being introduced into the market.[3] There are process innovations in how things are made and done. There are innovations arising from discoveries made in research, and others from new concepts in design. There are innovations in marketing and logistics, in business models, in organizations, and in the social institutions that regularize human arrangements and relationships. Some innovations may be narrowly focused affecting only a few people, and others may be so broad and deep in their impact that they literally change the world. Some innovations open the door to much more change; they serve as platforms on which further innovation can be built. Still others arise from ways that people respond to new needs of all kinds, and some innovations

---

[3] In this book, the words 'products' and 'production' will always embrace both goods and services, wherever that makes sense, even though they differ in many fundamental ways.

are the fruits of imagination alone – indeed, innovations arise from creativity and imagination shown by people in any domain of human activity. But whatever the details, innovation always involves the same two things, namely having a new idea and putting it into practice. Just having the new idea is not innovation.

Because it occurs in so many different ways, it is useful to think of innovation as a generic term. By analogy, 'wheel' is a generic term that always refers to a circular object that can rotate around its centre, whatever its context or use. There are truck wheels and train wheels, steering wheels and grinding wheels, bicycle wheels and roulette wheels. They appear in different contexts, vary greatly in detail, have different uses and are important in different ways to different people, but they are always circular objects that can rotate. The many circular objects that cannot rotate are not wheels. It's the same with innovation. It always refers to a new idea that is put into practice. The many new ideas that are not put into practice are not innovations.

This means that inventions themselves are not innovations. A particular invention might meet a significant need, and it might be ingenious, elegant, and proven to work successfully. But it becomes an innovation only when it is actually put into practice. That occurs when a customer chooses to buy it and use it, in preference to competing options. The distinction between invention and innovation is basic, and it has important policy implications that will be discussed in later chapters.

Today, innovation receives a great deal of attention from leaders in government and industry, policy makers and commentators and, as a result, the public is becoming more aware of it too. Academics have made it a subject for detailed study – the field is called Innovation Studies. To be called 'innovative' is received as praise; to be on the wrong side of an 'innovation gap' is to be missing something essential. Innovation is treated as an unquestioned good thing, something to do more of, a key to greater prosperity, and the way to improve the human condition in general. Sometimes the language used makes innovation seem an end in itself.

But innovation is not an end in itself; it is only a means to an end. It is a purposeful act of change to achieve some goal. The goal can be to grow market share for an established company, or to create an entirely new venture to take advantage of new knowledge. It can be as dramatic as improving the health outcomes of patients brought to hospital Emergency Rooms, or as benign as developing a new game 'app' for a smart phone. It can be constructive, or it can be purposely destructive; it can be a new tool or a new weapon. It can be mainly aesthetic, or purely functional, a new ornament or a new mechanism. It can be the new societal capacity to meet some existing human need that wasn't being met adequately before, or the creation of a new societal demand for an existing resource. It can be the new solution of some old problem that has so far defied solving, or a response to new circumstances. And any goal of innovation always has the potential of being of benefit to some people and against the interest of others. Innovation is change, and change disturbs the *status quo*, so people who feel they have something to lose will resist it.[4]

The resistance to innovation may range from organized action in defence against perceived potential harm, through foot-dragging, to the momentum of the *status quo*. Obvious examples of active resistance are the opposition to genetically-modified foods (GMF) in Europe and the NIMBY[5] movements in Canada to block proposed infrastructure projects, such as generating stations, garbage dumps, highway expansions, and more recently wind-turbine farms. Frequent and very visible examples of active and organized, but totally expected, opposition arise in legislative assemblies when new laws are proposed. Examples of foot-dragging resistance to innovation occur when legacy policies, regulations, standards and practices continue to be applied even though they are obsolete and may be counterproductive in current circumstances. Foot-dragging must also include the failure to implement new policies, regulations, programs and practices that have been demonstrated elsewhere to be effective in promoting and supporting necessary innovation. And sometimes the current way of doing things has so much momentum – is so deeply and widely rooted in society – that it is too difficult and too expensive to implement an obvious simple improvement. The textbook example of this is the QWERTY keyboard. The problem for which QWERTY was the solution disappeared when the

---

[4] People who resist technological innovation are sometimes called 'Luddites,' after a group of artisans in 18th century Britain who tried to destroy the machinery that would put them out of work.
[5] Not In My Back Yard! (NIMBY).

mechanical typewriter gave way to the word processor,[6] and a far more convenient keyboard layout is now only a matter of a simple software application. However, so many people have been trained on QWERTY, and it is so widely used, that the readily available more convenient layouts have not been adopted. These are all examples of barriers to innovation that are much more social than technical.

But there is another obstacle to innovation that is much less obvious, and may seem paradoxical at first glance. Any particular potential innovation has only a small chance to see the light of day simply because too many potential innovations are being proposed, and too many ideas are competing for financing. Good ideas and inventions are relatively cheap, but putting them into practice is much more expensive. The volume of attractive inventions in any domain is so great and the cost of commercializing any one of them is generally so large, that resources are found to pursue only a small fraction of even the most promising ones. The competition for such resources is very stiff. Venture capitalists reject most projects proposed to them for funding, and even the most innovative companies bring to market only a small percentage of the projects on which they start working. As a consequence, some companies have large portfolios of patents that they have not used to make things. More generally, abandoned potential innovations in various stages of completion can be found in both the private and public sectors. The ability to make good investment choices in this very competitive context is essential to success in the management of innovation.

The current widespread interest in innovation stems largely from its potential positive economic impact. The thesis presented in the first part of this chapter deals with just this. Innovation is increasingly seen as the key to prosperity in today's global

---

[6] The letter placement on the QWERTY keyboard was designed to slow down typists using the early mechanical typewriters. In these machines, the individual characters were mounted on long swinging arms activated by hitting the letter keys. All the arms swung toward the centre to deliver the type into one narrow guide so that all the characters would hit the inked ribbon and make an impression on the paper on the same line when the carriage moved sideways. The adjacent arms in this mechanism would jam against one another when the typist hit the keys too quickly, so the QWERTY layout was designed to put a delay between keystrokes for letters that often appeared close together in the text.

knowledge-based economy. That puts innovation in the same basket of concerns as gross domestic product (GDP) growth and productivity rates. The reason for this is that some kinds of innovation are very directly related to economic growth. Innovation by business in the form of new products that succeed in the market creates new value added. Value added creates wealth, both private wealth (wages and profits) and public wealth (taxes) in the total amount of the value added. And since GDP is the sum of value added throughout the economy, this contributes to GDP growth. The producers of innovations – new products that are different and available from one or only a small number of producers – can earn high margins because they can set their prices. On the other hand, the producers of commodities, or undifferentiated products that are available from many producers, can't do that; they must depend on market demand and take the current market price.[7] But the innovator's advantage doesn't last forever; most innovations have a short shelf life. Competitors quickly learn to produce similar products, and today's innovations become tomorrow's commodities. That competition breeds more innovation, because the only way to maintain the innovator's advantage is to counter commoditization by repeated innovation. Necessity may be the mother of invention, but competition is the father of innovation.

It is important to remember, however, that governments' interest in this complicated process arises from their assumption that successful innovations lead to new wealth creation in their place of origin. But in a globalized economy that need not be the case. Innovations diffuse locally, nationally and globally. A new product may be based on an invention arising out of research

[7] To see this difference in action, compare the current advertised price of an iMac desktop computer with that of a desktop PC from HP or Dell that has similar specifications in terms of speed, memory, etc., or the price of an Apple MacBook with that of a laptop PC from Acer, HP, Dell, Sony or some other 'PC clone.' The Apple computers are much more expensive than their PC counterparts. Apple Computer is a very innovative company, a master of design-based innovation. It rolls out a stream of new products, generally differentiated by their design – the look, feel, user interface and operating system. The internal components in Apple computers are pretty much the same as in all other computers, and are themselves commodity products. Apple's design-based innovations enable the company to set the price for its computers. In contrast, the PC is a commodity product and PC producers must take the much lower market price.

done in one place; it may be developed somewhere else, and produced in yet another place with components that originate in many places. And that refers just to the supply side. The benefits may be as great, or possibly much greater, on the demand side, where the new product might be used to create wealth half a world away by people who had nothing to do with supporting its original development. There is not much that governments can do about this. Protectionism would not work in an open global economy. All that a local government can do is, on the one hand, to help its industry to produce successful innovations and, on the other hand, to help them learn how to develop new uses and create wealth using innovations from everywhere in the world. In brief, government support for innovation is needed on both the supply side and the demand side.

Innovations that may have an economic impact are the focus of this book. While our general discussion will consider many kinds of innovation, many of the detailed examples will deal with four kinds: product innovation (introducing a new or improved good or service in the market); process innovation (making a good or offering a service in a new way); marketing innovation (bringing products to the customers in a new way); and innovation in business models (devising new commercial relationships to create and capture value in a new way). Note that product and process innovation will always be understood to include both goods and services, even when they are not mentioned explicitly. For brevity, these four kinds of innovation will be referred to as the 'canonical' four, but there are not four recipes for innovation. Any one kind can occur in very many different ways.

The discussion of the canonical four kinds of innovation will include Canadian examples, with international comparisons where instructive. It is worth noting that the four are not always independent; they may appear in various combinations depending on the circumstances. And the distinctions among them may not be absolute but more a matter of perspective. For example, a company that makes production machinery might develop and sell a totally new kind of tool as a product innovation. For a company that buys that tool to make its own products in a new way, the use of that same tool becomes a process innovation.

The goal of this book is to help the reader understand the complex and important process of innovation in a way that is useful to potential innovators, to students, to managers, to investors, to policy makers, to regulators, to researchers and many others. The objective is to produce a big-picture description of innovation, to see who does what and how the pieces fit together, with a deeper look at some details that are well described by data and theory. Where such knowledge is lacking, topics that need to be learned are identified. The emphasis in the book will be on four kinds of innovation that have the potential to produce a clear and direct economic impact, but other kinds of innovation will, of course, not be ignored and they will appear in the discussion as appropriate.

To assist in this discussion, a set of consistent definitions of key terms will be assembled in a section of chapter 4 on the language of innovation.

## The business of innovation

Business success through innovation brings many benefits, but getting there is risky. First, there must be a business model for creating and capturing value that is appropriate to the particular innovation. Value-added and wealth creation depend on sales; without sales there is no value added and no wealth creation. That means that market intelligence and high skills in commerce are necessary for business success in innovation. And since even the most attractive innovation may fail in the market for reasons that have nothing to do with its own merits, even more is required. Many things can undercut the sales of a promising innovation, and therefore its economic benefits: possibly a competitor's innovation that shifts market demand in an unexpected direction, a change in the economic climate, a new law or regulation, a policy decision, or even a single event. For this reason, the business of innovation requires people with special abilities and aptitudes. These are creative and tenacious people who have the ability to find and seize new opportunities to create value, and have a high tolerance for the risks in doing that. They are called entrepreneurs. That term will be used here whether the locus of the entrepreneurial activity is an established firm or a new venture.[8]

---

[8] The term 'intrapreneurs' is sometimes used for entrepreneurs working within established firms.

As has already been pointed out, even the most successful innovation doesn't stay an innovation forever. Any product innovation that succeeds in the market is sure to be imitated by competing producers, and eventually reduced to a commodity product that is available with very similar functionality and quality from many sources. The digital camera provides a current example. "Point-and-shoot" digital cameras are now a commodity product, and the more recent digital single-lens reflex cameras (DSLR) are in the process of being commoditized. When the innovation has become commoditized, its producer has lost the ability to set the price and earn high margins, and must take the always lower market price for what has now become a commodity product. This process of commoditization can be fast or slow, depending on the industry sector and on the applicable form of intellectual property (IP) protection. The one sustainable response to product commoditization is repeated innovation. As indicated, a company that keeps bringing innovations to market as fast as their earlier products are commoditized by competition will maintain the innovator's advantage of price-setting and high margins. That process is sometimes called 'keeping the innovation pipeline full.' The successful innovative companies are the ones who manage to continue to do that.

This is the place to recall the generic definition of innovation as having a new idea and putting it into practice. In product and process innovation, the new idea is an invention and putting it into practice is bringing it to market, or commercialization. One can, therefore, think of product or process innovation as: innovation = invention + commercialization.[9]

An invention is an idea conceived to meet some specific need, together with the practical means by which it can be implemented. And, once again, the same word can also be used for the process that leads to it. While the comic strip image of invention might still be a light bulb going on over the head of

---

[9] This idea was introduced by C. Freeman. 1974. *The Economics of Industrial Innovation*. Toronto and New York: Penguin Books, and has been useful in many applications since. For example, the process of innovation in Canada, based on inventions arising from the results of university research, is described in terms of an invention system and a commercialization system in T.A. Brzustowski. 2006. "Innovation = Invention + Commercialization: a systems perspective," *Optimumonline*, 36 (3): 1-8.

a lonely genius working in his garage, the reality is far more complicated. Invention is a difficult and demanding process. It requires defining very clearly what specific need is to be met and how the new idea will meet it, and then estimating what the market might be for the new solution. It requires a thorough knowledge of prior art. It also requires inspiration, imagination, persistence and an intuitive understanding of how people might react to the new solution. It draws on knowledge from many formal and informal sources, including the latest developments in related technologies, and it calls for a variety of skills and experience at a high level in many areas, including specifically design. And it depends on access to the appropriate materials, tools, equipment and facilities to try things and to keep trying. In light of all these demands, significant inventions are much more likely to come from well funded, well equipped and experienced teams than from individual inventors working in isolation. Does that mean that the brilliant new gadget from the inspired inventor working in his garage is a thing of the past? Let's hope not, but we shouldn't count on it to enhance our national prosperity.

The ideas and knowledge embodied in an invention are the inventor's intellectual property (IP). The inventor's rights to it are protected by various combinations of two elements: time and legal instruments. The choice depends on the dynamics of the sector and the market. For example, in some free-wheeling areas of consumer electronics and software, a six-month lead in the market can provide a sufficient financial return to the producer so that no other protection is worthwhile. At the other extreme, in the very highly regulated pharmaceutical industry, a patent for 20 years is granted very early in the development of a drug. If that drug successfully passes several years of clinical trials and then a long process of approval by government for patient use, and by drug-plan payers for reimbursement, the producer may have no more than 10 years of patent protection left to benefit from being its exclusive supplier in the market. The sales revenues during that period must first recover the research and development costs of the successful drug, including the cost of failures and dead ends explored along the way, and only then begin to make a profit for investors. And once the 20 years are up and the patent expires, the drug is quickly commoditized, as cheaper generic versions of it appear on the market.[10]

The legal instruments for the protection of IP rights are patents, copyrights, trade secrets and trade marks. A patent does not enable the inventor to do anything; it only prevents others from copying the invention while it is in force. The basic idea of the patent is to promote the diffusion of new technologies through the economy. The inventor has to disclose the invention in detail: describe what it is supposed to do, how it works, how it's made and, in return, the state grants a monopoly to the inventor for a fixed period of time. By the time the patent expires, other producers will have learned to produce competing products, and the price will drop to the benefit of the consumer. In theory, then, patents promote commoditization, but guarantee the inventors a fair return for their efforts. In practice, patents are relatively inexpensive to obtain and maintain, but become much more expensive to defend and even more expensive to enforce.[11] Many companies are now embracing open innovation and following patent strategies that treat patents as assets that can be used in a variety of ways. For example, if they own many more patents than they have the capacity to use, they can derive substantial revenues from selling them or licensing them to other companies, possibly including their own spin-offs created for the purpose. Conversely, if they need to strengthen their IP position in some area, they might obtain the necessary IP by buying or licensing the useful patents that appear in the IP market or by acquiring a firm that owns them.

[10] It is no surprise, therefore, that extending the intellectual property rights to 24 years, as is the case in the EU, is an issue on which the Canadian pharmaceutical industry has been active in lobbying government.

[11] While patent suits and massive settlements involving Apple, Motorola, RIM and other well-known companies have been in the news recently, legal action in this area is nothing new. Some of history's giants of innovation battled over patents for years. Examples include Alexander Graham Bell and Thomas Edison (Charlotte Gray. 2006. *Reluctant Genius – The Passionate Life and Inventive Mind of Alexander Graham Bell*. New York: HarperCollins) and Alfred Nobel, the man better known for endowing the Nobel Prize than for inventing dynamite (Stephen R. Bown. 2005. *A Most Damnable Invention – Dynamites, Nitrates and The Making of the Modern World*. Toronto: Viking Canada).

There are circumstances, of course, when it is to the innovator's great advantage to prevent the commoditization of the innovation at any time. (Think of the 'secret formula' for the syrup of Coca-Cola that has been protected for over a century.) The instrument intended to prevent commoditization is the trade secret, implemented through non-disclosure agreements and security practices that are the very opposite of the patent's requirements for disclosure and description. Far removed in the IP spectrum from both the patent and the trade secret is the 'open source' (OS) movement in which a basic technology is freely shared and, in return, users undertake to keep improving it and sharing the improvements. The commercial activity in the OS world is the custom adaptation of OS technology for specific use. At the present time, the OS approach is most strongly established in software, but the concept is spreading to other domains as well, and may eventually lead to new approaches for dealing with IP more generally. Since IP rights (IPR) are an important part of the business climate for innovation, the differences among national IPR regimes can loom large in the decisions that companies make on the location of their R&D activities.

The process of commercializing an invention can be very different in different circumstances, but it is always difficult and expensive. This can be illustrated with two extreme examples. Consider first a large technology company with established product lines, market share and customer base. In that case, the commercialization process is a filtered stream of projects and proposed innovations that originate from the company's own labs, from customers, from acquisitions and other sources. The company knows how to commercialize its products, and there are established procedures and experienced people in market intelligence, financing, R&D, marketing, sales projections, finding lead clients and beta test sites, supply chain development, manufacturing, distribution, etc. The projects flowing in 'the pipeline' compete for limited resources as they reach milestones, pass through gates, receive management approval to continue, etc.; most are filtered out and eventually some small fraction of them – perhaps just a few percent – proceed to the market.[12]

---

[12] Readers familiar with fluid mechanics will recognize this process as 'Eulerian' in its form, analogous to describing the local weather at some location as the wind blows clouds past it. For the research-based new venture, the

The rest may be abandoned, shelved, licensed, sold outright or handed off to new spin-offs of the parent company. The factors at play obviously include the technical quality of the invention itself, the product strategy of the company, market conditions, etc. Many people are involved in this process, much time is spent on it, and it all adds up to an expensive business. Conventional wisdom has it that most of the cost of innovation lies in the cost of commercializing the invention. It can be many times greater than the initial cost of the project that led to the invention, and in some sectors (e.g., pharmaceuticals) even several hundred times greater.

Now consider the very different case of a new venture set up to commercialize an invention that was suggested by the results of recent research, possibly in a university or research hospital. In this case, there is one invention and no pipeline. The challenge is to find investors to provide adequate amounts of needed financing at the various levels of risk that occur so that one invention proceeds to market through proof of concept, tests for robustness, scale-up, prototype design and construction, testing (or clinical trials in the health areas), design for manufacture, etc. The seed and early-stage funding may be relatively easy to obtain, but the special challenge is finding a financial bridge over the so-called 'valley of death' between proof of concept and a product offered in the market. Here the amounts needed are significantly greater, but the risk is still high, and venture capitalists (VC) are reluctant to invest. In theory, the whole process seems straightforward, if difficult and, at first glance, linear. In practice, however, things are often very different. First, for many researchers, commercialization is an afterthought, and commerce is generally (and wrongly!) assumed to be much easier than research – and therefore not requiring as much attention. If the researcher whose work suggested the invention in question is also the inventor, and then becomes the CEO of the new venture, then success depends on one individual having three

commercialization process is much more 'Lagrangian,' analogous to following what happens to a particular cloud carried by the wind from place to place. The point is that many detailed differences in the commercialization processes under these two sets of circumstances can be explained by the fundamental differences in their form.

different sets of skills at a very high level: skills in research, in invention, and in entrepreneurship. Such people are very rare. The researcher-inventor-CEO is likely to be preoccupied with finding financing to continue perfecting the new product, at a time when the new company should be working hard to secure the first customer.[13] Such new ventures obviously need outside help, and they are starting to find it from institutions called 'innovation intermediaries' that are appearing in the Canadian innovation system.

The situation is different in the case of established firms that innovate in response to their customers. These companies are fully engaged in commerce. They know their clients and they create value by offering products that meet their clients' needs, with mutual trust established by years of fair dealing. Their innovations are likely to be product improvements, often in response to feedback from customers. They are achieved through an R&D effort that includes a lot of design and relatively little research. Since they already have their organizational structure in place, customers who know them, and a flow of sales revenues, the 'valley of death' is much less of an issue, and the goal of their CEO is not so much to find financing as to keep their customers satisfied.

Obviously innovation is not some homogeneous uniform process; it has structure. It occurs differently under different circumstances. Different firms do different things to produce innovations, and they follow different strategies. In these circumstances, an organizing framework is a useful aid to understanding. One clear-cut taxonomy is obtained by dividing the innovation space into four quadrants, depending on whether the invention is research-based (new use of new knowledge) or design-based (new use of prior knowledge), and whether it is being commercialized by a new venture or by an established firm. This is useful because the business issues are largely

[13] Douglas Barber and Jeffrey Crelinsten have identified this as the cause of failure of many tech start-ups in their paper, "Understanding the Disappearance of Early-stage and Start-up R&D Performing Firms," The Impact Group, 2009, presented among other places at the Waterloo Workshop "From the Research Lab to the Marketplace," Faculty of Engineering, University of Waterloo, April 20, 2010. They interviewed the CEOs of 18 technology companies that went out of business to discover why.

different in the four quadrants. This taxonomy of innovation is very different from a classification of innovation behaviour mainly by firm size or by industry sector, since it emphasizes the business situation of the innovators rather than their size or the nature of their business.[14]

The 'research-based/new venture' quadrant is the locus of many start-ups, commercializing inventions suggested by research in universities and government labs. The hope is that such innovations might prove revolutionary, become 'game changers' as platforms for many more innovations that create new markets and set new directions, and create a great deal of wealth as a result. In Canada, this group seems to receive more attention in government policy than do the three others.

The 'design-based/established firm' quadrant is almost the polar opposite on every dimension. It is the locus of larger companies operating more or less steadily who depend on design far more than research, as they innovate to improve their products in response to customer needs. Their innovations are much more likely to be incremental than revolutionary, and much more likely to be sustaining their current business than disrupting it.[15]

The 'design-based/new ventures' are companies set up to exploit new configurations of existing components. They may include design boutiques, as well as start-ups or spin-offs in the digital media, software, clothing, furniture, entertainment, etc. The Cirque du Soleil was a perfect example. The large 'research-based/established firms' that depend on research for their innovations include, most notably, the pharmaceutical industry mentioned above and parts of the information and communications technology (ICT) sector. In reality, the distinctions among the companies are never as hard and fast as this quadrant model suggests, and they may never apply to entire complex organizations. Nevertheless, a classification exercise of this sort is valuable, since there are useful similarities in the process of commercialization carried out

---

[14] T.A. Brzustowski. 2011. "A new business-based taxonomy of innovation," *Optimumonline*, 41 (3): 30-37.

[15] Incremental innovation seemed to be in the process of being rediscovered in the spring of 2011. It appeared in the speeches of influential people, and in the title of a dedicated conference. This may be a reaction against the earlier preoccupation with the 'research-based/new venture' innovation quadrant.

by companies lying in the same quadrant, and significant differences among quadrants.[16]

Up to this point, the discussion of the connection between innovation and prosperity has focused on the wealth-creating private sector, but innovation is also essential in the wealth-consuming public sector that produces mainly services, and in the not-for-profit sector as well. In the public sector, the goal of innovation is to maximize both the effectiveness and efficiency of the services offered. This means achieving the greatest amount of whatever public good is produced in the sector (e.g., good health outcomes of health care, competent and well-informed adults in the case of education, etc.) at the cost of the least possible consumption of the nation's wealth. It makes the nation's existing prosperity go farther in supporting a good quality of life. In the public sector, most innovations are in programs, processes and methods, of which the most successful ones are actively disseminated as 'best practices' without IP protection. However, science and engineering research in the public sector may also generate some IP, and its treatment is more complicated.[17] Some is openly published in scholarly journals, or otherwise communicated to the international research community, as a contribution to knowledge. But when the research in the public sector leads to IP that has the potential to become a wealth-creating innovation, namely a new traded good or service, it is protected as in the private sector and may be licensed to industry or become the basis of a new venture. In the not-for-profit sector, there may be both wealth-consuming and wealth-creating activities within one organization. The former behave much as the public sector, and the latter much more like the private sector. The net effect must, of course, be zero profit.

### To innovate or not to innovate

Time out for a reality check! The discussion so far may have suggested that all companies innovate as a matter of course in order to be competitive and profitable and to grow. But, in reality, very many Canadian companies don't engage in much

---

[16] The four quadrants could also be considered as the elements of a two-by-two table.

[17] University, college or hospital research funded by public grants, and research in government labs.

innovation, and that has had an important impact on the economy. The impact is sufficiently important that the Government of Canada asked the Council of Canadian Academies in 2007 to set up an expert panel to find out why. The report of the Expert Panel on Business Innovation is a significant document that provides important new insights into innovation from the perspective of Canadian business.[18] It treats innovation in economic terms and examines its impact on the long-term performance of the Canadian economy.

Their overall conclusion is expressed in terms of the multifactor productivity (MFP):[19] "Canada's weak growth of MFP indicates that the country's lagging productivity growth is largely due to weak business innovation." The panel then goes on to examine the factors that influence a company's choice of innovation as its business strategy, and conclude:

> The principal factors that influence the business innovation decision can be categorized broadly as (i) particular characteristics of the firm's sector; (ii) the state of competition; (iii) the climate for new ventures; (iv) public policies that encourage or inhibit innovation; and (v) business ambition (i.e., entrepreneurial aggressiveness and growth orientation). The relative importance of these factors will vary from sector to sector and over the life cycle of individual firms [emphasis in the original].[20]

While these five factors are discussed in various appropriate sections of this book, it is the thesis stated in the preface that is most affected by the Expert Panel findings. The panel has made it clear that there isn't any dammed up wave of innovation ready to sweep across the Canadian economy, raising productivity and wealth creation in its wake. Instead, firms that have chosen not to engage in innovation will have to be convinced to reconsider – they will have to be given compelling reasons why they should innovate. This will require leadership, persuasion

---

[18] Expert Panel on Business Innovation. 2009. *Innovation and Business Strategy: Why Canada Falls Short*. Ottawa: Council of Canadian Academies, June.

[19] Expert Panel on Business Innovation. 2009. *Innovation and Business Strategy: Why Canada Falls Short*. Ottawa: Council of Canadian Academies, June, p. 4. Discussed in detail, but briefly, in chapter 5.

[20] Expert Panel on Business Innovation. 2009. *Innovation and Business Strategy: Why Canada Falls Short*. Ottawa: Council of Canadian Academies, June, p. 6.

and incentives, of course, but most importantly it will require attention to the five factors that influenced these companies' decisions in the first place. Innovation will have to become seen by the firm as the means of making it more competitive and profitable. In addition, the companies for whom innovation will be a new activity will likely need help in learning how to do it. We shall return to these matters in the final chapter on an innovation policy for Canada. In the meantime, we shall resume the discussion of how innovation happens.

## Productivity, R&D and export sales

Productivity is a very important business indicator, and innovation affects it. A nation's productivity increases when its workers produce more value per hour of work.[21] That can be done in three ways: by reducing the number of workers through the use of machinery, by increasing the volume of what they already produce, or by producing more valuable products. The first strategy can raise the productivity of a company, but its impact on the productivity of the nation may be negative, depending on what happens to the laid-off workers. The second strategy seems much more attractive at first glance, since Canada's current prosperity has greatly benefited from the export of commodities by the natural resource sectors. But there is uncertainty in that one as well. First, there is the basic uncertainty of commodity markets, and now there are the additional emerging issues of sustainability and the environmental and political costs of increased resource extraction, so that the long-term success of this strategy is not assured. On the other hand, conditions are starting to come together in Canada to enable success with the third strategy – selling more valuable products to the world. Widespread industrial innovation can shift the balance of production in all sectors toward a greater proportion of higher value-added products. In the 21st century, many of the high value-added products are knowledge-intensive, the fruits of R&D that takes advantage of new research results and new design concepts, and they are traded globally. That means

---

[21] This refers to the productivity of labour. Another widely used measure, the total factor or multifactor productivity (MFP), increases when the economy produces more value than can be accounted for by increases in the labour and capital employed in the economy. Both productivity measures are discussed in chapter 5.

that a national productivity increase which reflects a move of the economy to higher value products through innovation requires both technical excellence in science and engineering, and refined business skills in international trade. We now have the first, but we may not have enough of the second.

R&D is the acronym for research and development, a very important element in technological innovation, since it is the source of the imbedded new knowledge that creates value in new technology products. R&D is generally used as a singular noun that is silent on the relative proportions of its two components.[22] The order of the R and D words is consistent with research-based innovation, but the same expression is also used for design-based innovation in which development can precede research or proceed without research at all.

Research and development are two related but very different activities, carried out for different reasons by different people. Research involves mainly scientists and is undertaken to create new knowledge. Development is done mainly by engineers. It is undertaken, literally, to develop new products. Design is an early and important part of development. When the term R&D is used in connection with universities, hospitals and government labs, it refers almost entirely to research. When it is used in connection with industry, it involves mainly development, with perhaps some applied research. In research-based innovation, development generally follows research and invention. In design-based innovation, design comes first, followed by development of the first product and then by applied research, as needed, to provide any additional detailed knowledge needed to improve the product.

The proportion of sales revenues spent on R&D is a good indicator of a company's involvement in innovation. This quantity is called 'R&D intensity' with the acronym RDI, and is usually expressed in percent.[23] Established technology companies that

---

[22] One occasionally encounters attempts to give relative weight to the two components of R&D in expressions such 'big R, little d' referring to research institutions, and 'little r, big D' referring to industrial R&D.

[23] The term 'R&D intensity' is sometimes also used for the amount spent on R&D as a percentage of value added, but the acronym RDI is not used in that case. Since value added is sales revenue less the cost of purchased inputs, the R&D intensity based on value added is always a greater number than RDI.

maintain a full pipeline of innovations generally operate with RDI near 10 percent. Established producers of natural resource commodity products show much lower values of RDI, in the range of 1 percent or less, but because of their huge revenues this low RDI may still represent substantial annual R&D investments, in the tens of millions of dollars, focused largely on cost reduction in their processes and on developing new sources of raw materials.

In this connection, Manning[24] and Hawkins [25] have argued that Canada's resource industries are far more innovative than is widely recognized. Because their RDI is low, it has become conventional wisdom that these are not innovative companies. Hawkins and Manning argue that, in fact, they are very innovative, but their innovation takes place in the field and not in the lab, and it doesn't fit as well with the definition of R&D used in the SR&ED tax-credit program as does lab work. They point to the research base of many of these innovations and to the demand that the resource companies exert on the specialty service sectors and on the manufacturers who must supply the state-of-the-art equipment needed in the field. These are compelling arguments, and they demonstrate that there are some serious measurement issues in this area. If these measurement issues were resolved, and a much more comprehensive definition of R&D were adopted, Canadian resource companies might become eligible for more SR&ED tax credits, and it might even become conventional wisdom that they are very innovative. But we would be closer to solving Canada's prosperity problem only if and when the contribution of these companies to GDP increased significantly as a result.

At the other extreme of the RDI spectrum, there are companies operating at RDI of more than 100 percent, and some at very much more.[26] Their revenues are low or non-existent and

---

[24] Preston Manning, several public speeches as well as published columns and letters on innovation in 2010, 2011, 2012.

[25] Richard Hawkins. 2011. "Looking at Innovation From A Uniquely Canadian Perspective: The Case For A New Alliance Of Practice, Policy And Scholarship," *Perspectives*, Institute for Science, Society and Policy (ISSP), University of Ottawa, November.

[26] Some of these companies have no revenues at all, and therefore an infinite RDI. Such companies are often referred to as 'pre-market' or 'pre-revenue' companies. Obviously, the RDI is not a useful indicator in such circumstances.

they are financed to do R&D to develop their products. They consume wealth. These companies are not sustainable, and they will either produce a successful product and grow or use up their financing and disappear. Nevertheless, even if they have no positive economic impact today, they deserve serious attention from government because they are the source of the large, new innovative companies of tomorrow.

Canada's current prosperity has made it possible to invest in the public research that is the base for excellent science and engineering, and to bring it to an internationally competitive level in both quality and intensity of activity. That excellence in science and engineering leads to the capacity for high-quality R&D. But as a nation, Canada still has a lot to learn about connecting that capacity with wealth creation through innovation in the private sector, and doing that on a scale large enough to make a substantial difference in the economy. We will know that is happening when GDP growth takes off on a sustained trajectory noticeably steeper than 'business as usual.' But while it is known in theory what must be done to enhance Canada's wealth creation enough to restore the recent decline in prosperity (GDP/capita) and eliminate the deficit in productivity growth, in practice Canadian productivity and prosperity continue on a gradual decline.

Canada has a relatively small population (34 million) and that implies a limited domestic market for many new technology products. That means that Canadian technology companies depend heavily on export sales to recover their R&D costs, make a profit and grow. To succeed in world markets, they aim for 'first in the world' innovations that are based on inventions arising out of recent research results, on adaptations of new technology from abroad, on new designs that make use of new components available on world markets, or on combinations of them all. Canadian companies that operate domestically with low R&D costs might, of course, succeed with 'first in Canada' innovations, and in some sectors 'first in the company' innovations might bring success as well. While 'first in the world' innovation might rank higher than 'first in Canada' and higher than 'first in the company' on the scale of bragging rights, the important question for any kind of innovation is whether it increases the value added and wealth creation by the company that implements it. If it does, then it's a success that matters.

Innovation leads to enhanced prosperity when producers sell more valuable products that are new in the market. They can set the prices for these new value-added differentiated products and earn margins high enough to pay for the R&D that went into them, and to invest in more R&D toward the next new product. As each successive innovation becomes commoditized with time, they can maintain their wealth creation and profitability only by innovating repeatedly so that they always have an innovation in the market.[27] In contrast, the producers of undifferentiated or commodity products spend relatively much less on R&D, and what they do spend is focussed on improving their processes to lower their costs rather than developing new products. They must take the world market price for their products, but they can remain profitable if they keep their production costs low. However, their capacity to raise their value added by unilaterally raising their prices is virtually nil.

And there's more to it than that. Value added is a market compromise, not a supply-side decision. Value added occurs only when there are sales, and its magnitude depends on the price the buyer will be prepared to pay; without sales there is no value added and therefore no wealth creation. That means that high skills in commerce, in the marketing and sales of new products and in getting the price point right are key links in the chain connecting innovation with enhanced prosperity. But marketing and sales where? Let's return to the fact that in many knowledge-based industries, the Canadian market is small, far too small to recover the high costs of R&D and the other costs of the commercialization process. In those cases, the success of the Canadian producers will depend on their success in making sales in world markets. Exporting cannot be an afterthought; it must be in the business model of tech companies almost from the first day – they must be 'born global.' In fact, some successful Canadian tech companies have started to refer to themselves as the '5/95,' meaning that only 5 percent of their business is in Canada. The remaining 95 percent is done abroad. And there are even some that call themselves '1/99.' Clearly, growing more such companies and keeping them in Canada is a challenge for governments here.

[27] Michael E. Porter and Scott Stern. 2002. "Innovation: Location Matters" in *Innovation – Driving Product, Process, and Market Change.* Edward B. Roberts (ed.). New York: Jossey-Bass, p. 239.

## *Time scales of innovation*

Innovation can take a lot of time and cost a great deal, but it can also be very fast and inexpensive; the costs and time scales of innovation range over many magnitudes. For example, a new application (app) for a smart phone might be produced by a software developer in just a few months and at a cost of tens of thousands of dollars. At the other extreme, a pharmaceutical company might take almost ten years and spend many hundreds of millions of dollars to develop a new drug. Some product innovations may achieve market success in a few months, as the iPhone has done, but other 'enabling' innovations that lead to widespread change may take decades or even generations to reach their full impact. The use of steam to provide propulsion in transportation is one example. It took more than half a century, starting in the early eighteen hundreds, for steam locomotives and marine steam engines to become ubiquitous and reduce the challenge of distance in trade, industry and the daily life of millions. During that time, the steam engine was made much safer (boiler explosions became rare) and much more efficient (a ship could carry enough fuel to cross the Atlantic), and redesigned for use in the new ships and locomotives that were themselves evolving at the time. These developments were the work of engineers using mainly prior knowledge. They involved many new designs and inventions and many lessons learned from failures, and they were spurred by competition among many manufacturers.

But some innovations can be slow to have an impact even after the research has been done, inventions made, and new products developed, approved and distributed for sale. In such cases, it is the slow process of adoption, limited by human and societal considerations, that sets the pace. A good example is the long delay between a wave of business investment in information technology in the US in the 1980s and 1990s and the expected improvements in productivity. The delay was long enough that people began to do research on the 'computer paradox,' as the absence of productivity improvements began to be called. The improvements in productivity have now arrived. The delay was the slow pace of change in business processes, practices and organizations that were needed to take advantage of the new information technology (IT).[28]

But innovation can be delayed by management problems as well. A big and complex technical project can run into problems, even when the research has been done, designs completed, new technologies developed and new processes put in place. The Boeing 787 Dreamliner is a case in point. Deliveries of the plane are about three years behind schedule, mainly because of difficulties in coordinating the timing and quality of the work of the suppliers of major components from several nations.

A very useful approach to the time scales of innovation is attributed to Forgacs,[29] who suggested that the life of a product in the market is inversely proportional to its R&D intensity (RDI). This can also be stated as the frequency of innovation being directly proportional to RDI.[30] Forgacs' conjecture is empirical, suggested by aggregate industrial data. It suggests that companies operating at an RDI of 10 percent produce innovations at a rate of about once in every one and a half years. Companies operating at RDI of 1 percent innovate ten times less frequently, about once every decade and a half. Companies operating at RDI of 100 percent – ones that are being financed to do R&D to develop products – come up with something new, make some significant change, or reach another milestone, every couple of months. And the ones operating at RDI above 100 percent do it even more frequently. These companies experience very frequent change and are generally short of both time and money, which means that they need a more responsive policy and program environment than the much more stable companies that innovate far less often.

An entirely different approach to the time scale of innovation proposes a historical framework. This is introduced by Sundbo,[31]

---

[28] Erik Brynjolfsson and Adam Saunders. 2010. *Wired for Innovation – How Information Technology is Reshaping the Economy.* Cambridge, MA: The MIT Press.

[29] O. Forgacs. 2004. "Who spends money on R&D and why?" lecture, Conférence de Montréal, June 7.

[30] T.A. Brzustowski. 2006."Innovation in Canada: Learning from the Top 100 R&D spenders," *Optimumonline,* 36 (4): 48-56. Otto Forgacs originally suggested that the lifetime of a product in the market was inversely proportional to RDI. The two statements are equivalent.

[31] Jon Sundbo. 1998. *The Theory of Innovation – Entrepreneurs, Technology and Strategy.* Toronto: Edward Elgar.

and is related to the long wave, or Kondratiev, analysis of economic cycles. These 'K-waves' are in the range of 50 years in length; there have been four of them since the start of the industrial revolution, and we are now in the fifth. One suggestion is that there is a new way of innovating in each K-wave. For example, in the third Kondratiev from 1892 to 1948, the determinant of innovation was entrepreneurship and the creation of new ventures, many of which grew into major companies that have persisted to this day. Another way of looking at a historical framework of innovation is by the dominant material source of technical change. So the first Kondratiev might be identified with the age of steam, the second with the age of electricity, the third with oil, then the fourth with electronics, and perhaps today we could claim to be innovating in the age of biology.

And there may be still another way of looking at these 50-year long waves. It may be more than coincidence that they span three generations. The first generation develops a new enabling technology (say the digital computer), the second generation (25 years later) keeps improving it and developing new uses for it, and the third generation (another 25 years later) has never seen a world without it, and takes its widespread availability and utility for granted. That growth from appearance to widespread impact adds up to about 50 years.

## The many kinds of innovation

The fact that innovation is a generic term can lead to confusion when the word is used without modifiers. In this book we shall focus on four main kinds of innovations, namely in products, processes, marketing and business models, all of them in both the goods and the services sectors. For precision, these canonical four can be further classified by the use of pairs of opposing modifiers whose meaning is usually obvious. So these innovations can be technical or social, incremental or revolutionary, sustaining or disruptive, research-based or design-based, and supply-driven or demand-driven. The corresponding process of innovation might also be open or closed. In addition to the four canonical kinds of innovation, we will on occasion also need to refer to institutional, organizational and complementary innovations, just to name a few. It is important to realize, however, that each of these kinds of innovation can be realized in many different ways, depending on the people involved and on the circumstances in which they function.

It turns out that one of these contrasting modifier pairs, research-based vs. design-based, is particularly important because it refers to innovations of great current interest that are fundamentally different in many ways. Research-based innovations begin with basic (or curiosity-driven) research to create new knowledge.[32] If the research is successful, then inventions suggested by that new knowledge may follow. When such inventions are developed into new products through engineering and then commercialized successfully, they become research-based innovations. Their commercialization is difficult because it is driven by technology push rather than market pull. The producer claims, "I've got a great idea that you should buy!" There's no customer calling, "I've got a great problem, and I'll pay you for the solution." In very broad terms, this sequence of activities can be thought of as a linear progression from science to market, and is sometimes called the 'linear model' of innovation – a term much disliked within the discipline of innovation studies. In practice, of course, there are always plenty of feedback loops, surprises and dead ends along the way, and the detailed path of progress from research result to research-based innovation is anything but linear. Examples of research-based innovation can be found that started with research in the universities, in some government laboratories, in small new ventures, and in the R&D labs of some major corporations, particularly in the pharmaceutical industry.

Design-driven innovation is very different. It is the result of engineering very much more than science. It starts with a problem to be solved, or a customer's need to be met, and uses existing and often incomplete knowledge from many sources to design the solution – and some of the knowledge used may

---

[32] The goal of the research may be only to gain a new understanding, or it may be to gain a new understanding that also suggests a new use. In the former case, the research has been placed in 'Bohr's Quadrant' and in the latter in 'Pasteur's Quadrant' in the book by Donald Stokes (1997. *Pasteur's Quadrant.* New York: Brookings). The names are associated with Niels Bohr, the Danish scientist whose only goal was to understand the structure of the atom, and Louis Pasteur, considered the father of biomedical research, where the goal is to gain an understanding of how some detail of the human body works and use that new understanding to address some medical condition.

have existed for a very long time. The conditions under which the design must operate define the constraints on the solution. The design concept is then analyzed, modified, tested, improved, etc. using proven tools and possibly also relying on applied research where detailed information is lacking. Eventually, a solution that works acceptably well under all the constraints is produced, sold and put into practice, and that's the point when one can say the design-based innovation has been realized. There is a chronological order from the statement of the problem, through the design, to the solution that is finally implemented, but there is nothing like a linear progression from science to product. In fact, design-driven innovation provides many examples of the reverse – of engineering giving rise to the science. Perhaps the most obvious example is the practical development of the steam engine that preceded the scientific basis for the Second Law of Thermodynamics[33] by some five decades, and the First Law by three quarters of a century.[34]

There is another fundamental difference between research-based and design-based innovation. Briefly put, "a scientist studies what is; an engineer creates what never was."[35] The consequence is that a design-based innovation intended to meet a particular need is not unique; different engineers might design entirely different solutions using different materials in different configurations and with different operating principles, but all of them of course governed by the same laws of physics, chemistry, biology, mathematics, etc. In research-based innovation, the range of possible innovations is far smaller; they all derive from the same research result, or item of new knowledge.[36] This reasoning

---

[33] The Carnot cycle was introduced in 1824 by Sadi Carnot in *Reflections on the Motive Power of Fire.*

[34] Rudolf Clausius. 1850. "On the moving force of heat and the laws of heat which may be deduced therefrom," paper published in *Annalen der Physik.*

[35] Theodore von Karman quoted by Henry Petrosky, a distinguished American engineer who writes very informatively and eloquently on this subject, in his latest book, Henry Petrosky. 2010. *The Essential Engineer.* New York: Knopf. That book has two chapters entitled "Research and Development" and "Development and Research" that are particularly relevant to the present discussion.

[36] For potential investors in a research-based innovation being commercialized by a new venture, this traceability of the innovation to a particular documented research result may offer a welcome validation of the idea.

also suggests that a design-based innovation might become commoditized more quickly than a research-based innovation. Once the need has been defined and a product that meets it introduced in the market, engineers working for competing companies might design a great variety of different ways of meeting the same need that would not violate the patents of the lead producer, and different competing solutions – rather than imitations – begin appearing on the market. In research-based innovation, on the other hand, an imitator would have to come up with a way of achieving the same effect with different science, or wait for the patents to expire.

In striving for precision in dealing with the many kinds of innovation, we will take the time to introduce the language of innovation. We shall use common 'words that everybody knows,' but give them the precise definitions needed for present purposes. We shall define 'invention' and show how it differs from innovation. Three words that are often confused in popular writing, namely 'science', 'engineering' and 'technology,' will each be defined, revealing both the differences between them and the connections among them. The activities or processes of 'research', 'development', and also the hybrid acronym 'R&D' will be specified in detail and contrasted. We shall look into the meaning of 'creativity', 'imagination', and 'design', as well as 'entrepreneurship', 'commercialization' and 'marketing', and show the differences and complementarities among them. Careful definitions of these and other terms are needed because they each play a role in the complex process of innovation, and we need to understand precisely how their different roles fit together.

### Innovation systems

Innovation doesn't happen as an isolated act. First, there has to be a new idea, and then it must be put into action. The new idea may be the work of one person or just a few, but putting it into action usually requires the complementary contributions of many different players in many different organizations who bring the necessary range of expertise, and it can take a lot of time. The actors (individuals, institutions, organizations, etc.) and actions involved in this process and the influences at play, are often grouped for discussion under the general label of an 'innovation system.' In fact, it will become clear that it is difficult to talk about innovation apart from an innovation system. The innovation system may be internal to an organization, local in the community, regional or national, depending on what unit of analysis is appropriate.

For example, the OECD has proposed an innovation system that has seven subsystems: a system of companies interacting with the education and research system through a system of intermediaries, a system of global demand to which the companies respond, a system of supporting infrastructure on which the companies depend, and a political system that creates a system of framework conditions that creates the environment within which the companies operate.[37]

But the whole idea of a national innovation system has its critics who say that there can be no such thing because the actions of the companies are managed 'bottom-up,' whereas the institutions and national policies to channel and support them are managed 'top-down.'[38] The policy makers and funders think they control the process, but in reality 'nobody's in charge!' The governance issue may seem of limited relevance at first glance but, in fact, it is important in producing a good match between policy and need.

At a more immediate and practical level, the idea of a Canadian national system of innovation that responds positively to good government policies and incentives is excessively optimistic. This is a country of strong provinces, and distinct regions within them, and the federal and provincial governments are two important sources of influence, but they exist among many others. The global economy is another source of influence, and a particularly important one for companies who do most of their business abroad. Moreover, local companies are very much affected by local factors, such as local culture, the local investment community, educational institutions, labour pool and many others. That means the national innovation system in Canada should perhaps be thought of as a national collection of regional innovation systems.

---

[37] OECD. 2005. "A Generic National Innovation System (NIS)," cited by Guy Stanley in his lecture "Cardwell's Law & Canadian Innovation," Telfer School of Management, University of Ottawa, November 25, 2010.

[38] Gilles Paquet. 2005. *The New Geo-Governance*. Ottawa: University of Ottawa Press.

With such qualifications, the term 'innovation system' will be used here to mean the collection of actors, actions and influences potentially affecting innovation at a particular place and time. We identify an 'innovation ecosystem' as all the components of the innovation system that actually relate to a particular innovation or innovator, so there may be multiple innovation ecosystems functioning within the same innovation system. We will show that both macro and micro views of the innovation system can be useful. An innovation system that produces a stream of innovations that significantly enhance wealth creation will be considered healthy; it will be deemed weak if the innovations are sporadic and enjoy only little success in the market.

A term related to the innovation system is the 'innovation cluster.' Cluster is a suggestive and intuitive term, but we will define it narrowly. An innovation cluster will be taken to mean a grouping of innovating companies and supporting organizations that is concentrated geographically, and focused on one sector of business or industry. The world's best known high-tech cluster is, of course, Silicon Valley, CA but there are many others in many countries and working in many sectors. The reason is clear – companies clustered in close proximity to one another enjoy substantial benefits. First, they find their competitors close at hand, and that means that not only is competitive information 'in the air' but also that local cooperative measures that benefit them all might be feasible. Second, their concentration creates demand that attracts dynamic services, such as the venture capital industry, IP law offices, innovation intermediaries, specialized business consultants, etc. Third, some companies may become one another's customers and suppliers as supply chains are developed. Fourth, employees of the clustered companies communicate easily and frequently, often in the context of local social activities. They also frequently change jobs among the companies. This aids in the diffusion of new technology and in collaboration on projects, and creates a natural environment for open innovation. It also helps build up a stable reservoir of highly-qualified people (HQP) that is a resource to all members. The stability derives from the fact that if their particular company fails, the HQP are likely to find new jobs within the cluster. Moreover, the IP of the failed company is known and is therefore likely to be acquired and put to use quickly.

But clusters don't just happen. Many are located close to strong research universities because students or faculty started some of the early companies. Once again, Silicon Valley is a great example, with Stanford University as the anchor university and Hewlett-Packard as the iconic innovative company. In other cases, the cluster formed not only close to a university, but also near a large anchor company. An example of this is the high-tech cluster in Ottawa that grew up around Nortel Networks (and its predecessor companies). Nortel is now gone, but that cluster still benefits from the presence of two universities and a concentration of national laboratories. And clusters don't happen quickly. The Waterloo cluster took about fifty years to emerge. It has both an anchor university (University of Waterloo) and an anchor company (RIM). It also enjoys the advantage of being located in a community that has traditionally been both very enterprising and cooperative.

Recognizing the local and national economic advantages of successful clusters, governments try to give them a quick start. Placing a government laboratory near an existing university, and adding some financial support programs for new ventures seems to be the standard approach. However, it is still too early to see if that alone is sufficient to achieve long-term success, or whether that success also requires some favourable combination of local historical, cultural and sociological factors that is easier to see in hindsight than to predict.

## Last words

Most of the topics raised in this overview have been studied in detail by economists, sociologists and other scholars in the new discipline of 'innovation studies,' and have given rise to an extensive scholarly literature. We will draw on some of this in the book. Broader studies, more oriented to producing a more practical understanding and action have been undertaken by think-tanks, governments, consultants and others, with a policy orientation, and often with useful results. However, this 'grey' literature is scattered, and of variable quality, since it is not generally peer-reviewed. We will draw on that literature too, exercising both discrimination and caution. One important example that spans both groups is the recent report of the Expert Panel on Business Innovation of the Council of Canadian Academies to which we have already referred. It is a big-picture study that draws extensively on the scholarly literature as well as on important references in the grey literature, and it has itself been subjected to detailed expert peer review.

# CHAPTER 2

## THE CASE FOR MORE INNOVATION IN CANADA

*Moving to a higher level of national prosperity is not like scaling a mountain. It is much more like climbing up the down-escalator. You have to keep at it; if you want to get higher, you must go faster. You may never get as high as you want to go, but if you slow down, you'll go backwards.*

### Introduction

This chapter argues that Canada needs more innovation. The case is made that more innovation in the Canadian economy is needed to deal with our immediate economic challenge – note that it's 'challenge,' not 'crisis,' and that calls for strategic measures and not an emergency response. So innovation isn't a buzzword, or a 'nice to have,' or the policy of a particular government. It's something we need for the most important of strategic reasons – to maintain the quality of life of people in this country. It's purposeful change that must succeed because its purpose is essential for Canada's future.

The second main point in the chapter is that Canada has much of what it takes to succeed. We are a well educated and diverse population, living in a country richly endowed with natural resources, and strong in the knowledge and skills of science and engineering that are essential to creating value in today's economy. The best of Canadian businesses have put these factors to use and enjoyed some spectacular successes both in Canada and abroad, and what we need now is many more such successes. There is no need to search for any 'secret sauce' to produce the winning recipe. The answer is right in front of us – it is to develop a national strategy that focuses our recognized strengths on solving the problem, and then execute it skilfully. We need to overcome the fragmentation that we keep complaining about – the jurisdictional, political, cultural, geographic, sectoral, disciplinary, institutional and all the other kinds of fragmentation that divide our efforts and weaken our chances for success. We need to identify our successes and build on them, learn from our failures and then walk away from them. We need to bring the resources of our private and public sectors together, align them in a common thrust, and use them consistently. We must recognize that we are competing with the world, and stick with it for how ever long it takes.

To describe this pressure for more innovation in Canada we begin with a paradox. Canada is a very wealthy country, one of the wealthiest in the world. Our prosperity, as measured by gross domestic product (GDP) per capita, is about 3.4 times the world average,[1] and close to that of most industrialized countries. And there are many reasons to be satisfied with our quality of life. But, surprisingly, it is turning out that Canada is not prosperous enough. Evidence is mounting that our current prosperity is insufficient to meet all the truly important needs that are being identified across the land. There is a growing number of well-documented pressing needs and serious problems that we are not able to meet adequately. We can't afford to fund the necessary solutions fully, or quickly enough, or at all.

The necessary remedies range from the social, such as a significant reduction in child poverty, to the physical, such as the restoration of crumbling infrastructure in our big cities.[2] But

---

[1] In 2011, Canada had about 0.5% of the world's population, and about 1.7% of its GDP. Those numbers combine to suggest a GDP/capita that is 3.4 times the world average. In 2005, that number had been close to 3.6.

[2] Readers can assemble the lists of such needs for themselves just by paying attention to the media for a couple of weeks. In addition to health and education that are dealt with separately in the text, here is one list (in no particular order) of what is needed, what has been promised, and what isn't being funded adequately: reducing child poverty; providing safe water in every community; improving the standard of living in Aboriginal communities; reducing homelessness; upgrading dwellings to cut energy consumption; reducing the environmental footprint of a broad range of industrial activities; increasing the training capacity of the Canadian Forces; adding essential east-west connections to the electric power grid; eliminating landfills for urban solid waste; acquiring a modern fleet of fixed-wing search-and-rescue aircraft for Northern Canada;

looming above them all is an even bigger and more threatening challenge that is an inevitable consequence of demographics.

Our population is aging, people are living longer, and the proportion of those of working age is declining, in spite of the inflow of immigrants. The percentage of Canadians no longer in the work force is rising and the percentage of those working, on whom the economy depends, is falling. We are entering an era when the proportion of the population that consumes wealth will grow relative to the proportion that creates wealth, and this discrepancy will continue increasing.[3] More than that, the growing population of old people creates a new kind of demand on the health care system, a demand for which it was not designed – the management of chronic diseases for an increasing number of elderly people who will live with those diseases for a longer time.

Public spending on health care has been growing for years, and already represents the largest item of public expenditure of the provincial governments. The second largest item, spending on education, has been growing much more slowly, and is already proving inadequate in many ways. The threatening challenge is a trade-off between the two. Will education of the young have to be starved to feed health care for the old, or will health care have to be starved to feed education? That would be a terrible decision for a society to face, and we must do all we

building research facilities and icebreakers for the Arctic; repairing and upgrading bridges and tunnels and improving the transportation infrastructure to make it safe and remove traffic hazards and bottlenecks; transferring 0.7% of GDP as foreign aid to emerging nations; restoring and protecting natural environments at risk; increasing the availability and use of mass transit to reduce urban traffic congestion and energy waste; putting Canada's cultural institutions on a sustainable financial basis; bringing passenger rail transport into the modern age; expanding broad-band access to the population of rural Canada; building up a strong and functional diplomatic and trade presence in strategic locations; ending the dumping or spilling of untreated sewage into inland or coastal waters; etc., etc. Funding for these things is required from both public and private sources in various proportions and arrangements.

[3] The "dependence ratio" is the number of youth (ages 0 to 19) and seniors (ages 65 and older) per 100 people of working age (20 to 64). Statistics Canada http:// statcan.gc.ca [accessed August 7, 2012] shows that in 2006 there were very nearly 20 youth and 40 seniors per 100 people in the working ages, for a total dependence ratio of 60. This number will rise to 65 in 2022, 70 in 2017, 75 in 2030, and 84 in 2056, made up of 34 youth and 50 seniors. This will represent a 25% increase in the proportion of seniors.

can to become prosperous enough to avoid the necessity for such a trade-off, because the nation is responsible for the well-being of its people of all ages.

Fortunately, there is a way out. It is to resolve the wealth paradox. Yes, Canada is relatively very wealthy, but we cannot afford to be complacent. We must become even wealthier. If we are to live within our means – which we must do to keep our prosperity sustainable – and our means are not sufficient to meet all our important needs, then we must increase our means. There is no other way. We cannot meet our needs by doing more of the same and getting deeper in debt. The interest on our current debt is already eating up a lot of what our work now produces, and we cannot afford to have it eat up more. We must create more wealth so that there might be enough to buy both good health care for the elderly and good education for the young, and also to do all the other things that need doing, including reducing the debt we already carry. At the macroeconomic level, this calls for a sustained enhancement in economic growth, a sustained rate of GDP growth well beyond the 'business as usual' trend. Critics will say that there is nothing new in this. Enhancing economic growth has long been a preoccupation of governments and economists, and the target of both macroeconomic and microeconomic policies. That is true, of course, but it is the 'business as usual' that got us where we are. The new approach described here is to increase innovation specifically to accelerate GDP growth.

Innovation comes into the picture when we consider the microeconomic view of how individual enterprises might go about increasing their wealth creation. We will argue that there must be more innovation in the private sector to keep increasing the creation of both private and public wealth. At the same time, there must also be more innovation in the public sector where wealth is consumed, to keep raising the effectiveness and efficiency of meeting society's needs with the resources available.

However, the means to increase wealth creation in Canada do not lie wholly within our borders, and are not wholly within our control. Canada is a trading nation within an open and increasingly knowledge-based global economy. We need to know how Canada is positioned in that world economy, what opportunities that position offers, and how they might be seized. That is a huge subject, of course, and the work of many experts in many disciplines. However, in what follows, we will produce a simple but useful big picture by combining three perspectives. First, we will look at a few basic atlas-level data about the world's largest 25 economies, as well as seven small industrialized countries that are often held up to us as models, to see what they show and what they suggest about Canada's prospects. Secondly, we will look at relative prosperity of many of these economies and their capabilities in science and engineering. Third, we shall look at the important flows between Canada and the global economy, and the needs and opportunities for innovation that they imply. And finally, we shall put these things together to argue that enhanced innovation in Canada is a necessity.

## *Canada's place in the world, in a few numbers*

We begin with some very basic data about Canada and see what they tell us about our prospects and our challenges. The numbers suggest some of our potential and describe some of the conditions under which Canadians must operate. They are facts that need to be taken into account when we try to learn from comparisons with other countries. Table 2.1 shows data for 2011-12 for the world's 25 largest economies.[4] The table also includes data on seven small industrialized economies that are often held up as models for Canadians in one or another aspect of economic performance. On the basis of 2011 GDP in $ (PPP),[5] Canada has the 14th largest economy. We were 11th in 2005. Our membership in the G-8 is a courtesy, of course, but by coincidence our GDP per capita is the eighth highest in the table.

At 34.3 million, the Canadian population is smaller than 20 of the big economies and much larger than any of the seven small ones. That population turns out to be too small to create the domestic market to pay for commercializing many of the modern products that we have the technical capacity to invent. This suggests immediately that Canadian firms making technology products must depend greatly on export sales. Exporting can't be an afterthought; the products and the companies must become

---

[4] Data from the *CIA World Factbook* [accessed on the Internet, May 4, 2012].
[5] Local currencies converted to US dollars on the basis of purchasing-power parity.

export-ready at the earliest possible stage. They must be 'born global.' This can be done; the economies in Table 2.1 that have populations even smaller than our own have been doing it successfully for years in many sectors. Their success stories are a treasure trove of lessons for Canadians to learn.

The data of Table 2.1 don't show anything about the make-up of the populations. Canada's population is very diverse; it includes significant numbers of people who have community or even family connections with all our trading partners, and many of them are students in the Canadian post-secondary system. This presents an opportunity to develop support for Canada's international trade with extraordinarily well informed and culture-specific marketing on a massive scale, an opportunity that could provide the basis of a substantial advantage for Canadian exporters. At the moment, however, there is no national effort in place to exploit this advantage in a strategic way.

In area, Canada is huge, second only to Russia, and larger than each of the US and China by an area about the size of Germany or Japan. The enormous area immediately implies great quantities of a great variety of natural resources, but also great distances. Canada is a northern land that spans 4.5 time zones in longitude and more than 40 degrees in latitude, from about 42 deg. N. to the high Arctic. Eighty percent of the population live in just three large cities and a dozen medium and smaller ones that are widely spaced in a thin strip close to our southern border with the United States. The country faces challenges of long-distance transportation of people and goods between its centres of population and industrial activity, of difficult access to far-flung small communities, of remoteness of the natural resources from their markets, and of effective environmental stewardship over a vast and varied land. Combined with a climate that ranges from moderate to severe, these physical factors make Canada an expensive country to operate. Our fixed costs are very high.

## TABLE 2.1 Positioning Canada by the numbers, 2011

| country | GDP (2011 PPP) $ trillion | pop. 2012 est. million | area 000 sq.km | coastline km | GDP/capita 2011 PPP $ |
|---|---|---|---|---|---|
| US | 15.04 | 313.85 | 9,631.42 | 19,924 | 48,100 |
| China | 11.29 | 1,343.24 | 9,596.96 | 14,500 | 8,400 |
| India | 4.463 | 1,205.10 | 3,287.59 | 7,000 | 3,700 |
| Japan | 4.389 | 127.37 | 377.80 | 29,751 | 34,300 |
| Germany | 3.085 | 81.3 | 357.02 | 2,389 | 37,900 |
| Russia | 2.38 | 138.08 | 17,075.20 | 37,653 | 16,700 |
| Brazil | 2.282 | 205.72 | 8,511.97 | 7,491 | 11,600 |
| UK | 2.25 | 63.05 | 244.82 | 12,429 | 35,900 |
| France | 2.214 | 65.63 | 547.03 | 3,427 | 35,000 |
| Italy | 1.822 | 61.26 | 301.23 | 7,600 | 30,100 |
| Mexico | 1.657 | 114.97 | 1,972.55 | 9,330 | 15,100 |
| S. Korea | 1.549 | 48.86 | 98.48 | 2,413 | 31,700 |
| Spain | 1.411 | 47.04 | 504.78 | 4,946 | 30,600 |
| Canada | 1.389 | 34.3 | 9,984.67 | 202,080 | 40,300 |
| Indonesia | 1.121 | 248.22 | 1,904.57 | 54,716 | 4,700 |
| Turkey | 1.026 | 79.75 | 783.56 | 7,200 | 14,600 |
| Iran | 0.929 | 78.87 | 1,648.19 | 3,180 | 12,200 |
| Australia | 0.918 | 22.02 | 7,686.85 | 25,760 | 40,800 |
| Taiwan | 0.885 | 23.11 | 35.98 | 1,566 | 37,900 |
| Poland | 0.766 | 38.42 | 312.68 | 440 | 20,100 |
| Argentina | 0.71 | 42.19 | 2,780.40 | 4,989 | 17,400 |
| Netherlands | 0.706 | 16.73 | 41.53 | 451 | 42,300 |
| Saudi Arabia | 0.677 | 26.53 | 2,149.69 | 2,640 | 24,000 |
| Thailand | 0.601 | 67.09 | 513.12 | 3,219 | 9,700 |
| South Africa | 0.555 | 48.81 | 1,219.09 | 2,798 | 11,000 |
| Sweden | 0.379 | 9.103 | 449.96 | 3,218 | 40,600 |
| Switzerland | 0.341 | 7.66 | 41.29 | 0 | 43,400 |
| Singapore | 0.314 | 5.35 | 0.697 | 193 | 59,900 |
| Norway | 0.265 | 4.71 | 324.22 | 25,148 | 53,300 |
| Israel | 0.235 | 7.59 | 20.77 | 273 | 31,000 |
| Finland | 0.197 | 5.26 | 338.14 | 1,250 | 38,300 |
| Ireland | 0.182 | 4.72 | 70.28 | 1,448 | 39,500 |

Source: *CIA World Factbook* [accessed on the Internet on May 4, 2012].

Data on the EU treated as a single economy are not included. Note that the numbers given for GDP/cap are not exactly the ratio of the tabulated GDP to the tabulated population because the individual estimates are not perfectly aligned. For example, the world totals given are: population of 7,022 million, GDP of 78.95 $ trillion, and GDP/capita of $11,800, but the GDP and population numbers would combine to give $11,240.

Canada's coastline is by far the longest in the world, almost four times Indonesia's which is the second longest, and more than five times longer than Russia's. On that basis alone, one might expect that Canada would be a strong maritime nation, but that is not the case. We have a small and declining fishery, a small shipbuilding industry, and only a modest amount of off-shore extraction of oil. Whatever economic opportunities are presented by our coastlines along the Atlantic, Pacific and Arctic oceans remain largely unrealized. Today much of that coastline is frozen, that is in the Arctic islands, but climate warming is changing that. That may or may not make it easier to develop new off-shore resources, but it will certainly produce changes to coastal communities that may require significant (and expensive) adaptation.

And our geography has political and cultural implications as well. Regionalism is strong in Canada, with big differences from east to west and strong local connections across the border from north to south. Indeed, it often seems that north-south thinking comes more naturally to Canadians than does east-west thinking. That makes the United States our obvious and largest trading partner, and the greatest current source of economic and cultural influence. But the north-south bias is something that will have to change if Canada is to become a true participant in the global economy in which both Europe and Asia are emerging as great economic blocks.

At first glance, Table 2.1 is good economic news. Canada's GDP per capita, which is a good measure of prosperity, was exceeded significantly in 2011 only by those of Singapore, Norway, Switzerland, Netherlands, and the US, and only slightly by Australia and Sweden.[6] But the comparison with earlier data shows a trend that is less encouraging.[7] Canadian GDP/cap grew by 23 percent from 1995 to 2011, a number slightly below the middle of the pack. The corresponding numbers for Australia and Germany grew by 28 percent, China by 35 percent, Brazil by 36 percent, Sweden by 37 percent, Israel by 40 percent, Taiwan by 42 percent, Mexico by 51 percent, and Russia and South Korea by 56 percent. That performance by the Canadian economy is not reassuring, for all the reasons described at the beginning

[6] Refers only to the economies listed in Table 2.1; if we include some smaller economies not listed in that table, then Luxembourg, Belgium and the United Arab Emirates would have to be added.

[7] For example, the corresponding table for 2005, published by T.A. Brzustowki. 2008. *The Way Ahead: Meeting Canada's Productivity Challenge*. Ottawa: University of Ottawa Press, p.17.

of the chapter. We are not in a crisis, but we do face a challenge in the relative decline of our prosperity. We have no room for complacency; strategic measures are called for.

## The prosperity-competence nexus

Is there a connection between a nation's excellence in research in science and engineering and its prosperity? Yes, there is, but it's not nearly as direct as one might assume. All research costs money and it consumes wealth, largely public wealth. Even the best of research that is taken up by industry is a cost to society, until it eventually leads to new wealth creation with new products that succeed in the market. Even then, their producers begin to create net private and public wealth and contribute to prosperity only when the new products have earned enough sales revenue to recover the costs of the R&D and commercialization. Simply put, a nation's research excellence in science and engineering is a necessary condition for its prosperity, but it is far from sufficient.

The prosperity-competence context of innovation in Canada is shown in Figure 2.1. The vertical axis is national prosperity relative to the world average (data for 2005 converted to dollars at PPP).[8] The horizontal axis is an indicator of national excellence in science and technology. That indicator is the number, per million, of general population, of the published research papers in science and engineering that were among the 1 percent most often cited papers in the world in a four-year period ending four years earlier. (This seems to be a reasonable time lag between the publication of research and its economic impact.) It is based on an important paper by David King,[9] when he was Science Advisor to the government of the United Kingdom (UK). One can think of it as a quality-adjusted measure of the intensity of a nation's research activity.

It would be naïve to suggest that the publication of excellent research papers directly increases national prosperity. Wealth is created by the private sector, so the capabilities of the scientists and engineers doing research to create new knowledge must somehow be transferred to the scientists and engineers in industry

[8] The prosperity data come from the *CIA World Factbook* [accessed on the Internet, June 2006].

[9] David A. King. 2004. "The scientific impact of nations," *NATURE*, 430 (July): 311-316.

who will use that new knowledge. That diffusion of science and engineering research excellence and its transformation into science and engineering competence in the economy occurs in many ways. The most obvious and most important is the employment of graduates who are taught by professors who do research. They arrive on the job with an understanding of the fundamentals of the key technologies, an awareness of some recent developments in their field, and an idea of where to look for more. More direct contacts between universities and industry in the form of research partnerships, research contracts, and faculty consulting are very important as well. For these reasons, an indicator based on the excellence and intensity of research publication is a good indicator of national competence in science and engineering.

But the diffusion doesn't stop at national borders. Research is international. The laws of physics are the same in all countries. Research papers are published openly in international journals. International peer review is the principal instrument of quality control in most disciplines, and it is also an effective instrument for the international diffusion of new knowledge. Engineering and science education is international as well. Students are mobile, both at the graduate and undergraduate levels. The leading textbooks are translated into many languages. Patents are published describing how inventions work and how they are made, and patent applications are usually filed in more than one country.[10] Multinational companies diffuse their technologies through foreign direct investment; there is outsourcing of production and even of R&D, and international supply chains are routine. This is what it means to have a global knowledge-based economy: people everywhere have access to knowledge from everywhere, and smart people everywhere can learn to use it for innovation. This, of course, includes both design-based innovation, namely new use of prior knowledge, and research-based innovation, namely new use of new knowledge. An obvious consequence is that any national advantage in science and engineering competence is not permanent; it must be actively maintained, and one way of doing that at the upstream end is through excellent research and postgraduate education.

[10] For example, patents for the same invention granted by the US, EU, and Japan are common and referred to as 'Triadic patents.'

## FIGURE 2.1 Correlation between nations' relative prosperity and quality-adjusted intensity of their research in science and engineering

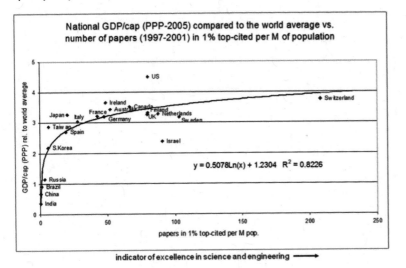

Source: T.A. Brzustowski. 2007. "National prosperity and excellence in science and engineering research," *Optimumonline*, 37 (2): 25-36.

Canada is obviously competitive with the major economies.

Figure 2.1 shows a strong correlation between prosperity and competence in science and engineering for 21 of the economies listed in Table 2.1. It is a snapshot in time of the global knowledge-based economy. Canada is in the mainstream, towards the top of the G-8 countries. But correlation is not causality. The data include several countries that have no natural resources to speak of, and others that are richly endowed. They also include countries that have a long history of science, engineering, and industry and others where they are much more recent.

Cause and effect are different in all these cases. For Canada, the historical dependence of our prosperity on the natural resource industries, and the relatively recent emergence of broad Canadian research excellence in science and engineering, suggest that our wealth from natural resources has allowed us to build up the research excellence, and not the other way around. But whatever its genesis, high competence in science and engineering is now in place in Canadian industry, and available to be used to enhance wealth creation. The direction of the causal arrow between prosperity and research excellence now needs to be turned toward prosperity.

### Key cross-border flows in the knowledge-based economy

Figure 2.2 shows the context of innovation in Canada in terms of the flows of knowledge, capital, and traded goods and services between Canada and the rest of the world.[11] The economy is open to the world and the flows of knowledge are more important than ever before, so calling the economy open, global and knowledge-based makes sense, even though commodities continue to be important.

The arrows[12] at the top show the flows of codified new knowledge – mainly published, refereed research papers – arising from research in Canada, predominantly in universities, research hospitals and government laboratories. Canadians publish about 7 percent of the world's research papers,[13] but the other 93 percent are available to us in the international research literature. Since the Canadian 7 percent cover most of the important areas of advancing knowledge and meet international standards set by the peer review process, Canadian researchers are able to understand the other 93 percent and to build on that knowledge as well. In effect, our 7 percent is the admission ticket to 100 percent. This is a very strong argument for spending public wealth to support excellent research that might today seem to have no connection with new wealth creation. History shows that such connections may emerge indirectly, unexpectedly and only after a long delay, and that even if they don't in specific cases, the cultural impact of excellent research on the intellectual competence of the nation is always positive.

The arrows at the 3 o'clock position show the flows in and out of Canada of highly qualified people (HQP) who carry tacit

[11] Modified slightly from Figure 4.1 in T.A. Brzustowski. 2008. *The Way Ahead: Meeting Canada's Productivity Challenge.* Ottawa: University of Ottawa Press, p.62.

[12] The width of the corresponding arrows is intended to convey the relative proportions only in a very rough sense.

[13] These are clearly the best papers and the ones that matter the most. The Canadian 7% includes 5% published with international co-authors. Source: http://www.Science.gc.ca – Higher Education [accessed October 26, 2011].

knowledge – education, understanding, experience, know-how, etc. The two arrows are shown as equal, because the balance of 'brain drain' vs. 'brain gain' shifts from time to time. The inflow of tacit knowledge can have a big impact on innovation in Canada if skilled new arrivals find opportunities to use their skills. This applies to HQP who arrive with an advanced education, as well as to entrepreneurial economic immigrants who see new opportunities to create wealth in this country. Unfortunately, the record seems to be that many HQP immigrants to Canada find barriers against using their skills to the fullest. This will have to change because worldwide competition for talent is already emerging as an important feature of the global economy.

### FIGURE 2.2 The Flows of Knowledge, Capital, People and Trade Between Canada and the World

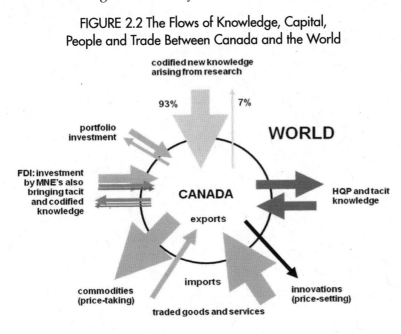

Source: Modified from Figure 4.1 in T.A. Brzustowski. 2008. *The Way Ahead: Meeting Canada's Productivity Challenge*. Ottawa: University of Ottawa Press, p. 62.

A better picture would have a greater flow of innovations in the Canadian exports. These might include entirely new products, as well as commodities made more valuable with additional processing.

The flows of capital, tacit knowledge and codified knowledge associated with foreign direct investment (FDI) are shown in the triplets of arrows at 9 o'clock. This is a very important activity since it builds up the receptor nation's economic capacity. For example, when Toyota built its assembly plant in Cambridge, ON, there was an inward flow to Canada of capital that paid for building and equipping the plant. There was also an inward flow of codified knowledge: the documentation of the technology in the products, the manufacturing processes, the tools and training manuals, etc. As well, there was an inflow of tacit knowledge in the form of Japanese managers and workers experienced in Toyota methods, trainers for Canadian workers, etc. All three have added up to a new industrial capacity in Canada. The corresponding outward flows occur when a Canadian company makes a direct investment abroad.

Inbound FDI provides both a challenge and an opportunity for innovation in Canada. The Canadian branch plants of multinational enterprises (MNE) that receive the investments must compete for projects with the other branch plants of the same MNE. The best of them develop new ways of creating value in the firm, they win product mandates – sometimes for the whole world – and they grow. The quality of the Canadian workforce and the national competence in science and engineering are important factors in such success.

The single arrows at 10 o'clock show the flows of capital associated with a very different kind of investment, namely portfolio investment. This represents people abroad buying shares in Canadian businesses, and vice-versa. It involves no flows of knowledge *per se*, but managed wisely, the inflow of this kind of investment capital can support the growth of the capacity of Canadian firms for wealth creation.

Finally, at the bottom we have the flows which enable Canadians to pay our way in the world, and buy all the imports for which we have a great appetite. These are our exports in traded goods and services out into world markets. The import flows are shown as well. For simplicity and emphasis, the traded goods and services have been divided into two mutually-exclusive categories: commodities and innovations. Commodities are goods or services available from many sources that are not differentiated. They don't differ appreciably in functionality, quality, availability, etc. Innovations are new products, or products differentiated by functionality, performance, quality, etc., that are available from only a very small number of producers.[14] For present purposes, it is important to note that the producers of commodities must take the market price for them. In contrast, the producers of innovations can set their own prices – with high margins to recover the costs of R&D – and invest in developing the next generation of products.

Canada's exports are now and have been, historically, much more commodities than innovations. Oil, gas, grains and oilseeds of various kinds, beef and pork, lumber, wood pulp, coal and other products of our natural resource and agricultural industries have long been the mainstay of our commodity exports. The BlackBerry smart phone, Pratt & Whitney Canada aircraft engines, SMART Technologies whiteboards, Bombardier aircraft , CAE training simulators, and Open Text software are examples of recent spectacularly successful Canadian innovations sold to the world, but there are too few of them.

Canadian imports are much more in the form of innovations than commodities. Consumer electronics provides the most visible innovations, but other areas include many of the high-end items available in specialty boutiques and department stores. The commodity imports include various foods and much of the stuff that fills the shelves of department and discount stores. Ironically, our imports also include just about all the new tools, machinery and process equipment for the natural resource industries on which so much of our wealth depends.

This is not a good balance between exports and imports for Canada as an industrialized country. In theory, a better balance would have more innovations and fewer commodities in the export mix, and fewer innovations and more commodities in the import mix.[15] But in practice, it is unlikely that Canadians' tastes for the great range of desirable imported goods available from around the world will change any time soon. And except maybe for the wine industry, Canada doesn't have, and probably never did have, the domestic producers that could

---

[14] A more detailed discussion of the definitions of commodities and innovations is presented in chapter 4.

[15] That would show up in Figure 3.1 as a thicker export arrow on the innovation side, and a thinner export arrow on the commodity side, and vice-versa on the import side.

compete successfully with imports that are most attractive to consumers. That means that the best strategy might be to concentrate on the export mix, on increasing the value of what Canadians sell to the world. Two ways of doing that seem clear. First, given Canada's great endowment of natural resources, we should develop and export more innovations based on our natural resources. Instead of shipping raw or only lightly processed materials, Canadian producers should ship more valuable, new intermediate goods or finished products. And second, Canadian industry should take advantage of the country's strengths in science and engineering, and develop entirely new products with new scientific and engineering knowledge embedded.

## The link between innovation and economic growth

The case has now been made that there is a need to increase Canada's prosperity, and that at the macro level one can see opportunities for doing that. Innovation enters the picture when we begin to consider just how that might be done at the micro level.

The link between innovation and economic growth has been one of the important topics of economics for a very long time, and the subject of a great deal of research and scholarship. In this section and in the rest of the book, the issue will be approached in practical terms at the micro level. We will discuss what companies actually do to create wealth, and what they might do to create more. At that level, we will encounter examples of technological growth that seem endogenous to the local innovation system, with new technologies and capabilities originating from scientific and engineering research and education within the system. But we will also see examples of ready-made technologies imported into an innovation system from an outside source, and subsequently used to develop new products unique to that innovation system, a scenario with elements more suggestive of adaptation and design.

Recall that prosperity was defined as GDP/capita.[16] In turn, the most helpful definition of GDP for present purposes is that GDP is the total of value added throughout the economy in a given period of time, usually a year. The dimension of time is essential in this discussion because the challenge of raising prosperity then becomes transformed into the challenge of increasing the rate at which value is added in economic activity. At the micro level, that rate can be thought of as the sum for all products of value-added per unit of product multiplied by the volume of product sold.

It then follows immediately that the rate at which value is added can be increased in two ways: by increasing the volume sold, or by increasing the value-added per unit. Doing both at the same time is even better, of course. Innovation comes into the picture in both approaches, but innovations that increase the unit value-added of product often turn out to be the more important.

A detailed discussion of value added and innovation follow later in the book, but for the moment a few examples might suffice to illustrate some issues.

First, consider increasing the rate of value added by increasing the volume produced, with no change to the product. Imagine a producer who sells a proven but undifferentiated product, with unused plant capacity to produce significantly more, and a market that will absorb more volume at the current price. In this idealized case, the producer need only open the tap wider to grow the rate of value added, and increase the rate of wealth creation. It would be hard to imagine that in such circumstances any informed producer would not already be operating at full capacity.

Now imagine the producer of a similar kind of product facing strong competition and struggling to retain market share in a limited market. With no change in the product, what might it mean to increase the volume? Increasing the volume produced,

---

[16] There is considerable discussion today about the appropriateness of the GDP/capita as a measure of prosperity, and many proposals exist for better gauges of the well-being of the people of a nation. Such proposals take into account values that are important in determining the quality of people's lives that cannot easily be expressed in economic terms. For present purposes, however, the traditional definitions of GDP and of prosperity as GDP/capita will suffice. This definition of prosperity has stood the test of time; it is woven into the first few pages of Adam Smiths great opus "… on the Wealth of Nations".

or even shipped, need not necessarily increase the volume of the sales on which the value-added depends. There might, in fact, be some short-term gain in sales volume, relying on retail promotions and the like, or an accumulation of unsold inventory in the hands of retail dealers, but in the long term a new equilibrium in the market would be established at a lower price. This would mean a lower value-added per unit of product, and no guarantee that the total rate of value-added by the enterprise would be increased.

So what else could be done? A third approach would be to continue to leave the product unchanged and try to grow market share at the expense of the competitors by buying more advertising, but this would involve a new purchased input cost that could eat into the total value added if the revenue increase were not sufficiently large. Another approach might be to try to develop new markets for the existing product, but once again that would cost money, and it might benefit the competition as well. It is worth noting that both these approaches to increasing the sales volume without changing the product would constitute marketing innovations for that particular producer. In this example and the ones above, the market and competing producers are taken to be global, unless special circumstances dictate otherwise.

Let's move on to another variation. The producer facing the same situation as in the last two examples decides to buy some new technology to reduce the cost of making the product. Once this new technology is installed, commissioned and paid for, and the workforce trained to use it, the input costs decline and the value-added per unit of the product rises. If sales price and sales volume were maintained, the result would be an increased total rate of value-added as a result of a process innovation. The producer taking this step would contribute more to prosperity, but not gain any lasting competitive advantage, since the same production technology would be readily available to the competition.

Now consider a very different situation, the extraction of a natural resource that is sold in the world commodity market as a raw material almost without any processing, like coal. The commodity market is deeply cyclical, with large fluctuations in both market demand and market price. An obvious strategy for increasing the value added in these sectors is to extract and ship more product at the time of commodity booms. However, a new set of considerations is starting to intrude in this area. In some sectors, all the resources that were easy to extract have already been used up. Further extraction is more difficult and expensive, and it may also carry a growing political cost if it leads to negative environmental impacts. As a result, increasing the rate of value added in these sectors by increasing the volume of shipments is not as easily done as it once was, and it could become even more difficult. Protecting this option for the future undoubtedly requires, among other things, process innovations that reduce the long-term environmental impacts of the extraction processes.

So much for increasing the volume but leaving the product unchanged. Now consider changing the product to increase its value-added per unit sold. One approach might be to differentiate the product slightly, making it more attractive to customers than the competition but still maintaining its traditional identity and market niche. Such a 'new and improved' model with some new features could be developed and offered at a higher price. The best outcome would be that the sales of the improved product increase, its unit value-added increases as well, and the total rate of creating value-added increases proportionately even more. This example combines a product innovation with a marketing innovation. Once again, it enhances prosperity but it produces only a temporary advantage for this particular producer, since product improvements can be made quickly and advertising campaigns mounted fast.

Now let's take a bigger step. The producer of a technology-rich but undifferentiated product invests in developing an entirely new 'next generation' follow-on product for the same market. The new product has game-changing new features and functions, offers the customer entirely new possibilities, and moves the market to a new level. It is offered at a premium price. This next generation product uses a new design incorporating new technology from suppliers, and is manufactured in a new simpler and cheaper process that also produces improved quality and leads to very high margins. The innovation takes the market by storm, and quickly achieves impressive growth in sales volume and market share, allowing the producer to take the earlier generation of cheaper products off the market and free up capacity for more new generation products. This producer has replaced a commodity product by a design-based innovation that, in turn, incorporates product innovations from suppliers, as well as process innovations. Both the unit value-added and the volume sold have increased, and this producer's rate of value added is much increased. This move enhances prosperity and gives the particular producer a competitive advantage that will last until competition from other producers has commoditized this product as well.

All the illustrations so far have dealt with established firms. Now consider a new venture created expressly to commercialize a new invention suggested by the results of research or by some new insight into market needs. If the commercialization succeeds, and the innovation finds a market and generates sufficient sales volume for long enough, then it becomes a new source of value added and wealth creation in the economy. This happens once the accumulated sales revenue exceeds the total costs of R&D and the other aspects of commercialization. Intellectual property considerations are key in determining how quickly this kind of product innovation becomes a commodity under the relentless competition in the market.

## The deal maker

At this point, we leave it to the good business sense of firms with established products to do what they need to do to grow by increasing their sales and reducing their costs through marketing and process innovations. The discussion will go on to concentrate on increasing wealth creation by creating and selling more valuable products. It is there that we will make the connection between more innovation and greater prosperity.

The definition of innovation that will drive our thinking in doing this is developed in more detail in chapter 4. It is:

• **Innovation** is a new way that value is added or created.[17]

Product innovation is a transient process. In the successful case, an idea emerges, an invention follows, a product is proposed, commercialization is launched, and eventually a product reaches the market where it appears as an innovation. That usually takes years, rather than months. If the innovation succeeds, the positive cash flow of sales revenues will eventually

---

[17] This definition is worded in such a way as to emphasize that an innovation is a new idea that has been put into practice. The easier wording 'Innovation is a new way of adding or creating value' does not suggest as strongly that the idea is implemented. A new way of doing something may or may not be put to use.

recover the cost of the original R&D, of the commercialization process that includes the failures and the exploration of dead ends along the way, as well as of the first product improvements. After that, the sales begin to return a net profit. However, at some point along the way, other companies in the sector realize that there's something new and good out there and set out to compete with it.

In doing that, their job is easier than it was for the original producer. Depending on the nature of the beast, and the protection of the intellectual property (IP) embodied in the original innovation, they will copy it, or imitate it somehow, or design around it to deliver the same value to the customer in an entirely different way, or perhaps leap-frog it entirely and shift the market. In any case, their job is easier, because they have the original as a target to guide them.[18] The result will be that sooner or later the original expensive innovation in the market will become a cheaper commodity product, undifferentiated in function or quality from the many competing products that have followed its lead. When that happens, the producer of the original innovation will no longer be able to set the price and enjoy the high margins of the innovation, but will have to take the lower commodity market price. A familiar illustration of this process is the commoditization of the digital camera that has been taking place for the last six years.

So what can an innovative company do to remain profitable in such a competitive environment? The advice is given in a short and powerful paragraph by Porter and Stern:[19]

> The defining challenge for competitiveness has shifted, especially in advanced nations and regions. The challenges of a decade ago were to restructure, lower cost, and raise quality. Today, continued operational improvement is a given, and many companies are able to acquire and deploy the best current technology. In advanced nations, producing standard products using standard methods will not sustain competitive advantage. Companies must be able to innovate at the global frontier. **They must create and commercialize a stream**

---

[18] Perhaps helped by the process called reverse engineering.

[19] Michael E. Porter and Scott Stern. 2002. "Innovation: Location Matters" in *Innovation – Driving Product, Process, and Market Change*. Edward B. Roberts (ed.). New York: Jossey-Bass, p. 239.

*of new products and processes that shift the technology frontier, progressing as fast as their rivals catch up.* [emphasis added]

...provided, of course, that they also maintain the capacity to manufacture and market these products on a sufficient scale to meet the demand for them where and when it arises.

The last sentence in the quotation answers the question posed. Innovation is a transient process, and for long-term success it must also be a repeated process. The only remedy for commoditization is repeated innovation. The innovative company has to keep producing innovations faster than the competition can commoditize them. It will then always have some products on the market that are innovations for which it can set prices high enough to pay for the next round of innovation, in this way creating the economist's virtuous cycle, or the engineer's positive feedback, to feed its growth.

---

**The only remedy for commoditization is repeated innovation.**

---

## Innovation and competition

The statement by Porter and Stern quoted above has another very important implication. It describes the influence of competition on innovation. It is competition that drives the need for repeated innovation. Rival producers at home and abroad commoditize any innovation by eventually producing competing products that are very similar. That competition drives the original innovator (or any one of the rival companies) to produce another innovation that earns high margins, and the cycle continues. But what happens to the original innovation after it has become commoditized? On the supply side, the original innovator works to reduce production costs, and the rivals do the same. On the demand side, the consumer sees a growing selection of the (now) commodity product, with marginal improvements and a declining price.[20] This is a

---

[20] A clear illustration of this process at work is offered by the recent history of the digital camera. The basic 'point-and-shoot' digital camera has been commoditized over the last half dozen years, to the point that the color of the camera body has now become an important distinguishing feature in the market. And the field has moved on. Today, it is the digital single lens reflex

very attractive situation for consumers that continues until the product becomes obsolete, and is neither produced nor given technical support by the manufacturers.

What would happen in the absence of foreign competition in some particular sector that the nation decided to protect from competition by trade policy? If there were no foreign competition, there would be less pressure for commoditization, and less pressure to reduce costs or to create new and improved products. There would be little need to innovate. This would give the original producer the continuing advantage of a high margin, and little pressure to invest in R&D – in many ways a nice deal for the supply side, but at the price of serving a domestic market that wouldn't grow. And things would not be great on the demand side. The consumer would see little improvement in the product and no reduction in price, and few new products entering the market – all in contrast with a much more attractive situation in other countries.

In such a scenario, Canadian producers in a protected sector would find it difficult to enter foreign markets. Perhaps some would choose to develop a double structure of one arm serving the domestic market and a second arm serving the global market. But that second arm would have to be competitive and innovative to world standards, and would probably be set up outside of Canada.

We do have some protected sectors in Canada, (e.g., telecommunications, dairy industry, etc.) so what would happen to producers in such a sector if their protection were lifted? An immediate consequence would be the arrival of foreign competition on their doorstep. Their margins would fall, and they would have to start innovating successfully or fail. Would they succeed in making the change if the protection were phased out slowly enough? What would be the impact on the national GDP? Innovation would increase, but would wealth creation in Canada increase as well? The answers to these questions are not obvious, and might go either way depending on the details of what was done.

camera (DSLR) that is in process of being commoditized, with the prices dropping and the models offered by the competing manufacturers becoming more and more alike.

Since the national goal is to solve our prosperity challenge by enhancing innovation and creating more wealth in Canada by increasing the value of goods and services sold to the world, then from this point on our discussion will be limited to the sectors of the Canadian economy that are not protected and are open to global competition. With that qualification, we can start on the recipe for growth by increased innovation.

## *The recipe for growth by increased innovation*

In the sectors of the Canadian economy that are open to world trade and not protected:

- Companies that have not usually innovated should start innovating to sell more valuable products, ranging from current products that are made more valuable by additional work or downstream processing, all the way to entirely new 'value-added' products.
- Companies that have a record of innovation should step up their innovative activities to increase the flow of new products from their so-called 'innovation pipeline.'

This is a common-sense and obvious recipe, but at this point it is still seriously incomplete. It overlooks the fact that innovations don't just happen. They require the effort of some very special people who can spot opportunities to add or create value in new ways, and then seize and exploit these opportunities. Such people are called entrepreneurs. Entrepreneurs may have advanced skills in many different fields, but their common attributes are a rich imagination, a high tolerance for risk, a very deep understanding of people's needs in the markets they know, high personal energy, and great persistence. Their role in innovation is essential. For that reason, our definition of entrepreneurs is closely tied to the definition of innovation given above.

- **Entrepreneurs** are people who have the ability to see, seize and exploit opportunities to add or create value in new ways, and can tolerate the risks involved.

Another way of putting it is that:

- **Entrepreneurs** are people who see, seize and exploit opportunities for innovation in the face of risk.

There is no limit on the kinds of innovation involved. Entrepreneurs may innovate in products, processes, marketing, or business models, or any other means of creating value. This definition is far removed from labelling anyone who owns a (small) business as an entrepreneur, even though that usage is common. Nevertheless, the people who play the very different role stated in the above definitions are also generally referred to as entrepreneurs, and no other label seems preferable to that one. This ambiguity will be a challenge when policy makers or researchers make statements about entrepreneurs; clarity may require and effort. And there is another slight twist. Entrepreneurs may exist within established organizations, or they might be independent. Some writers use the term 'intrapreneurs' for entrepreneurs working within organizations, but that term does not seem necessary when the above definition is used.

The essential role of entrepreneurs in innovation completes our recipe for growth by increased innovation, but it is difficult to capture it in one sentence. Certainly budding entrepreneurs should be encouraged, and given the opportunity to learn by doing. Entrepreneurship education should be promoted among creative people in all fields. Supportive government tax and procurement policies are needed too. Risk and growth capital must be available to them at the right times, in the right amounts and under the right conditions. Many other detailed measures might be important from time to time and place to place, but perhaps the most important would be for government to state explicitly that entrepreneurship is very important for the Canadian economy, and that great care must be taken by both business and government to avoid stifling entrepreneurship wherever it might occur.

## Conclusions so far

The topics raised in the last section of this chapter are discussed in much greater depth and detail in the rest of the book. Nevertheless, it is useful to conclude this chapter with just a few overall observations that might be easy to remember as we pursue the details:

- Canada is a huge country with a small population that enjoys some big-country economic advantages and suffers some small-country handicaps.
- Canada is a wealthy country, but not wealthy enough. We have many important needs that we can't meet adequately.

- If we want to live within our means, and also to meet the important needs that we can't meet now, we must increase our means. We need a larger GDP/capita.
- To achieve that we must increase the rate at which value is added in our economic activities, including export sales in the world market.
- Increasing prosperity by producing a greater volume of the same products is not always easy because of the reality of markets. A better strategy is to sell products of greater value.
- But in both cases, innovation of various kinds is required. Product, process and marketing innovation are all important.
- Canadian industry has the competence in science and engineering to create products of greater value and to develop improved processes.
- Innovation is not a one-time event; it fades with time and must be repeated regularly.
- Entrepreneurs are essential to the whole process.

There will be more to say about all these things in the later chapters, but for the moment a metaphor must suffice:

---

*Moving to a higher level of national prosperity is not like scaling a mountain. It is much more like climbing up the down-escalator. You have to keep at it; if you want to get higher, you must go faster. You may never get as high as you want to go, but if you slow down, you'll go backwards.*

---

Some might treat that as a hypothesis. I believe it is a fact.

# CHAPTER 3

## THE INNOVATION SYSTEM

*Innovation is change.*

I n this chapter, we begin to look at how innovation actually happens. We start with a theoretical view of innovation as a change process, with its inputs, outputs, outcomes and impacts. That discussion helps explain why it is not always easy to assess what impact an innovation is having. It also describes why we often have to describe change in terms of the inputs to it, when what we are really interested in is its impact. We then move on to talk about the actors and actions at the national level that contribute to innovation and we later bring that discussion down to the regional level. The details of what happens at the micro level of the entrepreneur come in later chapters.

The first words of the first chapter are: "innovation is change." Innovation is not spontaneous change; it doesn't just happen by itself. It is intentional change that requires effort. It takes time and it costs money, and it doesn't always succeed. Its goal is to achieve some specific impact, but for some kinds of innovation it may be difficult to determine to what extent the desired impact has been achieved. This chapter describes a systematic way of looking at such issues.

### Innovation as a change process

In the most general sense, innovation is change brought about by putting a new idea into practice. It is purposeful and managed change intended to have a desired impact to achieve some identified goal. To help in systematic thinking about change of this sort, we will use a bare-bones model of a change process, pictured as a chain of five elements in Figure 3.1. There is the change process itself – it is enclosed inside the box and not shown in detail, but we know how it works. Input into that change process results in a predictable output that, in turn, produces an expected outcome, which eventually produces a hoped-for impact. That impact would generally be the desired result of the innovation, but in certain cases the desired result might be the outcome, and its impact perhaps only an eventual unplanned consequence. One could also imagine cases where the output from the change process is all that one is interested in, and both the outcome and the impact are consequences one has to live with.

The simple model shown in Figure 3.1 will prove sufficient to show that a change process that looks very simple can actually be very complicated.

To begin with, it is assumed that the change process itself is understood and controlled, and that the box contains it completely. The change process is designed to produce the desired output, and is controlled through feedback to achieve that. (For simplicity that feedback loop is not shown in the diagram.) We show only one input, rather than many, and only one output to keep things simple. If the change is strictly technical, then things are straightforward. A new tire tread design reduces stopping distances, or it doesn't. A modified machine makes parts of the right size, or it does not. But when the goal is not strictly technical, and economic and social considerations enter the picture, things become more complicated downstream, in the realm of the outcomes and the impacts.

### FIGURE 3.1 A Managed Change Process

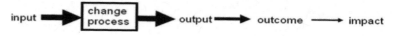

The changing arrows show the decreasing certainty of the causal connection as we move from output to impact.

Uncontrolled and even unknown influences come into play, time lags appear, and causal links become blurred. The output is clearly caused by the change process, but is the outcome what had been expected? Is it caused only by the output? Is it caused by the output at all? Was it going to happen anyway for entirely different reasons? In turn, the impact of the outcome is likely to appear even later, and is even less predictable. The longer it is delayed, the more it will be subject to other influences. That means that even if the output from the change process is exactly as it was designed to be, the eventual impact of the change may be far from what had been hoped for. And vice-versa, even if something close to the hoped-for impact is observed, it cannot be assumed that the change process is working as designed; the same impact might have been brought about by some other factors.

At first glance, such considerations might seem superfluous in dealing with the change processes involved in industrial innovation in products and processes. The changes there are strictly technical, are they not? No, there are many economic and social dimensions involved. Established innovative firms have experienced people and proven procedures to predict the duration and cost of innovation projects, to decide which ones to start, to monitor them, and to weed out along the way the ones that are least likely to succeed. The financial impact of these innovations is either set as a goal for the innovation process, or predicted when the goal is something else. When the contemplated changes are incremental, the expected return on investment (ROI) in process improvements and sales forecasts in existing product lines are considered reliable. But obviously, predictions of financial impact become more difficult and more risky for substantially new processes and for substantially new products that take a company into unfamiliar territory.

Once the innovation has taken place, measuring its financial impact also appears straightforward. For example, the impact of a successful process innovation shows up as an improvement in the productivity of a plant and in the corporate bottom line. Successful product improvements lead to increased sales revenues on the top line and to growth of market share, and they may also show up in more qualitative measures such as those describing expansion into new markets. Innovative companies also produce other useful indicators of their innovative performance. For example, some cite the percentage of current sales revenues attributed to products that are less than some small number of years old.

But this simple picture of the assessment of innovation in industry is, in fact, too simple. It leaves little room for considering – either in predicting what might happen or in analyzing what did happen – any unexpected influences beyond the company's control that may affect the outcome of a given output, or the impact of a given outcome. This is particularly important if the goal of the change process is to produce some desired impact. But it is also important if the goal of the change processes is some expected outcome because, in that case, the eventual unplanned impact might influence the company's future.

Figure 3.2 is an annotated version of Figure 3.1. For the moment, consider only the notes on the top of the diagram. They apply to the process of effecting change and should be read from left to right. The notes on the bottom should be read from right to left. They apply to measuring what the change process produces. We will come to them shortly.

Now consider the following illustration: A company in the commodity business has seen several years of declining profits, and the directors approve an investment to buy technology for process automation in a major mill in order to raise its efficiency and restore the company's profit levels. The innovation is the automation of the production process. The input is the investment in buying the technology to automate it. After the new equipment is commissioned, and the workforce trained to use it, the output is a decrease in the production cost per unit of the product as well as improved quality. The outcome is an increase in value added at the mill. The impact is an improvement in the company's profitability and in its prospects for long-term competitiveness. The simple picture of innovation in Figure 3.1 works just fine to this point. However, consider the case when the desired outcome of higher profits does not materialize in spite of the successful output, as the market price for the commodity produced in the mill collapses because of a worldwide drop in demand, and the mill is no longer profitable even with the newly automated process. In that case, a significant external influence disrupts the connection between output and outcome. The simple picture had nothing to say about that eventuality, but the plan to restore the company's profits might have been very different if the looming instability in the global market had been taken into account at the start.

The situation is even more complicated in institutional innovations. Consider this example: a new government program to support industrial R&D and innovation in order to create greater national prosperity is itself an institutional innovation.

Its input is a budget appropriation. Its output is money disbursed to industry according to the program rules. If its budget is fixed, then its cost is known, but if the new program is designed to support whatever amount of qualified activity takes place, then its budget is open-ended and the cost can't be predicted with any assurance. Its expected outcome is an increased volume of industrial R&D performed, but that raises the question of incrementality: how much of any increase might have happened anyway for other reasons? And can its impact be assessed at all? Since R&D is only one input to innovation, there's no guarantee that more industrial R&D will mean more innovations that succeed in the market and produce increases in wealth creation and in national prosperity. If the program is to be assessed by an increase in GDP growth, then that will show up only after a delay, but how long a delay, and to what extent will that new GDP growth be traceable to the increased R&D? To provide a framework for dealing with such questions, it is necessary to discuss innovation as a change process in the sort of detail that begins with Figure 3.2.

### FIGURE 3.2 Effecting Change and Measuring Change

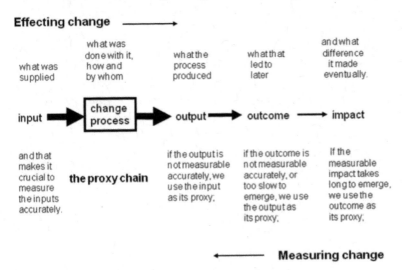

**Effecting change**

| what was supplied | what was done with it, how and by whom | what the process produced | what that led to later | and what difference it made eventually. |

input ➡ **change process** ➡ output ➡ outcome ➡ impact

| and that makes it crucial to measure the inputs accurately. | **the proxy chain** | if the output is not measurable, we use the input as its proxy; | if the outcome is not measurable, or too slow to emerge, we use the output as its proxy; | If the measurable impact takes long to emerge, we use the outcome as its proxy. |

**◀— Measuring change**

Measuring may be difficult, and we may have to take the inputs as a proxy for the impacts we really want to measure. The notes on top should be read left to right; those on the bottom from right to left.

Now consider an even more complicated hypothetical example of a social innovation. A ministry of education is alarmed at the low and falling completion rates of high school by boys, and what this might mean for their future in society. The boys who drop out face the prospect of very high rates of unemployment, family discord, trouble with the law, eventual poor health, dependence on social assistance, etc. Too many of them fail to become competent adults. Research points to the fact that boys generally require a great deal of individual attention in kindergarten to become cognitively and socially ready for learning at the elementary and secondary levels. The ministry decides to use this finding and deal with the situation by hiring more kindergarten teachers to increase the amount of individual attention given to all pupils. The change implemented in this case – the innovation – is the increase in the amount of individual attention given to children in kindergarten. The input is the larger number of kindergarten teachers. The output of this change process is a clear improvement in the social and cognitive capacity for learning that shows up in tests given to children entering grade 1. However, the outcome in the form of any increase in completion rates of high school by boys cannot become visible for another dozen years and, in the interim, the boys will be exposed to many other influences. And it will be some years after high school before their capabilities as adult males become evident. So any impact of the change in the number of kindergarten teachers on the competence of adult men would take many years to show up and, by then, the causal link would have become diffuse because of the many other things that happened to the boys and young men in the interim.

Such considerations make it very necessary to develop ways of evaluating innovations, particularly the expensive ones that may affect many people. Ways have to be found to do this, even if their impacts take a long time to emerge and become understood, perhaps years or decades in economic and social systems. In that case, the outcomes may have to serve as a proxy, or a surrogate, for the impacts. But, again, if the outcomes are also hard to measure or slow coming, the outputs must be used instead. And if there is a problem with measuring the outputs, the inputs become the proxy for the outputs and, in that way, for the outcomes and impacts as well. This 'proxy chain' is shown in Figure 3.2, and in the notes below the diagram that are read from right to left. This is why R&D spending is used as a key measure of industrial innovation, and why the student/teacher ratio is used as a measure of the quality of education. There are many similar examples where an input measure – however inadequate – has to be used as a proxy for output, outcome and impact simply because it is the only measure available in a timely way. This means, of course, that it is essential to have really good measures of the inputs to change processes.

Even so, the need to use the 'proxy chain' to assess the impact of an innovation is recognized as a very unsatisfactory state of affairs and, for that reason, a great deal of research is being done at the OECD, in national statistical offices and in many other places to learn how to measure the outputs, outcomes and impacts of innovation, and to develop indicators for them that will be generally accepted and understood by the international community. This is a difficult and challenging work in progress.

A closely related activity is program evaluation: a multidisciplinary professional activity requiring a deep understanding of government programs and their context. It is important to evaluate government policies and programs appropriately and accurately, since they can affect large numbers of people and involve massive expenditures of public funds. It is all the more important to do this because the links between cause and effect that underlie the design of many programs have to be assumed, as the nature of government programs generally precludes conducting controlled experiments to determine how best to design them.

### The national innovation system

From the perspective of public policy, it is useful to view innovation in the economy as the work of a system, comprising all the actors and activities involved in innovation in the private and public sectors. Freeman defined such a national innovation system as "the network of institutions in the public and private sectors whose activities and interactions initiate, import, and diffuse new technologies."[1]

[1] C. Freeman 1987. *Technology Policy and Economic Performance: Lessons from Japan.* London: Pinter quoted by Charles Edquist. 2005. "Systems of Innovation – perspectives and challenges," in *The Oxford Handbook of Innovation.* Fagerberg, Mowery and Nelson (eds.). Oxford, UK: Oxford University Press, p.183.

Another definition and model of an innovation system shown in Table 3.1 was developed by Statistics Canada to provide a basis for systematic measurement and analysis of innovation activity. It originated in the Science, Innovation and Electronic Information Division (SIEID) of Statistics Canada in the late 1990s, and has appeared in many documents from Statistics Canada and will be referred to here as Statistics Canada.[2]

**TABLE 3.1 National (or Regional) System of Innovation**

A national or regional network of institutions in the public and private sectors whose activities and interactions initiate, import, modify and diffuse new technologies. It is made up of units that interact through linkages and are shaped by various factors:

- **Units** include institutions such as private firms, universities, government laboratories, state corporations, government coordination agencies, government funding agencies and non-government coordination agencies.

- **Linkages** are legal, political, social, economic and business interactions that involve flows of information, money, materials, services and people.

- **Factors** are characteristics of the region that shape how units behave, and include markets, natural resources, technical interdependencies, collaborations and science and technology policies.

At first glance, this definition seems very complete, in the sense that the key terms 'units,' 'linkages' and 'factors,' are defined. Like Freeman's definition it refers to 'new technologies,' but the idea is easily generalized, e.g., to 'new ways of doing things.' A longer look reveals that there is no explicit reference to commercialization, adding value, selling and wealth creation. Maybe the words 'initiate, import, modify, and diffuse new technologies' are intended to include all those things, but that isn't obvious. One also assumes that R&D is included in the mix, but it would be a stretch to assume that design is also there. The emphasis is on new technologies, and it is not clear where

---

[2] Statistics Canada. 1999. "Science and Technology Activities and Impacts: A Framework for a Statistical Information System 1998," Catalogue 88-522-XIB. Ottawa: Statistics Canada.

product improvement and incremental innovation fit into the picture. Statistics Canada has provided a systematic definition of an innovation system, but it may not be sufficiently inclusive. However, their notion of units, linkages and factors is very useful and will be adopted in what follows.

Edquist himself defines the system of innovation (SI) in different terms, not as a network of institutions, but as "all important economic, social, political, organizational, institutional and other factors that influence the development, diffusion and use of innovations."[3]

The constituents of SI are both the components and the relations among them. The components are organizations and institutions. The relations among them are the various kinds of arrangements and relationships that exist in business: commercial, financial, collaborative, partnership, etc.

A very important part of Edquist's description of innovation systems is his list of their important activities.[4] Such a concrete list of things that they do elevates the innovation system from an abstract idea to something real. There are ten entries in this list under the headings of: provision of R&D; competence building; formation of new product markets; articulation of quality requirements from the demand side; creating and changing needed organizations; networking; creating and changing institutions; incubating activities; financing of innovation; provision of consultancy services.

The above ideas have guided the discussion of the innovation system presented below.

## The macro view

A macro view of the national innovation system (NIS) is useful for policy purposes. In this view, the NIS has a central role in creating greater prosperity. It responds positively to good public

[3] Charles Edquist. 1997. "Systems of Innovation Approaches – Their Emergence and Characteristics," in *Systems of Innovation: Technologies, Institutions and Organization*. C. Edquist (ed.). London: Pinter quoted in Charles Edquist. 2005. "Systems of Innovation - Perspectives and Challenges," in *The Oxford Handbook of Innovation*. Fagerberg, Mowery and Nelson (eds.). Oxford, UK: Oxford University Press, p. 183.

[4] Charles Edquist. 2005. "Systems of Innovation - Perspectives and Challenges," in *The Oxford Handbook of Innovation*. Fagerberg, Mowery and Nelson (eds.). Oxford, UK: Oxford University Press, p. 90-192.

policy and effective institutions, and is particularly sensitive to investments in education and science, and to direct incentives to business. The causal links are direct and unambiguous: more investment and better incentives lead to increased prosperity and a better life in the nation. This view is both simple and compelling, but it may be more hopeful than realistic.

In this simple macro view, the national system of innovation can be considered as a change process, as shown in Figure 3.3. Comparing Figures 3.1 and 3.3, we see that the inputs to it are smart public policy, good programs and the direct functions of effective institutions, as well as increased investments in education, research and public science, and better incentives for the private sector. If things work as hoped, then more wealth creation by business would be the output, greater national prosperity would be the outcome, and a better quality of life for more people would be the ultimate impact. The obvious feedback loops keep the economy growing.

Such a hopeful view from the outside is useful at the highest level. If these are the main factors at play and the causality is as shown by the arrows, then the challenge to governments is to create the smart public policies, good programs and effective institutions that will make the whole thing work as expected.

FIGURE 3.3 The National Innovation System –
A Hopeful Macro View

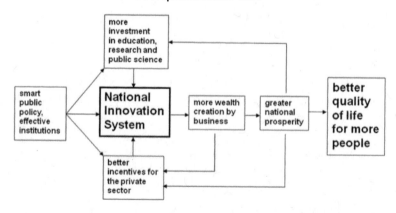

## *The not-quite-national system of innovation*

Zooming in on the national system of innovation shows that things are not as neat as Figure 3.3 suggests. A micro view of the internal structure of the national system of innovation reveals a 'soup' of companies of various shapes, sizes and ages in various sectors interacting with various supporting institutions and organizations, and doing business in their own best interests. It is their collective value added that contributes to the GDP, and the hope is to have them contribute more by innovating more. A close look shows that the neat causal links between public policy and wealth creation by business on the national scale are now replaced by influences to which the individual companies respond in their own ways. And only a few of the influences are exerted by the government and then not unilaterally. They will be shaped to some extent by consultation with the companies, by industry lobbying, by political reaction, etc. whose goal is to obtain the best set of incentives for business and remove the worst impediments. Moreover, the very notion of a strictly 'national' system of innovation becomes questionable, since many of the local companies are branch plants of multinationals, and since the influences on the whole soup of companies include those that come from the rest of the world.

In making their individual decisions, the companies are influenced by the goals, priorities, policies, programs, regulations and standards of the government, including particularly the tax and trade policies, and intellectual property rights (IPR), etc. They are also affected by the characteristics of the nation and its economy, such as the availability of people with the right skills, cost structures in the business environment, national institutions such as the education system, the nation's endowment in natural resources, its infrastructure, and many aspects of culture. Their decisions deal with their growth strategy, investments, outsourcing of production, amount and location their R&D, and possibly even on the location of the company headquarters. In making such decisions, they are obviously affected by the rest of the world. The opportunities they see are shaped not only by the trade policies and business climate of the trading partner countries, but also by world economic conditions as a whole.

The not-quite-national system of innovation is consistent with the view of Gilles Paquet who questions the whole idea of a national system of innovation from the point of view of governance.

*A presumption put forward very cautiously and tentatively by some scholars a few years ago suggested that the most effective way to analyze the innovation system and to intervene in it strategically would be to tackle the problem at the 'national' level. Yet much recent work has raised serious questions about this hypothesis. Too many forces at work in the world economy would appear to suggest that, as globalization proceeds, national disintegration occurs, and sub-national components gain more importance. Consequently, focusing on sub-national units of analysis would, in all likelihood, provide better insights into the workings of the 'real world of production', and better levers for policy intervention on the innovation front.[5]*

This idea takes us to the next step, and there is evidence to support it. There are good examples of sub-national regions where an effective innovation system has been identified. Silicon Valley, CA comes to mind immediately, and so does Route 128 around Boston, MA. In the late 1980s, four larger sub-national European regions identified themselves as 'The Four Motors of Europe,' i.e., economic motors. They were: Baden-Wurttemberg in Germany, Lombardy in Italy, Rhone-Alpes in France, and Catalonia in Spain. For a time, Ontario joined the group as a trans-Atlantic fifth motor.

## Canada's regional systems of innovation

The role of sub-national regions is, of course, very prominent in Canada where the Constitution dictates strong provincial governments, and the huge area and relatively small population dictate large distances and big physical differences among the various centres of economic activity. For these reasons, local factors at the level of the region or the city play a very strong role in Canada's innovation system. The federal government exerts influence through its policies, programs and regulations, but it is remote from much of the action both physically and in terms of jurisdiction. The provincial governments are closer to the action on the ground in jurisdictional terms and closer physically, and regional and urban governments are closer still.

[5] Gilles Paquet. 2005. *The New Geo-Governance - A Baroque Approach.* Ottawa: University of Ottawa Press, p. 129.

Strictly speaking, there is not one national innovation system in Canada; rather there are many different regional ones. Some of the local services that support innovation are offered by agencies of the senior governments, sometimes individually and sometimes in partnership, and many more are local ventures supported by the programs of these governments. However, such programs can't always provide the best fit with local needs because they must maintain a substantial measure of nationwide or province-wide uniformity. This means that it is the local people, institutions, organizations, conditions and circumstances that largely shape the particular local environment for innovation, and that is why there is a diversity of local innovation systems across Canada.

The idea of local influences on innovation is well established, and much has been written on the subject. Four books have been particularly useful. Saxenian's comparison of Silicon Valley with the Route 128 complex near Boston is an early example of studies documenting the importance of local cultural factors on the innovation performance of a region.[6] Porter's study of the basis for the competitiveness of nations brings in related local factors that affect innovation as well.[7] His so-called "diamond model" includes these four elements: the structure of local industry and the competition among companies, the nature of local demand, the array of local factors that affect company performance, and the availability of supply chain partners, supporting services, etc. The roles of government and of chance, or events, are included as well. A collection of 16 articles on local and regional systems of innovation provides both numerous examples of local innovation systems and various models for explaining how they function.[8] Most recently, Bowen has collected the recollections and advice of 33 entrepreneurs from the Waterloo area. Their success stories are rich in examples of local factors – the local innovation ecosystem in action – that contributed to their various successes.[9]

[6] A. Saxenian. 1994. *Regional Advantage: Culture and Competition in Silicon Valley and Route 128*. Boston, MA: Harvard University Press.

[7] M. Porter. 1990. *The Competitive Advantage of Nations*. New York: Free Press.

[8] John de la Mothe and Gilles Paquet (eds.). 1998. *Local and Regional Systems of Innovation*. Boston, MA: Kluwer Academic Publishers.

[9] James Bowen. 2011. *The Entrepreneurial Effect: Waterloo*. Ottawa: Invenire Books.

## FIGURE 3.4 The Regional System of Innovation – A More Realistic Micro View for Canada

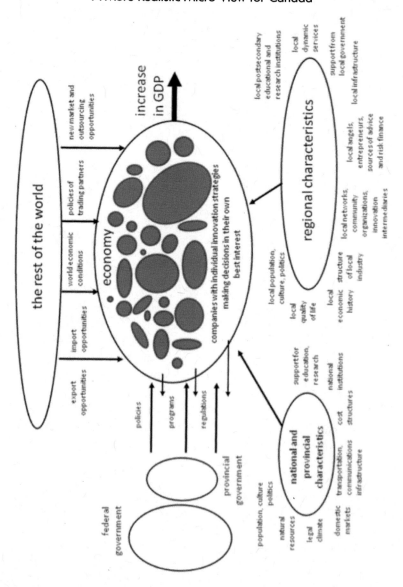

The national innovation system in Canada is a collection of different regional innovation systems like this one.

Figure 3.4 illustrates this regional aspect of the innovation systems in Canada. The difference between hope and reality is reflected in the fact that Figure 3.4 looks completely different from Figure 3.3. It is a busy but important diagram, and needs to be described in some detail. First, the economy is represented as a soup of companies of various sizes in various sectors, all adding value in different ways as they contribute to the GDP. The companies all have their individual innovation strategies, and make decisions in their own best interests. These companies are subject to influences from four sources: the senior Canadian governments (federal and provincial), national and provincial characteristics, regional characteristics, and the rest of the world. We will now proceed to describe these influences in greater detail.

### Senior governments

The federal and provincial governments influence the economy through their policies, programs and regulations. These might originate at one or another level of government, depending on the constitutional division of powers in the subject area. Even if the programs are offered through local offices, this still represents 'action at a distance.' Here are some examples:

- policies: economic, fiscal, tax, trade, competition, IPR, procurement ...
- programs: support for research in universities, hospitals and colleges; support for industrial R&D through tax credits and also IRAP; regional development agency programs; risk-sharing programs in advanced sectors ...
- regulations: health, safety, financial, transport, environmental, broadcast ...

There is always feedback from business on any government initiative that might affect it. This may take the form of participation in consultations and hearings, or private and public reactions, and possibly even opposition through political channels. The goal of this process is to obtain the best set of incentives for doing business and to remove the worst impediments. When initiatives are proposed in policies, programs or regulations, government and industry eventually reach an accommodation on their goals, on many aspects of their design, and on the way that progress toward the goals would be measured. It is then up to the two senior levels of government to work towards those goals, either separately or in alignment, depending on their respective jurisdictions in the areas affected.

However, the extent to which the two senior levels of government in Canada work in alignment is variable, as are the arrangements under which this is done. Here are three examples of good alignment: first, education is a provincial responsibility, and the policies, programs and regulations that govern the support and delivery of education are under provincial control. However, the federal government transfers funds to the provinces to help them support their educational institutions and indirectly influences their performance by setting the amount of the transfer. Second, the support of research is a federal responsibility and education a provincial one, but the provinces are perfectly happy that a large part of the federal research funding transferred to universities is actually spent in supporting students enrolled in programs of post-graduate education. Another example, another arrangement: the federal Canada Foundation for Innovation supports university research by providing major research equipment and facilities. However, CFI provides only 40 percent of the cost of approved projects; the universities must find the remaining 60 percent. As this program has evolved, it has become the practice that the provincial governments almost automatically match the federal 40 percent, leaving the universities to find only 20 percent of the project costs from other sources.

## The supply and demand sides of programs

It is sometimes too easy to forget that government programs have both a supply side and a demand side. This is particularly important for programs of industrial support. On the supply side, the government agencies delivering these programs need to be effective, efficient and accountable, and administrative systems are in place to help achieve that. On the demand side, however, effectiveness has some dimensions that may not be clearly seen from the supply side. They result from the fact that innovative companies, particularly SMEs and new ventures, are always short of time and money. Thus one measure of effectiveness is that support should be delivered in a way that imposes the least administrative burden on these companies. Another is that the form and timing of the support should match the need, e.g.: sharing the cost of buying a new piece of equipment tomorrow may be worth far more to a small growing company than receiving a larger amount of money as a tax credit a year later. And a third dimension of effectiveness as seen from the demand side is promptness in decision making and in delivering any approved support. There are time pressures in industrial investment decisions that must be met by governments, or else market opportunities might disappear. There is generally an urgent rhythm of business in firms that are trying to grow into established innovative companies, and government support for them must keep time with it. We will illustrate these ideas with data in the later chapters.

## *National and provincial characteristics*

The current policies, programs and regulations of government must do their work in the context of a set of more slowly evolving national and provincial characteristics that shape the long-term climate for business in the country. Some are shown in the lower left of Figure 3.4 and a fuller list is given below. The list is roughly in order of decreasing specificity and frequency of mention[10] rather than importance, since what is important to some may be less important to others:

- the cost structures, such as taxes, the minimum wage, and the cost to employers of health care for their employees;
- the legal climate and the rule of law in business, including specifically intellectual property rights (IPR);
- the quality of the transportation, communications and energy infrastructure, e.g., the quality of roads, the penetration of high-speed Internet, rail and air access, port facilities, plentiful, reliable and inexpensive electrical power, etc.;
- the bureaucratic burden of doing business, including the transparency and promptness of regulatory approval and judicial processes, etc.;

[10] Based on what the author has heard from speakers, panellists, facilitators, etc. at various meetings and conferences on innovation that he has attended in the last five years, and what he has read in the business press and research literature.

- the availability of prompt risk capital and angel investors, and the availability of subsequent larger amounts of growth capital from VC or other sources;
- the size, make-up and education of the population, from the point of view of both the potential consumer market and the potential workforce;
- the size of the domestic market and any applicable interprovincial trade barriers;
- the quality and extent of diplomatic support for international trade;
- the extent of support for education and research, and the quality being achieved;
- the quality and accessibility of national institutions, such as government science labs, data repositories, government bureaucracies, statutory tribunals;
- the endowment of natural resources;
- culture and the quality of life;
- the stability of the political system.

These are some of the national and provincial characteristics that, at their best, will combine to create the conditions for predictably profitable and stable business operations. Such conditions influence company strategies and investments, as well as decisions on the location of their activities. They attract foreign direct investment (FDI) of multinational enterprises (MNE), and they also make it attractive for Canadian companies to grow in Canada, even if much of their business is done abroad. The same conditions help the local branch plants of foreign MNEs to compete for world product mandates against their sister branch plants in other countries.

## Culture

The word 'culture' appears among the national characteristics, and it will appear among the regional characteristics as well. In fact, culture is implicit in many of the other factors. It may be most important at the local level, but can be very significant at the national and provincial levels as well. Culture, as we use the word here, does not deal just with the arts and entertainment, even though it includes them both. Rather, culture is what people consider important, what they are used to, how they express themselves, what they believe – perhaps unconsciously – and how they act as a result.[11] This is a good place to add culture to our accumulating list of definitions:

- **Culture** is what people consider important, what language and metaphor they use, what they are used to, what they believe, and how they act as a result.

The culture of the community affects the behaviour of its individual members, and many aspects of culture have implications for a community's openness to innovation. For example, if the community welcomes outsiders and values diversity, then the inflow of immigrant talent and connections with global partners and world markets are more likely to occur. Again, if the community is open-minded and celebrates creativity and excellence in any endeavour, then it is going to support creativity in business as well. If the culture is one of self-reliance, competition, and striving for excellence, then benchmarking local capabilities with the best in the world will not be seen as daunting or unusual. And if business failure is seen as a lesson on the way to success, rather than a stigma, then entrepreneurs will be attracted and encouraged, and the resources of failed initiatives will be quickly redeployed to new attempts.

## The rest of the world

The influence of the rest of the world is a major consideration for companies operating in a global economy. As this was being written, fiscal problems in Greece were on the verge of triggering a global debt crisis that would affect business in Canada and almost everywhere else. In more normal circumstances, global markets offer new export and import opportunities, and more. Companies that sell to the world make their foreign direct investments and locate their branch plants in any place in the world for which there is a compelling business case. And that may be right next door to corporate headquarters or halfway around the globe. Such companies pursue new market opportunities, as well as outsourcing opportunities if the costs of production in those new markets are sufficiently low and the logistics are manageable. In their decisions, they are influenced

[11] Douglas Barber has made a point of emphasizing the importance of culture in business, and he has discussed it many times in the author's presence. The definition above builds on his ideas.

by the economic policies of their business partners' countries, by the factors that shape their business climates, by their political stability and predictability, and by their own assessment of the risk of what they themselves have yet to learn. We have to be aware that a favourable combination of these factors in a location abroad could outweigh the advantages for a Canadian company of growing in this country, particularly if the company is already making most of its sales in global markets.

## The regional dimensions

Let us now look at the lower right part of Figure 3.4. Note that the word 'local' appears in every regional characteristic shown. The move from national and provincial dimensions to the regional and the local makes a company's participation in the innovation system more immediate and convenient. People meet more often and connect more readily, and conversations happen more easily. Companies, of course, continue to be influenced by senior governments and by the rest of the world, but many of their needs can now be met in their interactions with their neighbours. Their local proximity not only saves time and money, but it also makes it easier to seize any opportunities created by these interactions.

Much is known about the successful operation of the regional innovation system. Insights presented in books such as the ones by Saxenian (1994), de la Mothe and Paquet (1998), Porter (1990), Fagerberg, Mowery and Nelson (2005), and in the underlying research literature, in success stories of entrepreneurs such as those collected by Bowen (2011), in many government and agency reports, in presentations at conferences, in business media, etc. make it possible to describe in considerable detail the main characteristics of the regional systems that support innovation.

- *Local population and culture:* People are open, tolerant and creative. They are welcoming and cooperative. The population is diverse, with many newcomers. Education is supported actively, high standards are demanded, and the educational institutions produce a good balance of graduates among the arts, sciences, professional disciplines and the skilled trades. There are easy opportunities for people to mix across economic strata, across ethnic lines, across educational backgrounds, across generations and between newcomers and locals. People feel secure in what they do, and they have supportive attitudes to both growth and competition. They are prepared to find value in initiatives and support them, even if they may not understand their details and cannot participate in them personally. The region has vigorous community-level networks of people with common interests, and many active volunteer service organizations. The chamber of commerce is strong and active. The importance of all these characteristics has has been argued persuasively by Putnam,[12] Florida[13] and Senor and Singer[14] among others.

- **Local quality of life**: People like living in the region. The region attracts and retains well-educated, smart, creative people because there are interesting and valuable things for them to do in an attractive social and physical environment. Its natural environment is also attractive, and there are parks, hiking trails and bike paths. There are good facilities for recreation and entertainment – gyms, museums, theatres, concert halls – and good restaurants with a diversity of cuisines. Young singles leave the community for opportunities elsewhere, but other singles and young families are moving in. There are local teams in several sports and they have a loyal fan base. There are regular concerts, plays, art exhibitions both by local artists and by big names that come into the region. The community has at least one major hospital, good family medicine and many top-quality specialists. It also has good care facilities for the elderly.

- **Local economic history**: This is what has shaped today's structure of local industry, the level and distribution of local wealth, and the availability of business experience and investment capital. The local economic history has also shaped the attitudes of people in the region. The region has seen the decline of its earlier 'rust-belt' industry, and the subsequent growth of modern 'knowledge-based'

---

[12] Robert Putnam (with Robert Leonardi and Raffaella Y. Nanetti). 1993. *Making Democracy Work: Civic Traditions in Modern Italy*. Princeton, NJ: Princeton University Press.

[13] Richard Florida. 2009. *Who's Your City?* Toronto: Vintage Canada.

[14] Dan Senor and Saul Singer. 2009. *Start-up Nation – The Story of Israel's Economic Miracle*. New York: McClelland & Stewart.

companies. The local unemployment rate is not high, and the shortage of highly skilled people is noticeable but not a limit to growth. There are wealthy business leaders in the region who have led the evolution of their industries and are prepared to offer advice to today's innovators as well as acting as angel investors and providing early-stage risk capital. As well, there are local bank managers experienced in supporting innovation who understand the needs of growing innovative companies and have developed trust in the community.

- *The structure of local industry*: The region has a strong cluster of companies in at least one industrial sector, with a mix of established firms of various sizes, new ventures and a dominant anchor company that is a magnet for highly qualified people and ideas, and the source of many spin-offs. These companies are each other's potential customers, suppliers, partners and competitors, and they may become linked in each other's value chains. The regional companies export much of what they produce, and small firms have access to global market channels through the large firms. There is strong and sophisticated local demand for new and improved products at every level. There are also institutions[15] or projects in the region that demand goods or services that initially challenge and stretch local suppliers, but eventually lead them to produce differentiated products that they can then offer in broader markets.[16] To support the local industry, the region has dynamic modern business services (e.g., IP lawyers, specialty accounting firms) available locally. And there are various organizations in the region that act as innovation intermediaries. These are organizations that help in

[15] By institutions we mean stable organizations with a physical presence. This is a narrower meaning than is sometimes used in the literature where institutions may also include certain permanent arrangements and relationships. We will use the expression 'institutions and arrangements' when that broader meaning is intended.

[16] For example, the construction of SNO, the Sudbury Neutrino Observatory, a trail-setting ultra-clean particle physics lab two kilometers underground, stretched local suppliers in Sudbury, especially in deep excavation, underground construction and water treatment to achieve ultra-high purity. Once developed, these capabilities led to products sold in international markets.

innovation by providing companies with capabilities that they themselves don't have, ranging from helping them to make various useful connections all the way to providing a range of commercialization services under contract. Growth capital is available from the venture capital industry that has a local presence which includes some specialists in the strong local sectors.

- *Infrastructure*: The region has good infrastructure for the transportation of people and goods. Water and electric power are reliable and plentiful at reasonable rates. There is convenient access to air, rail and water transport, and road access is easy enough to enable just-in-time manufacturing of bulky items. Traffic congestion is not a problem. Access to major cities and airports is fast and easy. The region has adequate conference facilities and hotel rooms.

- *Local government*: The local government (regional or urban, or both) supports innovation, less through programs such as those of the senior governments, and more on the basis of individual projects. It participates in the planning of all important community projects and takes the lead in infrastructure and other projects where its leadership is both appropriate and required. The local government is active and effective in making the case for local innovation projects of many kinds to the senior levels of government.

- *Post-secondary and research institutions*: There are good post-secondary educational institutions in the region, and 'town and gown' relations are cordial and constructive, with good information flow in both directions. The universities are strong in research, and the community colleges in the skilled trades and various applications of technology; there is a substantial flow of their graduates to local companies. Collaborations between local industry and the universities are actively pursued in the forms of university-industry research programs, contract research and consulting by faculty. The colleges work with local industry to offer specialist education on demand, continuing education, and consulting services for small business. University research that leads to inventions that are then commercialized by new ventures is a source of new innovative SMEs for the region. Researchers in government labs, who have more time than university professors[17] to conduct contract research, have strengths related to the local industries, with specialized facilities that industry can access on a fee basis. Government labs may also have a capacity to act as innovation intermediaries and undertake the early stages of product development for industry.

- *Local champions*: The region has numerous prominent, enthusiastic, articulate and well-connected local champions among the leaders of local government, business and post-secondary education. These champions actively promote the region as a destination for business investment. They deliver consistent messages locally, nationally and globally. They eschew 'beggar your neighbour' approaches and create strategic partnerships and alliances for maximum effect.

## *The challenge to government*

The challenge to senior governments in Canada in dealing with innovation is to treat innovation as a change process on a national or provincial scale, while most of the action occurs at a regional or local level. Given the structure of the country, both in its geography and in its Constitution, they must work to achieve the optimistic macro goals of Figure 3.3 while dealing with a reality that looks much more like the micro view of Figure 3.4. To manage this, government policy makers have to take into account the continuing influence of the national characteristics of local culture and of the actions of the rest of the world on the decisions of individual companies in Canada. The policies and programs they develop should align with and build on these factors where possible, or compensate for them where necessary, with the capacity to change as new lessons are learned. The senior governments must evaluate the outcomes and impacts of their policies and programs as accurately as they can, and use reliable and persuasive indicators to signal the accomplishments to the public. And as they do all this, they must remember that, even though they can exert influence from Ottawa and the provincial capitals and spend money, what people will choose to do and how well they succeed in innovation will be determined to a great extent by local factors over which they have little control.

[17] Because the time of professors is split between teaching and research.

This increasingly common state of affairs is captured effectively in the writings on governance by Paquet and his collaborators.[18] In their language, Figure 3.3 would be an illustration of "Big G" government, the traditional hierarchical and directive form of governance in which a strong government has full information and all the power to decide on the goals, and then to mount programs designed to advance those goals. On the other hand, Figure 3.4 would be an illustration of "small g" governance in which information and power are distributed and the goals are specific to the various players. In this case, "nobody is in charge" and the system works by a variety of arrangements and accommodations, underpinned by continuous learning.

[18] For example: Ruth Hubbard, Gilles Paquet and Christopher Wilson. 2012. *Stewardship: Collaborative Decentred Metagovernance and Inquiring Systems.* Ottawa: Invenire Books.

# CHAPTER 4

## WEALTH CREATION, VALUE-ADDED
## AND THE LANGUAGE OF INNOVATION

*"It is often said that, in the information age, knowledge is the most valuable commodity. This is quite true, but it is also true that knowledge itself can be bought relatively cheaply. Wealth is generated most abundantly by producing tradable articles in which knowledge is embodied."*

John A. Schey

In making the case for more innovation in Canada in chapter 2, we started by pointing out the need for greater prosperity. This means a greater gross domestic product (GDP)/capita which, in turn, calls for a greater rate of creation of value added in the Canadian economy. Achieving that requires either increasing the volume of products sold, or selling products of greater value, or both. Several sample scenarios were offered, suggesting that raising the rate of creation of value added at the level of the firm requires innovation; product, process and marketing innovations figured in the specific examples. The scenarios also suggested that increasing the volume of products already being sold is not always an easy option. Selling more valuable products is better.

In chapter 3 we looked at innovation as a change process and identified the uncertainties involved in achieving the desired results, and measuring what happens. The idea of a national innovation system, only loosely defined up to that point, was used to introduce the public policy goals (in the hopeful view) and the challenges in meeting them (in the realistic view).

In this chapter, we develop some of the main ideas further, starting with wealth creation and the underlying concept of value-added. We then move on to definitions of innovation and innovation system, reviewing and commenting on the many definitions of innovation that can be found in the literature, and proposing one that seems particularly appropriate for our purpose. The chapter concludes with a discussion of the language of innovation that offers the definition of many other important terms.

## Value-added

Value-added[1] is the basis of one way of calculating the gross domestic product.[2] It is the most useful one for the discussion of innovation. Note that the GDP is usually expressed in dollars, but implicit in the number is the period of time over which the data are aggregated. Strictly speaking, the conventional annual value of GDP should be stated in dollars per year, but the 'per year' is taken for granted.

The concept of value-added is powerful, but straightforward. Equation 4.1 shows how value-added is created by a producer. This equation can be taken as its definition.

**value-added = sales revenue - cost of purchased inputs  (4.1)**

The producer's labour costs are not included among the purchased inputs in equation 4.1 because those inputs include only the finished goods and final services that the producer must buy from suppliers. However, they certainly do include the labour costs that the suppliers paid their own workers in producing those goods and services.

Equation 4.1 does not contain time explicitly, but the expression 'per unit time' is implicit in each term, and the time resolution must be the same for all three terms. That means, for example, that if equation 4.1 is used to describe performance in a quarter, then all three terms must refer to the same quarter. It also means that if equation 4.1 is being used to track a transient process, such as the introduction of a new product, the time

---

[1] 'Value-added' is an awkward term. It is treated as a singular noun. Various other combinations of the noun 'value' and the verb 'add' might be preferable in some contexts, but are generally not used. 'New value' is another equivalent expression, and it will be used below when it makes the idea easier to express. 'Value-add' is an unnecessarily terse expression and won't be used here.

[2] This is textbook material. Andrew B. Abel, Ben S. Bernanke and Gregor W. Smith. 1995. *Macroeconomics, Canadian Edition*. Toronto: Addison-Wesley, chapter 2.

resolution of value-added will be limited to the time resolution of the sales data, and then all terms will be evaluated for the same unit of time.

The value-added created according to equation 4.1 is used as shown in equation 4.2.

$$\text{value-added} = \text{wages} + \text{profits} + \text{taxes} \qquad (4.2)$$

where the wages now refer to the labour costs of the producer from equation 4. 1. Once again, all the terms are rates, with 'per unit time' suppressed.

The importance of equation 4.2 is that it provides the connection between value-added and wealth creation. The wages and profits contribute to private wealth, and the taxes to public wealth.

Equation 4.2 also connects GDP/capita with prosperity as experienced by the population. The annual GDP is the total of the value-added throughout the whole economy during the year. Therefore, it equals the total earnings of the work force plus all the profits of investors plus the entire tax revenues of governments. Anything that individuals and firms buy for themselves or that government provides for them is paid for out of the total of all those funds, and the more that people and governments can buy, the more prosperous the nation.

Equation 4.1 makes another very important statement. It highlights the importance of commerce. Bluntly put, there is no value-added and no wealth creation without adequate sales revenue. The world's best product is a money-losing proposition if it accumulates in the warehouse. The finest service organization in the world loses money when trained personnel sit around idle in the shop instead of providing paid services to customers.

According to equation 4.1, the value-added becomes negative when the sales revenue falls below the cost of purchased inputs. This unsustainable situation cannot be changed just by raising prices. Value-added is a market compromise, not a supply-side decision. Producers of commodities, that is undifferentiated products that are available from many sources, have very little freedom in setting their selling price. They must take the prevailing market price. On the other hand, producers of innovations, new and differentiated products, have much more freedom to set prices and secure margins high enough to keep their innovation pipeline full, but even they must approach price-setting as a strategic decision within their market.

A useful version of equation 4.1 is obtained by dividing both sides by an amount of product (e.g., kg, tons, units, barrels, etc.) that is appropriate to the practices of the industry in question. That defines the value-added per unit of product (e.g., $/kg, $/ton, $/unit, $/barrel, etc.). When this is multiplied by the sales volume of the product, in terms of the same measure of amount per some equally appropriate unit of time, (kg/hr, tons per year, units per quarter, barrels/day, etc.), the result is the rate of creation of value-added, an important measure of the rate of economic output by the particular producer. It may vary over time. When it is aggregated over the year, it becomes that particular producer's contribution to the annual GDP.

## Wealth creation

Wealth is the difference between assets and liabilities. That makes wealth creation the process of increasing assets relative to liabilities. This definition is linked to value-added through equation 4.2. Note that the distribution of the created wealth among wages, profits and taxes is an entirely separate matter that will not be discussed here. However, we will go a step further in interpreting equation 4.2 and take wealth creation and the creation of value-added to be the same, in the sense that:

• wealth is created where value is added;
• wealth is created when value is added;
• wealth is created in the amount of value-added.

What the definition does not say explicitly is that wealth creation in our economy is the business of the private sector.[3] The private wealth created is spent or invested by individuals or by corporations. The public wealth created is spent by the public sector to achieve the government's policy goals and service the national debt. Once created, private wealth and public wealth can be transformed from one to the other. For example, private wealth is transformed into public wealth by paying income taxes or making gifts to public institutions. Public wealth is transformed into private wealth when government and public institutions pay their employees, buy goods or services in the market, etc.

[3] In the few remaining cases of Crown corporations, we will stress the 'corporation' aspect of their operations over the 'Crown' aspect.

The concept of wealth creation through value-added in economic activity is central in economics. The case for more innovation in Canada depends on the contribution of innovation to enhanced value-added. In fact, one approach to defining innovation is to connect it to a new way of adding value. We will get to that definition after examining some others that have been used.

## Marketing

The dependence of value-added on sales points out the importance of successful marketing in wealth creation. Marketing is an element of commercialization. It is an array of activities that begins upstream with the value proposition for the product, and ends downstream with the sale – the acceptance of the product by the customer and the receipt of the price by the vendor. Marketing is successful when the needs of both parties are met in this exchange.

Marketing includes the functions of pricing, advertising, distribution, delivery, etc. and it is closely connected with the business model of the firm, namely the way in which the firm creates and captures value. Marketing also provides feedback into other parts of the commercialization process. In what follows, much of the discussion deals with innovations in products and processes, but innovations in business models and in marketing may also be necessary to make them successful. When reference is made in chapter 6 and beyond to the need of research-based new ventures to learn commerce, marketing is a large part of that.

## The language of innovation

A scan of its dictionary definitions shows that innovation involves more than having a new idea. It also includes putting the new idea to use. The new idea is 'introduced', 'used', 'put into practice', etc. – generally implemented in some way. Innovation can be either a process or the result of a process. The context makes it clear which meaning applies.

On that basis, the following generic definition of innovation will be used here.

- **Innovation is a new idea put to use, or the activity of developing a new idea and putting it to use.**

It is important to keep in mind that this is a generic definition. There are specific definitions in particular cases, but all the definitions of different kinds of innovation have the two basic elements: a new idea and putting it to use.

There are many kinds of innovation, and many corresponding specific definitions. For the moment, the discussion will be limited to four obvious kinds of innovation that are important in economic activity – call them the canonical four – namely innovation in products, in processes, in marketing and in business models. Note that each of the specific definitions given below has the twin elements of a new idea and of putting it to use. Each term can refer either to the activity or process of innovating or to the result of the process. For brevity, we express the definition in terms of the result, and it is understood that the process of achieving it is given the same name. Note also that products always include both goods and services.

- **Product innovation** is a new or improved product (good or service) that has been brought to market.
- **Process innovation** is a new or improved process (physical or procedural) that has been put into operation.
- **Marketing innovation** is a new way of securing customers and meeting their needs that has been put in practice.
- **Business model innovation** is a new commercial arrangement for creating and capturing value that has been implemented.

Note that every one of these definitions includes an unmistakable indication that the new element has been put to use.

In discussing product and process innovation in industry, the following quasi-definition of innovation is very useful because it clearly shows the difference between innovation and invention, and it explicitly introduces commercialization into the picture.

$$\text{innovation} = \text{invention} + \text{commercialization} \qquad (4.3)$$

On the right-hand side of the equation-like relationship (4.3), the invention is the new idea and the commercialization is the way it is put to use, or brought to market in this case. More precise definitions of invention and commercialization are:

- **Invention:** a new idea conceived to meet a need, together with the practical means by which it can be implemented.

Note that this corresponds closely to the two basic requirements for a patent application, namely to describe what the invention does and how it is made. And once more, the process of invention and the result are both called the same.

- **Commercialization:** the multifaceted process of bringing a product (good or service) to market to create wealth, including activities such as market studies, product design and development, design for manufacture, testing, production, supply chain development, pricing, distribution, marketing, etc. with feedback among various of these activities.

The relationship that equation 4.3 suggests is a way of thinking about commercialization that might help in the understanding of what is involved in innovation. This suggestion is aimed particularly at technical readers, such as engineers, scientists and students who might be inclined to think that all the creative work in an innovation is in the invention, and that the commercialization is the easy routine part. That is not the case, and that point needs to be made in a clear and memorable way. In fact, there is intellectual property in both parts of the innovation. First, there is the intellectual property embodied in the invention and protected as IP in one of the customary ways. And, second, there is the total effect of all the creative work that went into designing the right business model, defining the value chain, finding channels to market, creating a supply chain, marketing the invention, etc., ... etc. If this is not done very well, then the innovation will not succeed, regardless of the technical merit of the invention. The outcome of the creative activity in commercialization may not be protectable, and it may not even have a name. But if the creative content of the innovation were called 'total intellectual property (IP)', then perhaps its two parts could be called 'technical IP' and 'business IP.' That nomenclature would lead to the counterpart of equation 4.3, namely:

**total IP = technical IP + business IP**

The relationship (described in equation 4.3) is important in a historical perspective, as described first in the classic book on industrial innovation by Christopher Freeman[4] and

[4] Christopher Freeman. 1974. *The Economics of Industrial Innovation.* New York and Toronto: Penguin.

later expanded in its third edition by Freeman and Soete[5] who say:

> "[We] owe to Schumpeter [Austrian economist working in the first half of the 20th century] the extremely important distinction between inventions and innovations, which has since been generally incorporated into economic theory. An invention is an idea, a sketch or a model for a new or improved device, product, process or system. Such inventions may often (not always) be patented but they do not necessarily lead to technical innovations. In fact the majority do not. An innovation in the economic sense is accomplished only with the first commercial transaction involving the new product, process, system or device, although the word is used also to describe the whole process." [original emphasis]

The same thing is restated much more briefly by the same authors in the title of their sec. 8.1. "Innovation [is the] coupling of new technology with a market." The new idea is the new technology or invention, and coupling it with a market, or commercialization, is putting it to use.

Note that in chapter 2 we have used innovation in a somewhat different sense as a short-hand device to divide traded goods and services into two mutually exclusive categories: innovations and commodities. In that case, some of the attributes of industrial innovations provide the definition and the distinction.

- **Innovation** or **innovative product:** a new or improved product in the market that is significantly differentiated from other products in terms of functionality, performance, quality, etc., is available from only a very small number of producers, and cannot be substituted readily.
- **Commodity** or **commodity product:** a product that is not appreciably different from other products in terms of functionality, quality, properties, etc., is available from many sources, and can be substituted readily.

This distinction is important, since the producers of innovations can set the price for their products, whereas the producers of commodities must take the price offered in the market.

---

[5] Christopher Freeman and Luc Soete. 1997. *The Economics of Industrial Innovation,* Third Edition. New York: Routledge.

We conclude this section with another distinction in innovation, this time between technological innovation and social innovation. These two labels seem entirely intuitive. The first is obviously innovation driven by new technology; the second is innovation driven by some new arrangement or relationship among people. But nothing is that simple. The term 'social innovation' is taking on a very specialized meaning, and one that paradoxically links it with technological innovation. Here is the definition that is coming into use:

- **Social innovation:** the creation of networks of like-minded people committed to achieving a common goal, whose efforts are mobilized and managed with the help of the technology of social media

We shall discuss social innovation in chapter 11.

## Definitions of innovation in the literature – a diversity

The literature on innovation, including scholarly papers, books, reports and the popular press, presents many definitions of innovation that are different from the ones given above and reflect the perspectives of their respective authors. Some of these definitions treat innovation as a generic term, made specific with modifiers. Others attempt to make the concept of innovation more comprehensive by including various specific kinds of innovation right in the definition. However, including too many specific examples in a general definition sometimes has the result of a loss of focus.

What follows is just a small sample of definitions of innovation that readers may encounter in the literature, and some comments on them.

We begin with the most widely used definition of innovation, as given in the *Oslo Manual* of the Organisation for Economic Co-operation and Development (OECD).[6] This is the definition in the third edition of the *Oslo Manual*:

*"An innovation is the implementation of a new or significantly improved product (good or service), or process, a new marketing*

---

[6] OECD. 2005. *Oslo Manual: Guidelines for Collecting and Interpreting Innovation Data.* Paris: OECD/Eurostat, paragraphs 146 and 150 as cited with comments by Fred Gault. 2010. *Innovation Strategies for a Global Economy – Development, Implementation, Measurement and Management.* Northampton, MA: Edward Elgar and Ottawa, ON: IDRC, p. 42-3.

*method, or a new organization method in business practices, workplace organization or external relations."*

This is very close to a specific definition of our four canonical innovations, but with more stress on the organization than on the business model. The *Oslo Manual* says right up front that the ideas are new and they must be implemented, and then draws attention to that again later:

*"A common feature of an innovation is that it must have been implemented. A new or improved product is implemented when it is introduced on the market. New processes, marketing methods or organizational methods are implemented when they are brought into actual use in the firm's operations."*

An important source of information about the academic literature on innovation is *The Oxford Handbook of Innovation*. In an introductory chapter, Fagerberg offers a brief generic definition that embodies the element of priority.[7] This is an extract from his thorough discussion of what innovation is and what it is not.

*"...innovation is the first attempt to carry [an idea for a new product or process] out into practice."*

This raises the issue of degrees of novelty in innovation. Fagerberg apparently insists on absolute novelty; only the first attempt counts as an innovation. But is that first in the world, or something less absolute? Other writers accept more relative measures of novelty, such as first-in-the-industry, first-in-the-market, first-in-the-company, etc. These degrees of novelty probably rank differently on the scale of bragging rights, but it is their impact on the value-added and wealth creation by the firm that matters more, and that may depend on more factors than just priority.

In a very different approach, Padmore and Gibson define innovation in a way that stresses breadth over priority.[8]

*To us, an innovation is any change in inputs, methods, or outputs which improves the commercial position of a firm and that is new to the firm's operating market. In principle, we*

[7] Jan Fagerberg. 2005. "Innovation – A guide to the literature" in *The Oxford Handbook of Innovation*, Jan Fagerberg, David C. Mowery, Richard R. Nelson. Oxford, UK: Oxford University Press, chapter 1.

[8] Tim Padmore and Hervey Gibson. 1998. Modeling Regional Innovation and Competitiveness" in *Local and Regional Systems of Innovation*. John de la Mothe and Gilles Paquet (eds.). Boston, MA: Kluwer Academic Publishers, p. 48.

*accord comparable importance to innovation in areas such as management, marketing and finance as we do to technological innovation, reflecting the reality of the business world which can not afford to draw a line between different types of innovation.*

It is interesting that Padmore and Gibson include only a successful innovation in their definition, one that "improves the commercial position of a firm." (Is there no such thing as an innovation that fails?) They also make a point of not discriminating among "different types of innovation," and yet they limit their definition to four types that are of interest to business and industry. The breadth of the definition of innovation is an intriguing issue, and one to which we shall return shortly.

The Government of Canada recently (2007) set up the Science, Technology and Innovation Council (STIC) in order to enhance the country's innovation performance. In its first report[9], the council discussed the meaning that innovation had for them. Here is a direct quote from the third page of the report, entitled "Innovation, the Innovation System and Innovation Performance":

*Innovation is the process by which individuals, companies and organizations develop, master and use new products, designs, processes and business methods. These can be new to them, if not to their sector, their nation or to the world. The components of innovation include research and development, invention, capital investment and training and development. This wide definition includes the invention of new products, processes, services and systems, as well as their application, adaptation and diffusion in the economy and society. Agents of diffusion include individuals, companies and colleges and universities. These users and producers of innovation are part of the innovation system, which also includes governments as facilitators and regulators. Adoption and diffusion are encouraged by public policy including financial assistance in the form of direct support and tax incentives, intellectual property policies as well as other marketplace frameworks such as competition and regulatory policies. Venture capital firms and other private sector investors that finance innovation are*

---

[9] Government of Canada. 2009. "State of the Nation 2008 - Canada's Science, Technology and Innovation System," Ottawa, ON: Science, Technology and Innovation Council (STIC), April, (available online at www.stic-csti.ca).

*also part of the system. Innovation performance is influenced by multiple sectors and public policies on education, science and technology, industry and finance, developed by different levels of government. Immigration, international science and technology, trade and foreign investment policies also affect innovation outcomes.*

This statement actually goes far beyond defining innovation and says a lot about how innovation happens in Canada, but the first sentence limits its scope to innovation in business and industry. This is not surprising since the mandate of STIC is to promote the use of science, technology and innovation to enhance Canadian prosperity.

The Conference Board of Canada that has been running projects on various aspects of innovation for many years offered another definition that introduced (to this author at least) an important element:[10]

*The Conference Board defines innovation as a process through which economic or social value is extracted from knowledge – through the generation, development, and implementation of ideas – to produce new or improved products, processes, and services.*

The important thing about this definition is that it connects innovation with value. However, one can argue that the value is not extracted from knowledge. It is created with knowledge, and the difference is more than semantics. The source of value-added in products and processes is the knowledge embodied in them. In the case of many new products, that is achieved through R&D. On just this point, the words of John A. Schey, one of the world's great manufacturing engineers, already quoted at the head of this chapter, are worth repeating here:[11]

*It is often said that, in the information age, knowledge is the most valuable commodity. This is quite true, but it is also true that knowledge itself can be bought relatively cheaply. Wealth is generated most abundantly by producing tradable articles in which knowledge is embodied.*

---

[10] The Conference Board of Canada. 2003. "Trading in the Global Ideas Market," 5th Annual Innovation Report. Ottawa, ON: Conference Board of Canada, p. 5.
[11] John A. Schey. 2000. *Introduction to Manufacturing Processes*, 3rd editon. Boston, MA: McGraw-Hill, p.1.

Innovation by Canadian business was the focus of an expert panel assessment by the Council of Canadian Academies (CCA).[12] The council is a think tank supported by an endowment of public funds that assembles volunteer expert panels to produce independent assessments of the state of knowledge in areas deemed important by the Government of Canada. An assessment takes the form of an expert panel's response to one or more questions submitted to council from within government. Proposed questions are discussed between the government and the council, and may be amended, to assure both parties that they are unambiguous and capable of being answered on the basis of evidence.

The private-sector CCA Expert Panel that wrote the report on innovation adopted the *Oslo Manual* definition, but also proposed their own on the very first page of the Executive Summary.

*"Innovation is new or better ways [sic] of doing valued things."*

Their definition of innovation made the connection between innovation and value more precise, and took it another step in the right direction. They then went on to define radical and incremental innovation, both of which we shall discuss later.

The CCA Expert Panel assembled an impressive array of current and historical Canadian and international data for a study that was both thorough and deep. The CCA report turned out to be somewhat controversial in a very interesting way, since it included 'business ambition' as one of the factors that determined whether a company included innovation in its business strategy. This was a shock to some because, until then, discussions of innovation performance by Canadian business had always focussed on the role of factors exogenous to the firm. If only these factors were made more favourable, then innovation performance would undoubtedly improve. That had been the conventional wisdom, but now it was being challenged. An endogenous factor was at play as well. More will be said about this later, but for the moment this statement will serve to remind the reader that innovation is not uniformly perceived as a necessary or desirable activity in business.

---

[12] Expert Panel on Business Innovation. 2009. *Innovation and Business Strategy: Why Canada Falls Short*. Ottawa: Council of Canadian Academies, April (available online at www.scienceadvice.ca).

## *Definition of innovation for economic impact*

Finally, making the connection between innovation and value, and framing it in a way that recalls our interest in wealth creation and value-added, we now propose a further generic definition of innovation for those cases when innovation is intended to have economic impact.

- **Innovation** is a new way that value is added or created.

This is the definition of innovation that will be used or implied in most of what follows. The phrase 'value is added' applies to established patterns of business activity where the purchased inputs are clear. 'Value is created' could be used in those situations where they may not be. Note that the definition does not say 'new way of adding or creating' because a new way of doing something may exist but not be used.

Two additional comments need to be made about the various definitions of innovation that exist in the literature. The first has to do with inclusivity. There are many kinds of innovation, and it seems open-minded and generous to include more and more of them in broadening the definition of innovation.[13] But that breeds confusion; it makes innovation an increasingly vague concept that tries to be all things to all people. It is better to stick with one generic definition, and to develop different specific definitions for innovation that make sense for different areas of interest. But, of course, each of those specific definitions must include both the appropriate expression of the new idea and the appropriate form of its implementation.

Finally, we need to avoid a bias in discussing innovation. The bias may be in treating innovation implicitly as a supply-side concept. With a successful innovation, there is invention, then commercialization and then success in selling the product in the market, all producing economic benefits on the supply side where the product is made. But it is also important to keep track of what is done in the economy by those who buy the products. Tools, machinery, computers, trucks, etc. enable their purchasers to add value, often in new ways. Let's call this latter activity 'demand-side innovation,' which is not the same

---

[13] An unfortunate tendency in some popular writing about technical issues today is the confusion between vagueness and imprecision on the one hand, and flexibility and generality on the other.

as what some call 'customer innovation' that will be discussed in chapter 11. It may be tracked on its own as the purchaser's innovation, but it becomes demand-side innovation when it is linked to a prior enabling innovation supplied by the vendor. For example, the laser was an enabling supply-side innovation that has led to a vast range of demand-side innovations in which lasers are used in many different ways in many different sectors.

A very important feature of demand-side innovation is that the economic benefits deriving from it can accrue to those who bought and used that enabling product, possibly in very different sectors and very far away from where it was made. Such benefits on the demand side can outweigh the benefits to the supply side. One can easily point to examples, such as the use of computers vs. the manufacture of computers, where demand-side innovation has the much greater impact across the economy. If this is called a 'spillover,' a common term in economics, the term may wrongly suggest to a lay audience that the benefit on the demand side is incidental and minor and that the benefit to the producer is much greater.

The importance of demand-side innovation is recognized in the CCA report:[14]

> ...[M]ost of the innovation that is ultimately used in a particular business originates outside the business itself and is acquired through investment in machinery and equipment, and by adaptation of leading-edge knowledge that is circulating in business and academic environments.

If the goal of public policy is to encourage more innovation, then the distinction between supply-side innovation and demand-side innovation is important because the two need to be encouraged differently. For example, enabling innovations on the supply side are more likely to emerge from research, and constitute new uses of new knowledge. This process depends greatly on research support for public research institutions and technology industries. Demand-side innovations are more likely to be based on design, and constitute new uses of existing

---

[14] Expert Panel on Business Innovation. 2009. *Innovation and Business Strategy: Why Canada Falls Short*. Ottawa: Council of Canadian Academies, April (available online at www.scienceadvice.ca), p. 27.

knowledge. This is encouraged by tax credits to industry, equipment depreciation rates, etc. in all sectors.

## Some system perspectives

Innovation, as defined in the above discussion, is the output of the innovation system discussed in chapter 3. The word 'system' itself was not defined at the time, but it might be useful here to be reminded of just precisely what a system is.

A very clear definition is cited by Edquist in his excellent chapter on innovation systems in *The Oxford Handbook of Innovation*.[15] In that definition, a system has three attributes:

- "A system consists of two kinds of constituents: There are, first, some kinds of components and, second, relations among them. The components and relations should form a coherent whole (which has properties different from the properties of the constituents).
- The system has a function, i.e., it is performing or achieving something.
- It must be possible to discriminate between the system and the rest of the world, i.e., it must be possible to identify the boundaries of the system."

### Science, Technology and Innovation Council

In its first report already quoted above, Science, Technology and Innovation Council (STIC) deals with innovation system by expanding the *Oslo Manual*[16] definition of innovation to include a few of what could also be considered as elements of the innovation system. According to STIC, here are the requirements of a healthy innovation system:[17]

- *"A healthy innovation system requires the right conditions:*
- *Supportive Marketplace Frameworks* – Policies and practices that create strong, open, competitive domestic markets where ideas can be taken from conception to application.

---

[15] Jan Fagerberg, David C. Mowery, Richard R. Nelson. 2005. *The Oxford Handbook of Innovation*. Oxford, UK: Oxford University Press, p. 187.

[16] OECD. 1992. *OECD Proposed Guidelines for Collecting and Interpreting Technological Innovation Data – Oslo Manual*. Paris: OCDE/GD (92) 26.

[17] Government of Canada. 2009. "State of the Nation 2008 - Canada's Science, Technology and Innovation System," Ottawa, ON: Science, Technology and Innovation Council (STIC), April, section 3.1, p. 9, (available online at www.stic-csti.ca).

- *Engaged Citizens* - Individuals and businesses that demand better quality products and services, for themselves and their communities deriving manufacturers and service providers to become more innovative.
- *Highly-skilled people* – People who have leading edge research skills and people who know how to put new technology to work.
- *Infrastructure* – A modern physical and regulatory infrastructure to insure the free flow of goods, services and ideas.
- *Accurate Measures of Performance* – Statistics that better reflect plans, activities, linkages and outcomes of innovation so that we can determine the full impact of innovation on the Canadian economy, and measure how well we are doing against global competition.
- Underpinning these conditions is the vital need for collaboration. Greater cooperation and collaboration between the private sector, universities and colleges, all levels of government, and others at the regional and national levels strengthen a nation's ability to compete at the international level. Collaboration is also vital to foster multidisciplinary research, which is integral to the knowledge-based economy."

Many of the points in this list are implicit in the functioning of the regional innovation system discussed in chapter 3. But, remarkably, there is no reference to creating value-added and to commerce in any of this, and no connection made with wealth creation. That raises a question: Is the connection of innovation with value-added, and hence with wealth creation and prosperity, so well and widely understood that it doesn't need to be mentioned explicitly? Or, is the very opposite the case? It isn't talked about because it's not well understood. If it's the latter, then the implications are disturbing.

## Council of Canadian Academies (CCA)

As already pointed out, the CCA's recent report on innovation by Canadian business has been both influential and controversial.[18] It documents Canada's weak private-sector innovation performance, and proposes an explanation that suggests the roles of both business and government in influencing this outcome. Along the way, CCA cites the definition of innovation in OECD's *Oslo Manual*, and then breaks some new ground by classifying innovation as incremental or radical in terms of the different markets at which it is targeted.

- "[Innovation is] ...the implementation of a new or significantly improved product (good or service), or process, a new marketing method, or a new organizational method in business practices, workplace organization or external relations."
- **Incremental innovation is connected with established markets.** "Incremental innovation – in which developments are typically 'new to the firm,' or perhaps to a sector, but not 'new to the world' – is what drives productivity growth and firm competitiveness in *established markets*. Since established markets constitute the great bulk of economic activity, incremental innovation is directly responsible for the vast majority of labour productivity growth."
- **Radical innovation is associated with creating entirely new markets.** "The ultimate economic benefits (jobs and income growth) of a blockbuster innovation usually diffuse broadly and rapidly beyond the firm and location where the innovation originates."

The distinction between radical and incremental innovation in these terms introduces the important approach of looking at innovation in terms of its economic goals, rather than its technological attributes. In this perspective, innovation is an economic issue, not a technological one. This approach will be pursued, modified and extended in the chapters that follow.

---

[18] Expert Panel on Business Innovation. 2009. *Innovation and Business Strategy: Why Canada Falls Short*. Ottawa: Council of Canadian Academies, April (available online at www.scienceadvice.ca), p. 21-22.

## R&D and other "words that everybody knows"

Innovation is nothing new, but these days it's getting a lot of attention. Innovation is increasingly recognized as having the potential to help in dealing with Canada's economic challenge. As a result, conversations about innovation among government, the universities and business, and in the media are becoming more frequent. What bedevils these conversations is that the language of innovation is made up of common words. Everybody knows what these words mean – to them – but they may mean different things to different people. For example, we saw earlier in this chapter that different authors offer substantially different definitions of innovation itself, viewing it from different perspectives. In addition, as people with diverse interests learn about the immense scope of innovation, they want to make the terminology more flexible and inclusive, but sometimes the result is greater vagueness and imprecision rather than clarity.

For that reason, much care is given in this book to the precise definition of important terms. A common understanding of 'words that everybody knows' is not taken for granted. Definitions have been introduced throughout the text in those places where an intuitive understanding of the key terms might no longer suffice, and more will follow in the rest of this chapter. These definitions may not be unique, but they will be complete, comprehensive and consistent within the framework set down in this book.

We have already discussed the definitions of innovation, innovation system, invention, commercialization, value-added, entrepreneurship and culture. We now move on to the definitions of more terms that appear in the discussions of innovation and innovation systems. Most of them go beyond the customary dictionary definitions, in ways that reflect both widespread usage and the logic of the subject. They are largely based on the glossary previously offered by the author, with some sharpening up since.[19]

### Science and research

Science is much more than research. Debate is an essential process in science. When scientists openly debate some major findings, the criticism 'Science can't even get its act together!'

---

[19] T.A. Brzustowski. 2008. *The Way Ahead: Meeting Canada's Productivity Challenge.* Ottawa, ON: University of Ottawa Press, chapter 6 and glossary.

is a misinterpretation of that debate. And prediction is a major activity both within science and in its use by society. In research, observations are predicted from hypotheses, which are then either verified or falsified by experiment. And, once established, scientific facts provide the basis for predicting what can happen in the wider world. Here is the definition of science that includes these ideas:

- **Science:** the social system for creating new knowledge that involves three interrelated activities: **research** conducted according to the scientific method, **debate** within the scientific community to determine when results of research should be accepted as fact, and finally **predictions** based on facts. (The word 'science' is also sometimes used to mean the body of facts established by science).

As shown above, research is an integral part of science. It is defined as follows:

- **Research:** the process of learning what is not yet known, not by anyone, anywhere.

Let's call this the hard definition of research. It specifically excludes using the word (often as a verb) to describe the process of looking for existing information in a library, on the Internet, or in some other repository. That should generally be called information gathering, or a library 'search.' However, if the information gathered in this way subsequently led to a new insight or to an entirely new understanding, and something was learned that hadn't been known before, then research was done.

There are several kinds of research. Basic research comes to mind first.

- **Basic research:** research whose goal is only discovery, or seeking the answers to important unanswered questions about nature

Basic research is also called 'fundamental', 'curiosity-driven', or 'pure.' Of these terms, the first seems the most appropriate substitute for 'basic.' 'Curiosity-driven' is too vague. All research of any kind is driven by curiosity, but it may be curiosity about different things. 'Pure' suggests that some other kind of research might be impure, which seems like a gratuitous put-down. Note that the hard definition of 'research' has a particular consequence for basic research. Priority of discovery – answering the question that is still unanswered and publishing the answer before anyone else does – is a cherished goal and the principal measure of success among basic researchers.

Applied research differs from basic research more in its goal than in its methods. Even though applying research may be questionable in semantic terms, the term 'applied research' is widely used, and identifies an activity that is very important for industry.

- **Applied research:** research undertaken to answer detailed questions about a specific artifact[20], system, process, or natural occurrence, whose governing scientific principles are already understood at a general level

Here it becomes necessary to relax a bit the element of priority in research. The results of applied research, particularly in industry, may be kept secret for competitive reasons, or for reasons of national security. That means that others working in the same area may be trying to learn something that is already known, but not to them. In this case, the work should still count as research within the performing organization. Matters might come to a head only if the results of the work are later submitted for a patent or publication and someone else claims priority.

Another important modality, project research, is distinguished more by its format than its goals or content. Project research is particularly important when university research is undertaken to deal with an industrial problem. It is managed as a project, with a beginning, a middle and an end, and with timelines, budgets, scheduling, organization, intellectual property agreements, formal progress reports, etc. This approach is exceptional in the universities, where long-term programs of basic research are the norm, timelines are how long it takes, and reporting is usually done in the open, international, peer-reviewed research literature. Here is the definition:

- **Project research:** the research activity whose object is solving a specified practical problem that cannot be solved with existing knowledge, and whose form is a project with a schedule, a budget, a management structure, an IP agreement, regular reporting, etc.

Note that project research and applied research are similar in some ways, but they differ in two aspects. First, applied research

---

[20] The second vowel is optional. Some sources, including MS Word spellcheck, insist on 'artefact.' I prefer 'artifact,' namely something made by an artisan.

can be carried on as a program rather than as a project. And, second, in the case of project research the governing scientific principles may not all be known at the outset.

### Creativity and entrepreneurship

Creativity is another word that everybody knows. It is a human attribute that is often cited as being very important in many aspects of innovation. The problem is that it's very difficult to define. Many dictionary definitions of creativity seem circular – creativity is the state of being creative – that sort of thing. Imagination and originality sometimes appear in the definition loop, but not always. In general, people seem to use the adjective 'creative' much more often than the noun 'creativity,' even though they don't define it either. Instead, they talk about creative people, what they have been able to do, and how they seem to have done it.

The wonderful book on creativity by the Root-Bernsteins is an example.[21] Its sub-title is "The 13 Thinking Tools of the World's Most Creative People" and the noun 'creativity' doesn't even appear in the index. But their descriptions, and those by others, of what creative people actually do point the way to a definition of creativity. On the basis of many examples from many sources, the following definition of creativity is offered here:

- **Creativity:** the ability to look at something that others look at and to see something different than what they see, and then to make that new perception apparent to others – creativity is expressed in the arts and letters, in design, in research, etc.

As written, the definition seems to apply most closely to the visual arts, but its intent extends far beyond that. 'Look' and 'see' can be taken to have a very broad meaning, but different pairs of words might have been chosen instead. For example 'observe' and 'conclude', 'experience' and 'feel', 'hear' and 'understand.' The point is that creativity is the ability of some people to perceive something new that others don't perceive in the same situation, and then to communicate it to the others in some persuasive way. So, for example, a creative scientist sees a new pattern in data that

[21] Robert and Michele Root-Bernstein. 2001. *Sparks of Genius – The 13 Thinking Tools of the World's Most Creative People.* New York: Mariner Books.

others have looked at for years, and then manages to persuade the scientific community to accept it as a fact. A creative painter sees the interplay of shape, colour, light and shadow in a way that is new, and manages to convey that impression on canvas in a way that becomes accepted as beautiful. A creative writer finds new words to describe some aspect of the human condition and becomes quoted and influential, etc.

Creativity shows up in innovation in many ways. One important connection is through entrepreneurship which requires creativity of a particular sort, as already referred to in chapter 2. The definition of entrepreneurship given below echoes the definition of creativity. They both depend on seeing something that others haven't seen in a given situation. In the case of an entrepreneur, it's seeing the opportunity to add value and create wealth in a new way, and then seizing it.

- **Entrepreneurship:** the capacity to find and seize an opportunity for a new way of creating value; generally through a new venture set up for the purpose, but sometimes as a new activity within an existing organization. In that case, it might be called 'intrapreneurship.'

This is a focused definition of entrepreneurship. It's far narrower than calling the owner of any (small) business an entrepreneur, something that often appears in the literature. It is closer to, but still not the same as, tying entrepreneurship to the creation of a new venture.[22]

## Engineering, design and technology

Unlike science, engineering is a profession like medicine, law, architecture, etc., and engineering education is professional education. A degree in medicine makes one a doctor, a degree in law a lawyer, a degree in architecture an architect, but a degree in science does not make one a scientist. A scientist is one who engages in science, as defined above.

In the context of innovation, the difference between an engineer and a scientist is even more stark. It is perhaps best captured by the words attributed to Theodore von Karman and already quoted earlier in this book: "A scientist studies what is; an

---

[22] Graham Bannock, Evan Davis, Paul Trott and Mark Uncles. 2002. *The New Penguin Business Dictionary.* New York: Penguin Books, p. 120.

engineer creates what never was."[23] Consequently, the following definition of engineering is offered:

- **Engineering:** the professional activity of creating artifacts, systems and processes to meet people's material needs, with **design** as the central creative process, **scientific knowledge** and **economic considerations** as its essential inputs, and **public safety** as its overriding responsibility

The word 'professional' is very important in the definition of engineering. It goes far beyond being paid for what one does, as in 'professional sport.' Public liability is an important consideration because what many engineers do can affect public safety. For that reason, the profession is regulated by legislation and one has to be a certified professional engineer to supervise engineering work. Accordingly, public responsibility and professional ethics are important elements of engineering education.

Scientific knowledge is a necessary input into engineering, as are economic considerations. But the essential creative process in engineering is design. In that sense, design is to engineering what research is to science. We offer this definition of design:

- **Design:** the creative process of solving the problem of meeting a specified need under a set of constraints, such as limits on cost, compatibility with existing systems, safety regulations, ergonomic requirements, etc. The output of design is a proposed realization of an artifact, system, or process in terms of its function and its form. The quality of a design is measured by its adequacy in meeting the need and by appropriate attributes such as robustness, reliability, durability and aesthetic appeal.

While the essential form of creative intellectual activity in engineering is design, research may also be included in an engineering project if it is needed. Research in engineering is the same activity as in science, but it is more likely to be applied research than basic research.

Technology is a word with many shades of meaning. The definition offered here stresses the needs of industry.

- **Technology:** the set of designs, materials, tools and procedures, that predictably and reproducibly combine to produce a specified desired effect in the material world.

---

[23] Theodore von Karman. 2010. Quoted in Henry Petroski. *The Essential Engineer – why science alone will not solve our global problems.* New York: Knopf, p. 20.

This definition describes technology that can be applied and transferred. The key words are 'predictably' and 'reproducibly.' As a result, this is technology that makes all manufacturing and construction possible. It is interesting to note that the most familiar form of technology defined in this way is never referred to by that name; it can be found in the home in any cookbook of proven recipes.

While the above definition of technology addresses its most important aspects, the same word is used in other ways as well. Here are a few:

- Some use the word 'technology' for all relatively recent science-based artifacts, but the limits on that usage are vague. A digital TV would likely be described as a technology product, but a refrigerator probably not.
- An extension of this view includes not only artifacts but also their use, their governing scientific principles, their design and construction features, the details of their operation, etc. The most common example is 'information technology.'
- The phrase 'technology industry' is usually applied mainly to two sectors: Information and communications technology (ICT), and biotechnology.
- Technology is also the T of S&T (science and technology), an acronym uttered in one breath, generally in the context of public policy and government spending, but in this context "T" seems to have no meaning on its own. Government S&T spending includes spending on engineering and science-related activities in government departments, on industrial R&D, on research in universities and research hospitals and on graduate education in science and engineering.
- Technology is also sometimes confused with engineering, with expressions such as 'research in technology' and 'education in technology' referring to engineering in both cases. On the other hand, there is no confusion in the term 'technologist.' That is someone trained in the use of certain technologies, as defined above.
- The label 'STEM disciplines' is a label used in the US, and increasingly in Canada to describe science, technology, engineering and mathematics as fields of study. The meaning of technology in this is not clear. It does not refer to the education of technologists, since the label refers to

university studies only. A listing of the STEM subjects by the US National Science Foundation includes engineering, mathematics and science and some subjects in computer science, such as management information systems. So either the T is short-hand for IT (information technology), or it is there to make the acronym easier to say – or maybe just to confuse biologists who think about stem cells.

## R&D

R&D is the acronym for research and development, an essential element in technological innovation, since it is the means for embodying the knowledge that creates value in new products.

R&D is generally used as a singular noun that is silent on the relative proportions of its two components. The order of the R and D words suggests that research comes first, as in research-based innovation, but the same expression is also used for design-based innovation in which design and development come first.

Research and development are two related but very different activities, carried out for different reasons, by different people, at different levels of risk. Research involves mainly scientists and is undertaken to create new knowledge. Development is done mainly by engineers, literally to develop new products. Design is an early and important part of development, but it plays little or no role in research. When the term R&D is used in connection with universities, hospitals and government labs, it refers almost entirely to research. When it is used in connection with industry, it involves much more development than research.[24] In research-based innovation, development follows research and invention. In design-based innovation, design comes first as part of the invention process, followed by development of the product, with applied research as needed to provide any additional detailed knowledge. This is a simplification, of course, since there are many feedback loops in the process and many activities take place simultaneously,

---

[24] One occasionally encounters attempts to give relative weight to the two components of R&D in cute expressions such as 'big R, little d' referring to research institutions, and 'little r, big D' referring to industrial R&D.

but it is a useful way to describe the contrasting logic in the two cases.

We already have the definition of research. The corresponding definition of development is:

- **Development:** the multifaceted industrial activity, always involving design and testing, to produce a new marketable product from an invention or from an earlier product.

This is a very limited definition. It doesn't deal with development as it refers to real estate or to the opening up of natural resources as new sources of raw materials, even though innovation may be involved in both. And its biological meaning is entirely outside of this discussion.

Note that the phrase 'experimental development (ED)' sometimes replaces the 'development' of R&D for the simple reason that 'development' alone is common in the economic literature as the abbreviation of 'economic development,' and that is a very different thing.[25]

The differences between the R and D of R&D are clearly shown in a one-by-one comparison of their attributes in Table 4.1.

The comparison reveals that research and development are opposites or near-opposites on many dimensions, and demonstrates why they must not be confused in communications. In spite of that, R&D is often referred to imprecisely as a single activity. Even more confusing is usage such as 'R&D in universities' which suggests that university activities actually include a significant amount of development. But they don't. 'R&D in government labs' is somewhat more accurate, since in certain cases their work may include some development.

The listing of attributes in Table 4.1 is too unwieldy to serve as a definition of R&D. A manageably succinct definition would be:

- **R&D** is the set of activities that embody knowledge in a new product or process.

---

[25] An example is Canada's SR&ED tax credit – the Scientific Research and Experimental Development tax credit.

## TABLE 4.1 The Differences Between Research and Development

| Research | Development |
| --- | --- |
| • exploration and discovery to produce new knowledge; | • proprietary development of new products or processes based on inventions or prior art; |
| • long-term mainly publicly-funded programs building up answers to scientific questions often defined by the international research community, but it can also be pre-competitive industrial research funded by consortia of interested companies; | • short-term projects with specific objectives defined by the firm paying for the R&D, and often shaped by market feedback to existing products; |
| • the same questions may be pursued in many labs around the world; | • similar questions may be pursued independently by competing companies; |
| • in Canada done largely in the public sector; | • in Canada done mostly in the private sector; |
| • mainly the work of scientists, with technicians and some engineers involved; | • mostly the work of engineers and technicians, with some scientists involved; |
| • depends heavily on codified knowledge; | • depends on tacit knowledge in addition to codified knowledge; |
| • involves theory, experiment and verification; | • involves design, building of prototypes, testing and performance measurement; |
| • consumes wealth; | • consumes a lot of wealth, generally much more expensive than research; |
| • risk is scientific, and managed through scientific peer review; | • risk is financial, and managed through due diligence and good business practice; |
| • produces new codified knowledge, provides context for training of highly qualified people (HQP); | • employs both HQP and skilled trades, and produces new knowledge in the context of a new product; |
| • open publication of results and international flows of information are common, with competition to achieve priority of publication; in exceptional cases publication may be delayed when the research results suggest inventions that are to be protected by patents; | • information generated is proprietary and generally closely held for competitive reasons; IP is protected: there are many patents and trade secrets; |
| • successful research always leads to more research; it may also lead to important and revolutionary innovations, but they are rare and unpredictable. | • successful development projects are necessary to produce innovations and new wealth creation through sales of new goods or services. |

Source: Based closely on the author's earlier work: T.A. Brzustowski. 2008. *The Way Ahead: Meeting Canada's Productivity Challenge*. Ottawa, ON: University of Ottawa Press, chapter 6.

## A very short historical perspective on R&D

To understand better the role of R&D today, it is useful to take time out to look at it in the historical perspective. The Industrial Revolution started in Great Britain in the late 18th century when the leading technical innovators were individual, experienced craftsmen and entrepreneurs who kept themselves informed about their work. The craftsmen were learning about many aspects of the behaviour of matter and of the working of machines, and experimented to create new machines to do things that couldn't be done before. The entrepreneurs followed what the craftsmen were doing and visualized new products that could be important in the economy. The steam engines that drove pumps to keep the coal mines dry, and machines for the cotton industry are two well-known examples.

The Industrial Revolution advanced through much of the 19th century in the areas of steam power, railways, steamships, electricity and manufacturing through the competition of many firms who initially still largely relied on craft-shop operations. An important factor spurring that advance was that British businessmen and entrepreneurs continued to follow the work of natural philosophers – serious investigators, often of independent means – who were making discoveries in physics and chemistry and keeping the public informed. Today such people would be called scientists.

The advances in British technology diffused rapidly across much of Europe and to the United States, and the process of technological innovation spread and accelerated as well. Then, as Freeman argues in compelling fashion, the great surge in industrial innovation since the mid 19th century came about because of the professionalization of R&D.[26] People started to be trained and hired to do R&D. The model research-intensive university, generally attributed to Wilhelm von Humboldt, the Minister of Education in Prussia, was founded in Berlin in 1810. The Massachusetts Institute of Technology was founded in Boston in 1861, explicitly to translate new scientific discoveries into new technology and to teach engineers. Edison founded the

[26] Christopher Freeman. 1974. *The Economics of Industrial Innovation.* New York: Penguin Books and also Christopher Freeman and Luc Soete. 2004. *The Economics of Industrial Innovation,* Third edition. New York: Routledge.

first industrial research lab in Menlo Park in 1876. During this time, the engineering profession was expanding from just civil engineering, concerned with roads and bridges, into mechanical, electrical and chemical engineering as well.

At their peak, the best industrial research labs, such as the Bell Labs in New Jersey, General Electric Labs in Schenectady NY, etc. functioned in many ways like universities pursuing basic research, but were generally better funded and equipped. Their researchers showed general interest in possible uses of the findings, but little interest in specific applications, and some were only loosely connected with the business of the parent companies. That started changing in the 1960s, as corporations realized that these were very expensive activities, and began to bring the R&D labs back into closer contact with their business to justify the cost. Today, the R of most corporate R&D includes only short-term applied research closely related to the products under development. Companies now expect the long-term basic research to be done at public cost by universities and government labs around the world, and often relocate or expand their own R&D activities to be close to centres of strong research wherever they are found.

### Intellectual property

Intellectual property is a very important product of R&D, and we must be clear about its definition and what it implies. Many dictionaries don't have an entry for it, and encyclopedias tend to be excessively detailed. Fortunately, a practical and accessible definition is available in a little didactic volume on Canadian IP law:[27]

> *"Intellectual property: an intangible creation of the mind that can be legally protected. Not all intangible creations can be protected; the ones that can are considered IP... Intellectual properties are rights, not things. The owner of the rights can enforce them against any third party. The two most fundamental rights belonging to an intellectual property owner are: The right to use the property without interference from others, and the right to exclude others from using the property... You*

---

[27] Henri Charmasson, John Buchaca, Neil Milton and Diana Byron. 2009. *Canadian Intellectual Property Law for Dummies.* Toronto, ON: Wiley, p. 8-9.

*can use one or more of the following to secure your IP rights: patents...,trademarks..., copyrights...,industrial designs...Two other categories of rights are relevant to IP: trade secrets and contractual rights. ..[but] these can be enforced only against people with whom you have a contractual relationship."*

It is important to note that a patent secures the inventor's right to use the invention freely and exclusively for a given period of time. But that's all it does. Whether the inventor actually manages to use that invention productively is a separate issue. However, it seems to be the case that having a patent provides an important element of validation for the invention, and that may help the inventor in attracting the early investment for a research-based new venture.

There will be much more to say about R&D and IP in later chapters.

# CHAPTER 5

## INNOVATION AND PRODUCTIVITY

*Canada doesn't have a productivity problem; we have a prosperity problem.*

Productivity is a measure of what is achieved by the effort expended. In everyday life, the language is intuitive. When the objective of our action is fully attained, we describe the effort as fruitful or productive. At the other extreme, when an effort accomplishes nothing, we call it futile or unproductive. In what follows, the effort consists of the human labour and the capital invested in the economy, and the objective is the creation of value or wealth. Productivity again refers to how fruitful the effort has been, but now it takes the form of a quantitative measure.

Many distinguished voices have been telling us that Canada has a 'productivity problem' that we must fix or face dire consequences. Our productivity is, indeed, significantly lower than that of the US, and we are slipping further behind. However, I believe that Canada doesn't have a productivity problem; we have a prosperity problem, and the productivity gap is only a relevant indicator. As argued in chapter 2, Canada's prosperity problem is that, as a nation, we are accumulating important needs that we cannot afford to fund adequately.

In thinking about this, I find the following analogy helpful: The productivity of an economy is an indicator, analogous to the speedometer in a car. If your car has trouble keeping up with traffic on a long hill, you don't solve the problem by repairing the speedometer; you must fix the engine.

In this case, the engine is the economic activity that creates wealth; it happens to be where value-added is produced. To fix the prosperity problem, Canada needs more wealth creation in the economy. In making the case in chapter 2 for more innovation in Canada, we argued that this should be achieved by producing more valuable products than we do now – much more valuable or even only slightly more valuable – across the board, in all sectors. Since innovation is a new way of creating value-added, what Canada needs is more innovation. That will address the prosperity problem, and the productivity problem will be solved at the same time.

Two measures of productivity are commonly used: the productivity of labour and the 'total factor productivity' or 'multifactor productivity' (MFP). The productivity of labour is an intuitive direct measure. MFP is a more abstract measure derived from a theoretical model of the economy.

## Productivity of labour

An intuitive measure of productivity is the value produced per hour worked, measured in $/hr. This might apply to an individual worker or be the average for the entire workforce of a firm. The national productivity of labour is somewhat more complicated because it is averaged over the whole population of whom only a fraction – the workforce – is employed.

The defining relationship is:

$$\frac{GDP}{capita} = \frac{GDP}{hr} \times \frac{hrs}{capita} \qquad (5.1)$$

where $\dfrac{GDP}{capita}$ is the prosperity measured in $ per capita,

$\dfrac{GDP}{hr}$ is the national productivity of labour measured in $ per hour, and

$\dfrac{hrs}{capita}$ is the total number of hours worked by the nation's work force per capita of the general population.

Both $\dfrac{GDP}{capita}$ and $\dfrac{hrs}{capita}$ are annual amounts, but the phrase 'per year' has been cancelled on both sides of the equation.

Estimating the order of magnitude of Canadian productivity of labour for 2009 helps explain how equation 5.1 works. Take the population as roughly 33,000,000 in that year, and gross domestic product (GDP) as roughly $1,500,000,000,000 in current Canadian dollars. The number of hours worked per capita per year can be estimated assuming that a working year is 35 hours per week for 50 weeks and that the workforce is one half of the Canadian population.[1]

These numbers combine to give the estimates

$$\frac{GDP}{capita} = \$45,400$$

and $\frac{hrs}{capita}$ = 875 hours per capita per year. Dividing the first of these numbers by the second gives the productivity of labour for Canada in 2009 at roughly $52 per hour.

In reality, the calculation of the number of hours worked per year per capita is very much more complicated than what was done here, but this simple estimate is surprisingly close.

## Multi-factor productivity

The multi-factor productivity (MFP), also known as the total factor productivity, is a much more abstract concept than the productivity of labour. It arises from the basic philosophical assumption that the GDP depends only on the amount of capital invested and labour employed in the economy. Its mathematical form is the so-called production function that expresses GDP as a power function of the capital (K) and the labour (L). Denoting GDP by Y, we have

$$Y = AK^{\alpha}L^{\beta}$$

In order to provide an effect that economists call 'return to scale,' namely that a doubling of the labour and capital will double the GDP, the relationship must be made linear overall. That is done by making $\beta = 1 - \alpha$, with $\alpha$ taking values between 0 and 1. With that change, the above equation gives the Cobb-Douglas production function for the GDP as

$$Y = AK^{\alpha}L^{1-\alpha} \qquad (5.2)$$

The name of this equation derives from the names of two statisticians, Cobb and Douglas, who verified that it was a good fit to the data for the US in the first quarter of the 20th century.

---

[1] By coincidence, the Canadian workforce has been quite close to half of the population for several years.

The quantity A is the most interesting feature of equation 5.2. It is the total factor productivity. The larger it is, the greater the GDP created with a given amount of labour and capital invested in the national economy. This is where innovation comes into the picture and makes it possible to produce more value with a given amount of capital and labour.

The Cobb-Douglas production function is an empirical relationship that has been shown to be useful in practice. Its derivation is seldom shown, but it is instructive. Very briefly, it goes like this:

Assume that Y is a function of K and L, such that Y = Y(K,L) and then impose the perfectly reasonable intuitive requirement on it that the percentage change in Y should be a linear combination of the percentage changes in K and L. That means that

$$\frac{\Delta Y}{Y} = \propto \left(\frac{\Delta K}{K}\right) + \beta \left(\frac{\Delta L}{L}\right)$$

where the equation has been divided by 100 percent. In the limit of very small relative changes

$$\frac{dY}{Y} = \propto \left(\frac{dK}{K}\right) + \beta \left(\frac{dL}{L}\right)$$

which is the same as

$$d\ln Y = \propto d\ln K + \beta d\ln L$$

This relationship can be integrated immediately to

$$\ln Y = \propto \ln K + \beta \ln L + a$$

where **a** is a constant not dependent on K or L.

Taking the exponent of both sides gives

$$Y = AK^{\propto} L^{\beta} \quad \text{where} \quad A = e^{a}$$

To produce the so-called 'return to scale,' a linear relation between the output and the total of the inputs, $\alpha$ and $\beta$ must add up to 1, so that $\beta = 1 - \alpha$. When that substitution is made, the result is equation 5.2, the Cobb-Douglas equation for Y as a function of K and L.

Next, we want to see how the total factor productivity, or MFP, changes with time. This time all of Y, A, K and L are functions of time, such that Y=Y(t), A=A(t), K=K(t) and L=L(t).

So, taking the natural logarithm of both sides of the equation and differentiating with respect to time gives the result:

$$\left(\frac{1}{Y}\right)\left(\frac{dY}{dt}\right) = \left(\frac{1}{A}\right)\left(\frac{dA}{dt}\right) + \left(\frac{1}{K^{\alpha}}\right)\left(\frac{dK^{\alpha}}{dt}\right) + \left(\frac{1}{L^{1-\alpha}}\right)\left(\frac{dL^{1-\alpha}}{dt}\right)$$

Bringing the productivity term to the left side, taking a finite time interval and multiplying through by it, gives the expression for the relative productivity change over that period:

$$\frac{\Delta A}{A} = \frac{\Delta Y}{Y} - \left(\frac{\Delta K^{\alpha}}{K^{\alpha}}\right) - \left(\frac{\Delta L^{1-\alpha}}{L^{1-\alpha}}\right) \qquad (5.3)$$

Equation 5.3 shows how the change in total factor productivity (or MFP) A can be calculated from the data on GDP, capital and labour. Note that we have not had to discuss the units of K and L which are awkward to say the least. Whatever they are, they cancel in equation 5.3. All that is needed is that the data should be accurate and consistent. If the goal is to calculate the absolute value of the MFP, then the units of K and L must be noted, since MFP would be different for another set of units.

*Two examples*: The US GDP was estimated[2] as $Y = 1.1K^{0.25} L^{0.75}$. The units of Y, K and L are not given, but as pointed out above, they don't need to be if the object is to calculate only the relative year-over-year growth in MFP. All that's needed are consistent annual values of Y, K, L.

A very different example appears in a well-known macro-economics textbook.[3] The production function for Canada is given as $Y = AK^{0.3} L^{0.7}$. Here is an extract from a table that lists the annual values of the relevant quantities for the years 1990 to 1992, inclusive.

[2] G. Bannock, E. Davis, P. Trott and M. Uncles. 2002. *The New Penguin Business Dictionary*. New York: Penguin Books, p. 289.
[3] Andrew B. Abel, Ben S. Bernanke and Gregor W. Smith. 1995. *Macroeconomics, Canadian Edition*. Toronto: Addison-Wesley, p. 66.

## TABLE 5.1 Canadian MFP, 1990-1992

| Year | GDP (Y) $1986 billions | Capital (K) $1986 billions | Labour (L) millions of workers | Total Factor Productivity (A) (or MFP) | Growth in MFP % |
|------|------|------|------|------|------|
| 1990 | 565 | 479 | 12.6 | 15.05 | -1.67 |
| 1991 | 556 | 493 | 12.3 | 14.94 | -0.78 |
| 1992 | 560 | 500 | 12.2 | 15.08 | 0.87 |

Source: Andrew B. Abel, Ben S. Bernanke and Gregor W. Smith. 1995. *Macroeconomics, Canadian Edition*. Toronto: Addison-Wesley, p. 66.

Note that in this table the amount of capital (K) refers to year-end non-residential capital stock, while labour (L) is the civilian employment over 14 years of age.

The units of MFP are idiosyncratic: ($ 1986 billion per million workers)$^{0.7}$, and that's if we ignore the 'per year' part of GDP. It's neither useful nor necessary to look for a meaning of the MFP in some basic terms. Its only meaning derives from the production function. And there's no point trying to compare it with the productivity of labour discussed earlier. The important quantity is the growth in MFP shown in the last column.

A quick comparison of the production functions for Canada and the US might suggest that the Canadian GDP is more dependent on capital and less on labour than that of the US. That may, indeed, be the case but much more detailed data of better quality need to be used to determine if it is so, and why.

# PART II

## WHERE WE ARE NOW

# CHAPTER 6

## FROM GIGAPROJECTS TO SMALL POTATOES: THE COST OF INNOVATION

*You don't get much for a million dollars these days – a Megaproject is a small house in Vancouver. Any serious industrial venture is a Gigaproject.*

### Introduction

How much does innovation cost? The question seems obvious and important, but it's the wrong question. Some of the costs of innovation, such as patent applications, are fixed and in many cases unavoidable. But there are other costs that are highly variable. The basic functionality of the new product must be established when it is first introduced; bells and whistles can be added later. The necessary safety features must be incorporated right away; convenience features can be added as improvements later. An acceptable level of quality must be reached from the start; perfecting it can be done later in light of user experience. Ultimately, innovation costs as much as you are prepared to spend on it.

A better question to ask is how much was spent on a particular innovation. But even that question is difficult to answer. The right data are hard to get. The spending on individual innovation projects ranges from billions of dollars to very little. It differs between the public and private sectors, and among sectors in business and industry. For example, the corporate process of product innovation by a technology firm may be self-sustaining with annual spending in the hundreds of million dollars, or several percent of sales revenues to produce an important innovation every couple of years. It is self-sustaining when each new product generates revenues that recover all its costs, including commercialization, and provides both seed funding for the next generation of products and adequate profits. In a natural-resource company, a major innovation in process technology that exploits a new source of raw materials may be a very large up-front expense, likely in the billions of dollars. It is expected to pay for itself from new sales over decades. In a government agency, a service innovation may cost many millions annually, and the project may drag on for a long time. Its cost is expected to be recovered eventually from future efficiencies in operations. At the other extreme, many small businesses routinely introduce inexpensive incremental innovations – minor product or process improvements – and include them in their operating costs. These examples illustrate that the spending on innovation is strongly linked to the nature and operation of the innovating organization. The discussion that follows shows that it also depends on the nature of the innovation.

We begin the discussion with the private sector. To help make the discussion systematic, we start with a simple framework based on the kind of innovation involved and on the nature of the firm taking it to market.

## A framework for business innovation – the quad taxonomy

A quad taxonomy, also called a two-by-two table, serves as a useful framework for discussing many issues on the business side of innovation.[1] The innovations are divided into two kinds: research-based innovations which are new uses of new knowledge, and design-based innovations which are new uses of prior knowledge. The companies commercializing them may be either established firms or new ventures. The four combinations of innovations and firms constitute the four quadrants of the innovation space. These are: the research-based innovation by a new venture (R-N); its near opposite, the design-based innovation by an established firm (D-E); the research-based innovation by an established firm (R-E) and the design-based innovation by a new venture (D-N). Figure 6.1 shows this framework.

[1] T.A. Brzustowski. 2011. "A New Business-based Taxonomy of Innovation," *Optimumonline*, 41 (3): 30-37.

The useful feature of the framework is that the business issues are very different in the four quadrants, with different cost structures and spending patterns.

**FIGURE 6.1 The Quad Taxonomy of Innovation**

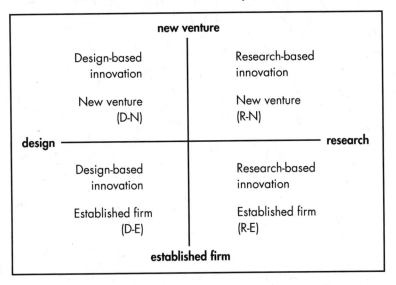

Source: T.A. Brzustowski. 2011. "A New Business-based Taxonomy of Innovation," *Optimumonline*, 41(3): 30-37.

Note: The business aspects of innovation are different depending on the kind of innovation and the state of the firm.

## *Research-based innovation, new venture (R-N)*

This quadrant of the innovation space is the realm of inventions that are suggested by the results of basic and applied research that is mostly publicly funded and done in universities, research hospitals or government labs that are then commercialized by new ventures. The scope of the inventions is generally narrow, typically a single, new technology, but the hope always is that it might become an enabler, a platform, a game-changer with tremendous impact – and every now and then it turns out that way. That hope is one reason why this quadrant receives the bulk of the media attention paid to innovation. It also receives the bulk of policy attention, since research in the Canadian post-secondary institutions and hospitals has been the beneficiary of major public investments over the last fifteen years, and is the focus of governments' expectations for a more prosperous future.

The underlying research is funded by grants, typically in the range of several hundred thousand dollars over a few years, but the funding criteria do not include invention. Funding is granted on the basis of the excellence of the research, as indicated by the principal investigators' publication records in international, peer-reviewed journals, and by the advanced education offered to their research students. Inventions, if and when they come, may be unexpected, but are likely to be more unexpected in the natural sciences than in engineering or the health sciences,[2] and more unexpected in basic research than in applied research. It is a consequence of the openness of the international research community that inventions made in Canadian laboratories might build on discoveries made in laboratories around the world and vice-versa.

When a new venture is formed to commercialize a research-based invention, it starts out as an small to medium-sized enterprise (SME), a risky small business without customers. It usually starts with a technical team that has no experience in management, commercialization or sales. It is faced with the expensive technical process of developing an invention into its first product, and, at the same time, developing the appropriate business model, finding the right market, and securing its first customers. To fund this work, it must assemble risk capital in the right amounts at the right times, starting with seed, start-up, then early-stage, and progressing eventually to growth capital. A particular challenge is to bridge the so-called 'valley of death.' This is the name given to the deep drop in the availability of risk capital needed to go from a working prototype to a product ready for the market, typically in the range from a few hundred thousand dollars to a few million per project. It must be remembered that this capital is private money that is exposed to business risk – high risk in this quadrant. The risk declines as the company achieves successive milestones, but it remains high by

---

[2] One explanation of the reason for this is offered in the book by Donald Stokes (1997. *Pasteur's Quadrant*. New York: Brookings). According to Stokes, research in the health sciences and in engineering is generally undertaken to develop both a new understanding and a new use. In the natural sciences, it is done only to develop a new understanding.

investment standards. In contrast, the public funds spent on the underlying research are exposed only to scientific risk, a risk that is well understood and is minimized by the established process of peer review.

So how much does it cost to produce an R-N innovation? At first glance, it seems that four amounts can be presumed known:

- The amount of research support provided to the laboratory where the invention occurred;
- The amount of risk capital raised by the new venture to start commercializing the invention;
- The amount spent by the new venture on R&D;
- The amount of any government grant to support commercialization.

The first amount is not uncertain, but neither is it very useful in determining the cost of innovation. In basic research, grants pay for a variety of activities, of which the invention might be only an incidental outcome.[3] An audit after the fact would be hampered by difficulties in identifying which activities contributed to the invention in question and which didn't. If the research is targeted and invention is a goal,[4] the audit is easier, but difficult questions remain. How far back does one start to take into account the support for research that eventually led to the invention? How does one deal with the cost of blind alleys, dead ends and failed attempts along the way? How does one take into account the research supported in other labs – perhaps even other countries' labs – that contributed to the necessary related knowledge?

The amount of risk capital raised – the second amount in the list – is much more straightforward. It can be found in the financial statements of the new venture. The third one is clear if the new venture is a successful applicant for the SR&ED tax credit.[5] Success in this program requires documentation of activities that meet the definition of R&D developed by the

---

[3] According to Stokes, basic research lies in Bohr's Quadrant, where the goal is a new understanding, but there is no concern with any new use. Donald Stokes. 1997. *Pasteur's Quadrant*. New York: Brookings.

[4] This would put the research into Pasteur's Quadrant where the goal is both a new understanding and a new use.

[5] This is the Scientific Research and Experimental Development program of tax credits administered by the Canada Revenue Agency. The program uses the OECD definition of R&D in the *Oslo Manual* to determine what activities qualify.

OECD.[6] While this amount is known to have been spent on R&D, it will not cover all the costs, because it takes much more than R&D to make an innovation. But in any case, the spending on R&D would likely be included in the second amount on the list, namely the risk capital raised, and therefore the third amount would provide no new information if only the total cost of innovation is sought.

Finally, the amount of any grants to support commercialization would be an unambiguous and separately documented component of the total cost of innovation in this case.

So how much does a typical R-N innovation cost? It varies greatly. Perhaps the best hint lies in the conventional wisdom that the cost of commercialization is usually many times greater than the cost of research. If that is the case, then a good estimate for the cost of an R-N innovation might be just the amount of risk capital that had to be raised to bring it to market, namely the second item on our list above, with the cost of research ignored as small. If there was a grant for commercialization that would have to be added. The amount of research support ignored in specific cases might instead be treated in aggregate as the funding that enables some component of the innovation system (e.g., a particular laboratory, an institute, a department, a university ...) to produce R-N innovations. All told, the amounts of research grants and the typical financing rounds suggest costs in the range of a few hundred thousand to several million dollars.

The big exception would be an innovation in the pharmaceutical area. In the case of a proposed new drug, the costs associated with clinical trials can raise the total amount into the hundreds of millions of dollars.

A more macro measure than the cost of a typical innovation, such as the number of research-based start-ups created per so many millions of dollars of research funding serves to compare the performance of institutions or jurisdictions, but since it also includes the research funding that has not led to innovations, it offers no information on the cost of any individual innovation.

---

[6] Organisation for Economic Co-operation and Development.

## *Design-based innovation, established firm (D-E)*

Next consider the D-E quadrant, which is almost the polar opposite of R-N on many dimensions. Most companies involved in D-E innovation are medium or large, but there may be some established small firms in this quadrant as well. This quadrant represents the bulk of industrial innovation, in which new use is made of prior knowledge, but it gets relatively little media or policy attention. It involves R&D that is primarily D. The company may have a separate R&D department or division, and may have a design department as well. If some new knowledge is needed for a project, the necessary applied research is usually contracted out to a university or a government lab. At the low end of the spending scale, D-E innovation includes incremental innovation and product improvement that may be routinely included under product support. At the high end, the innovation may be a huge project that is so important and expensive that the company is literally betting its future on its success. Obvious current examples are two Gigaprojects in the aerospace industry, namely Boeing's 787 Dreamliner and Bombardier's Series C jet.[7]

The term gigaproject emphasizes the very high cost of large industrial projects. A gigaproject is one that costs in the billion dollar range. Megaprojects (i.e., costing in the millions) are not as impressive as they once were. A megaproject today might be a small house in Vancouver.

The established company already has its product lines, its expertise and knowledge base, its markets and customers, its organizational structure for innovation, its supply chains, access to finance, technical expertise in its field, as well as corporate management experience. In sectors where innovation is frequent, there are established procedures and experience in gathering market intelligence, selecting the most promising innovation projects as they pass through the innovation pipeline and shutting down the rest, dealing with intellectual property (IP) issues, and generally managing innovation systematically. The large, expensive projects often have international supply chains in which the suppliers develop some of the needed technology. That can introduce two competing considerations.

---

[7] Giga is the prefix for billion.

First, an international supply chain involving suppliers who have substantial technological capabilities can distribute the project risk. But, secondly, it can also introduce the challenge of managing that international supply chain.[8]

Established firms pay for innovation mainly out of their sales revenues and raised capital. Needless to say, they seek tax credits from the SR&ED program wherever applicable, and also take advantage of any programs through which government shares the risk of new projects. However, sales revenues are the main source of funding for their innovations. We shall look at the actual data on this for specific firms in chapter 12.

Some elements of financing design-based innovation by established firms are illustrated in Figure 6.2. The diagram is a sketch only; it is not based on detailed data. It shows the rate of creation of value-added in a successful innovation project as a function of time. This is done for two kinds of products: a personal device in a fast-moving market, such as consumer electronics (top), and a very large and complex product with long time scales, such as a jet airliner (bottom).

The first thing to note is that the time scales are very different. At the top, the time is measured in months. At the bottom it is in years. There is an obvious similarity between the two cases: both projects initially lose money. This is shown by the negative value-added. As the product is being developed, inputs are bought and wages paid, but there is no sales revenue. The firm is burning through cash. In the case of a new jet, the development costs can be so great – in the billions – that substantial deposits from customers have to be collected as the order book is built up.

[8] This is a serious challenge. Deliveries of the Boeing 787 are about three years behind schedule. According to the business press, the delay was caused by problems in managing the complex international supply chain that provided some major components of the aircraft. Five years earlier, the delivery of the Airbus A380 was delayed for two years by problems of incompatibility in the design of the electrical wiring harness for the cabin between plants of the same company in France and in Germany.

## FIGURE 6.2 The Financial History of Two Innovations

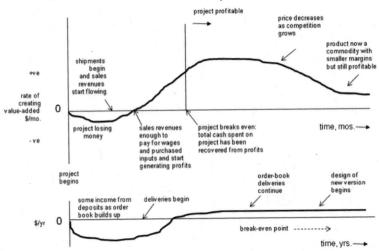

Note: Sketches of the rate of creation of value-added for a consumer electronic product (top) and a jetliner (bottom) - not based on data. Both innovations are financial successes, but on very different time scales. They both consume a lot of wealth before they become profitable.

After shipments and deliveries begin, and sales revenues start flowing, the value-added continues to be negative for some time. It crosses zero and moves into positive territory only at the point where the sales revenue first becomes sufficient to pay for the purchased inputs to the project and the wages of the people working on it. After that profit begins to be generated. At some later time, when the cumulative profits reach the amount of cash spent to date, the project breaks even and starts being profitable. That happens fairly quickly in consumer electronics, and much later in aerospace.[9]

What happens next reflects the different state of the competition in the two sectors. In consumer electronics, there are plenty of competitors with comparable technological capabilities, and competing products quickly begin to appear on the market. The original product and its competing products – which often include many of the same commodity components – evolve in

---

[9] In late August 2011, when the Boeing 787 Dreamliner was within weeks of its first delivery to a customer, and the order book counted about 850 firm orders, the company indicated that it was still unable to predict the point at which this new aircraft would become profitable.

the same direction. This competition leads to price reductions, and ultimately turns the original innovation into a commodity product, which nevertheless may still be profitable. Digital cameras went through this process recently, and it is now happening with smart phones.

The situation is very different in civilian aerospace. There are very few producers. For example, Boeing competes only with Airbus in the large jet market. The competition between them occurs when the order books are being built up, not when the product is being delivered. The product is exceedingly complex and production is slow, and customers often compete for delivery dates. There is no commoditization and the product is delivered substantially unchanged for many years, but with improvements, perhaps over a time period as long as a couple of decades. The design of a new version begins only after many years of operating experience with the original model.

The two examples presented in Figure 6.2 seem to be useful illustrations of innovation in the D-E quadrant. Their financial histories probably come close to bracketing those in many other sectors, even though some differences quickly come to mind. One is the auto industry, where the annual model change means that the product is sold only for a fixed period of time and then taken off the market. This means that the development process is generally longer than the market lifetime of the product. Another difference arises in the resource industries where an innovation project might often be the purchase and adaptation of a new process technology to reduce production costs. This can mean a large up-front investment followed by a long period of cost recovery through sales at modest margins that might have to last through several commodity market cycles.

### Research-based innovation, established firm (R-E)

In this quadrant of innovation space, there are many similarities to what happens in D-E but with some different business issues, particularly those involving intellectual property rights (IPR). We will illustrate this point by looking at three cases: (i) firms acquiring a new technology by licensing a single research-based invention, (ii) firms that hold portfolios of patents that they have originated or acquired, and (iii) the research-based pharmaceutical industry.

In all three cases, the corporate resources of the companies involved include the factors listed for the D-E quadrant. A company may license a research-based invention from a university, a research hospital or a government laboratory or perhaps from another company. It will usually seek an exclusive licence to the IP, but sometimes a licence exclusive in their market will suffice to meet their needs.[10] The technology acquired in this way becomes an input into the company's own R&D and innovation processes to be used in various ways. It may be commercialized as a stand-alone innovation. It may be added to an existing technology to strengthen it by filling a gap or opening the door to developments in a new direction. Or it may serve as a platform technology from which the company will develop its own related new technologies that it will then patent.

In this situation, the main issue in IPR is clarity of ownership. The licensee company must be sure that it obtains the licence from people who are authorized to grant it. In the case of a university, there is no ambiguity if the institution owns the IP. But in some universities, the inventor owns the IP, and that opens the possibility of someone – a former student or a one-time visiting researcher – coming forward late in the game and claiming to have contributed to the invention. Such a late entrance could lead to legal wrangling and produce expensive delays in the commercialization process. It can be avoided, of course, if the lead researcher concerned enters into explicit agreements with all members of the research team early enough in the game.

The time history of value-added in this case depends on the sector of activity, very likely falling somewhere between the two shown Figure 6.2.

Sometimes a patent is not used to make anything, but rather serves as an asset. Some companies, such as IBM, have substantial in-house research capacity and sell the patents that they don't intend to use. The companies buying these patents may use them, or they may also treat them as an asset. There have recently been many high-profile patent suits and countersuits among big-name companies in information and communications technology

---

[10] A reason why some owners of IP prefer to grant only licences restricted to one market is the belief that good entrepreneurs might find different ways to exploit that same IP in different ways, in different markets, and the prospect of multiple licences is attractive to the owner.

(ICT). An auction for the patent portfolio of the bankrupt Nortel Networks in the summer of 2011 fetched a price of several billion dollars. Some of the patents acquired this way may be used to develop new technologies, as described in the earlier case, but many might also be used to strengthen the new owners' position in any patent litigation. The idea is that there are so many patents in closely related fields in the ICT industry that patent infringement, intentional or not, is likely. The best defence against an infringement suit in that case seems to be a big patent portfolio of one's own, with a plausible allegation in return that the plaintiff has probably infringed some of them. The prospect of a successful countersuit may turn the parties from litigation to negotiation. That can save a lot of time and a huge amount of money

How much money? The legal costs are a few tens of thousands of dollars to prepare the patent application and file it, with an annual maintenance fee of a few hundred dollars after that. Signing a licence agreement is a matter of a few thousand dollars, unless there is something very complicated about it. But then the costs skyrocket, potentially rising to hundreds of thousands and even millions in defending the patent against charges of infringement – and that's not taking into account the potential cost of any judgments – and probably in the same range for enforcing one's patent and charging someone else with infringement. And a big award of damages is too uncertain to count on. Needless to say, an opponent with deep pockets is a serious threat on either side in any patent litigation.

The principal IP issues for these companies are the ownership and validity of the patents. The length of protection is less important because the field moves very quickly.

The research-based pharmaceutical industry is a different story. It is a special case in the R-E quadrant, in that it is a very tightly regulated industry, working to a timeline that is largely not under its own control. The sketch in Figure 6.3 tells the story. Strictly speaking, the timeline is under company control only in the initial period of additional R&D and clinical trials after the patent has been issued. That seems to take some seven years. The time required for all the approval processes has been growing as additional reviews have been added over the years, and now is about three years. Patent protection expires after 20 years, and the drug is commoditized very quickly when generic versions hit the market at much lower prices and take most of the sales. This means that the drug manufacturer will essentially have about ten years of market exclusivity in which to recover all the costs of the project and earn a profit on the new product.

For obvious reasons, the principal IP issue in the research-based pharmaceutical industry is the length of patent protection.[11] But there are other IP issues as well. The generic drug industry does not have to seek FDA and Health Canada approvals to sell their version of the same drug, and they don't engage in clinical trials, but they still spend a lot on R&D. This is mainly R&D on manufacturing processes because they must avoid infringing on any patents on the process by which the drug is manufactured. Such patents may be more recent than the patent on the drug, and may still be in force when the patent on the drug expires.

### FIGURE 6.3 The Financial History of an Innovation in the Research-based Pharmaceutical Industry

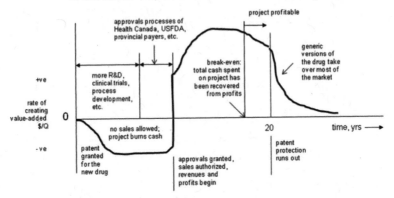

**Note:** (Sketch only – not based on data) The patent for a new drug is granted at t=0. There is research before that and its cost is included in the total cash spent on the project.

## Design-based innovation, new venture (D-N)

This quadrant is very different from the R-N quadrant with which we started. The innovations represent new uses of prior knowledge, and the knowledge may be in any domain. The companies are involved in a much broader spectrum of activities.

[11] As this is being written in September 2011, the issue of the length of patent protection is on the table in the free trade negotiations between Canada and the EU. The research-based pharmaceutical industry is lobbying for a longer term.

Success here can flow mainly from the ability of the entrepreneur to sense the needs and tastes of the public. The innovation may involve technology, new or old, but it doesn't have to. There may be R&D spending in some cases, but probably just on product development. Some innovations in this area may have primarily aesthetic appeal (e.g., in high fashion, entertainment, or a specialty restaurant), while others may introduce a new level of convenience to an established activity (e.g., a new application for a smart phone or a new personal service). Recent technology may be the sources of new value-added in this quadrant, but so may imagination, creativity, style, fashion and almost any outstanding individual talent and skill.

In many ways, these new ventures face the same problems as most other SME's. They are always short of time and money. But they are more risky, particularly if their innovation is a new kind of business. They can't offer the potential investor any results of research as the validation of their founding idea; their credibility and risk worthiness depends much more on the quality of the individuals in the enterprise. But the search for investment may be less of an issue than in R-N, and many of these companies probably don't face the 'valley of death.' One reason is that they may not require expensive specialized equipment; these days a laptop computer and an Internet connection provide enormous capacity for business communications. And in many companies, the labour costs of getting into business may be relatively low, because of the high amount of 'sweat equity' provided by the '3F' – the founders, their families and friends.

Many of the innovations may be local – first in the city, say – and many may involve the purchase and use of off-the-shelf technology. Many of these companies are likely to stay small, but some whose products catch the public's eye may enjoy spectacular growth. Export readiness may not be a pressing issue, in general, but an awareness of competition from abroad may be important. Finally, in terms of policy attention, this quadrant probably doesn't stand out from small business in general.

## *Canada's national spending on innovation*

In this concluding section, we will offer some summary numbers on R&D spending in Canada. R&D spending includes the cost of research and certain costs of product development that we will call the technical costs of commercialization. The remainder, namely the business costs of commercialization, are not included in R&D spending. And we have just seen in the discussion of the D-N quadrant that some innovation can occur without any R&D spending at all. All this is to say that the total of R&D spending significantly underestimates the spending on innovation.

Nevertheless, we will look at the numbers on R&D since they're all that we have. First we need to introduce some new language.

A nation's total expenditure on R&D is labelled GERD, short for gross expenditure on R&D. The ratio of GERD to GDP is an indicator of the nation's R&D intensity. The part of GERD provided by business out of its own resources is labelled BERD, short for business expenditure on R&D. Given the structure of Canadian industry that has many branch plants of multinational enterprises (MNE), some 15 percent of Canadian BERD comes from foreign sources, namely MNEs. If we label the total public expenditure on R&D as PERD, then PERD = GERD – BERD (minus charity-funded research). In turn, public expenditure on R&D has two components: the government's own expenditure on R&D called GOVERD, and the higher education expenditure on R&D, mainly in universities but in some colleges as well, called HERD. That means that PERD = GOVERD + HERD. Additional indicators can be formed by normalizing BERD, PERD and HERD by GDP.[12]

Table 6.1 lists the values of these quantities by source of funds in current dollars for 2009,[13] with GDP data from Statistics Canada. GOVERD includes both the federal and provincial governments.

---

[12] Is there another ...ERD acronym floating in this alphabet soup? NERD seems somehow relevant.

[13] Science, Technology and Innovation Council. 2011. "State of the Nation 2010 – Imagination to Innovation," Ottawa: Science, Technology and Innovation Council, p. 14, Figure 3.

## TABLE 6.1 Canada's Spending on R&D, 2009 ($ billion)

| | | |
|---|---|---|
| GERD = 29.854 | GDP = 1,527.258 | GERD/GDP = 1.95% |
| BERD = 16.955, including 2.783 from foreign sources | | |
| PERD = 11.906 | GOVERD = 7.231 | HERD = 4.675 |

Source: Statistics Canada, Provincial Economic Accounts, CANSIM: Table 384-0002.

Note also that for Canada in 2009, BERD/PERD is about 1.4. The emerging conventional wisdom[14] is that in countries whose industry is very innovative, BERD/PERD is near 3; numbers smaller than 3 suggest less industrialized and more commodity-dependent economies.

The STIC report shows that the Canadian national R&D intensity, GERD/GDP, is very close to the average for the OECD, but only about half of that of Sweden and two-thirds of the US value. A detailed discussion of the R&D intensity will follow in a later chapter, but it is worth noting here that Freedman points out that there may be a way of seeing the Canadian value as a glass half-full, not half empty.[15] He points out that Quebec and Ontario, the most industrialized provinces have values of BERD/GDP that are much above the OECD average. He also suggests that a low GERD/GDP need not be taken as a sign of low performance. It might be a sign of high efficiency in using the results of R&D, or the result of a surge in GDP.

It is worth reminding ourselves that the goal here is to discuss measures for increasing Canada's prosperity, as represented by GDP/capita. GERD/GDP is just an indicator of one way of getting there, and it's not unambiguous. In chapter 2, we showed that growing our prosperity calls for more innovation, or more new ways of adding value in the economy. If the rate of innovation is proportional to R&D spending, then a low GERD/GDP is a sign of a problem. On the other hand, if both the GDP and GERD grow, and the GDP grows faster, then

[14] Alan Cornford. 2011. "Canadian R&D innovative competitiveness in free fall – a new recipe is required," Re$earch Money, 25 (4): 8.
[15] Ron Freedman. 2011. "Could Canada's innovation cup be half full?" Re$earch Money, 25 (11): 8.

GERD/GDP will decline, but the result for the economy will be positive. The latter situation could arise if there was a surge of innovation in industries that do not depend heavily on R&D. In any case, the interpretation of the values and trends in GERD/GDP requires independent information about each component of that ratio and, without such information, it is risky to use that indicator as a single policy target.

The same point will be made later in the discussion of a company's R&D intensity, which is the counterpart of GERD/GDP at the level of the firm. The arguments are similar.

# CHAPTER 7

## FOUR MODELS OF INDUSTRIAL INNOVATION IN CANADA

*"One size fits all" doesn't fit any very well.*

The four models of industrial innovation discussed in this chapter correspond to the four quadrants of innovation space introduced in chapter 6. The four models are different because the business circumstances differ among the quadrants. With the understanding that the quad taxonomy provides, we now know that we shouldn't even try to look for the model of innovation that applies in all circumstances. "One size fits all" doesn't fit any very well.

However, some caution is called for. The models discussed here are not unique. They are only aids to understanding selected to emphasize and explain certain features of the innovation process that are important in the thesis of this book. With different objectives, models with different perspectives may be more useful. Moreover, the new understanding is far from complete. These models do not include explicitly the role of company culture. Figure 3.4 showed culture among the local factors in the innovation system, but that was culture in the community, not in the company. There are many examples of the culture of a community acting as a major influence in the performance of its local innovation system – perhaps an endogenous factor in that system, but an exogenous factor for any firm within it. But the internal company culture may be even more important. It may be what makes one company an innovation powerhouse, and another one of comparable technical capability, a laggard. It is now becoming conventional wisdom that community and company culture are both very important for innovation, but we have to leave it to researchers in innovation studies to refine that view and test it in detail. In the meantime, culture will be included in the discussion wherever it seems important.

## Models of innovation

A model of innovation is a representation of how innovation happens. Some models are theoretical, suggesting how their authors think innovation generally happens. Others are empirical, reflecting what their authors have learned about how it actually happens in particular circumstances. Some models are verbal, and some are graphical. Some show only the connections among the various functions in the innovation process; others also show the actors involved. At the level of detail in the models that follow, the internal organizational structure of the companies and their business and innovation strategies are not shown explicitly.

To start with, consider the model shown in Figure 7.1. This is the so-called linear model of innovation. It is worth looking at because it is the oldest and simplest model, and the most intuitive. But it is also wrong – in the sense that too many important elements of innovation are missing from it. Nevertheless, it is a good place to start because examining its shortcomings is instructive and provides a good introduction to better models.

### FIGURE 7.1 The Linear Model of Innovation

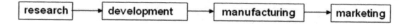

Intuitive and simple, this model omits many important features of how innovation happens, e.g.: feedback loops among the processes.

The linear model of innovation has been around for a long time, and is sometimes attributed to Francis Bacon in the 17th century. It occasionally appears with minor variations, such as a box labelled 'invention' just downstream of research, and another labelled 'design' between invention and development. But in any case, the linear model of innovation has been discredited by Kline and Rosenberg[1] and many other innovation scholars because it fails to describe what actually happens in the majority of innovations.

The linear model portrays a sequence of processes in series; each is completed before the next one is started, with the output handed off downstream. In very broad terms, the four processes seem to be in the right chronological sequence. The model shows that innovation begins with research, but very many innovations don't. In such cases, dropping the research box at the upstream end and starting with invention is an improvement, but it still doesn't fix the linear model. Its most serious flaw is the lack of interaction and feedback loops among the various elements. It also fails to take into account processes running simultaneously, dead ends and restarts, as well as the entire influence of the market. These deficiencies are corrected in the models that follow.

The linear model of innovation and its shortcomings in dealing with industrial innovation are thoroughly discussed by Kline and Rosenberg, as well as by Roger Blais[2] among many other sources. Unfortunately, the intuitive nature of that model makes it easy to understand and attractive in spite of its shortcomings, and as a result it is often presented uncritically in media stories and may sometimes even figure implicitly in policy making.

## *The four quadrants of innovation space*

Recall the four quadrants in innovation space that were introduced in chapter 6. They are defined by whether the invention underlying the innovation is research-based or design-based,[3] and whether it is being commercialized by a new venture or by an established firm. Recall also that 'research-based' means a new use of new knowledge, and 'design-based' means a new use of prior knowledge.

[1] Stephen J. Kline and Nathan Rosenberg. 1986. "An Overview of Innovation" in *The Positive Sum Strategy: Harnessing Technology for Economic Growth*. R. Landau (ed.). Washington, DC: National Academy Press, p. 275-306.

[2] Roger A. Blais (ed.). 1997. *Technological Entrepreneurship and Engineering in Canada*. Ottawa: Canadian Academy of Engineering, p. 151-155.

[3] Since innovation = invention + commercialization, this wording is accurate, but a bit lengthy. For brevity, we will refer to these as research-based and design-based innovations, and leave invention for more detailed discussions.

## The R-E quadrant and the Kline-Rosenberg Chain-Link Model of Innovation

We begin the discussion with the classic model, the "Kline-Rosenberg Chain-Link Model of Innovation" which is often cited as the clinching argument against the linear model. Figure 7.2 shows it slightly modified from the original version.[4]

The chain-link model fits in the R-E quadrant, namely research-based innovation that is commercialized by an established firm. It shows the internal innovation process of the firm and also its connections into external research.

### FIGURE 7.2 The Kline-Rosenberg Chain-Link Model of Innovation (1986)

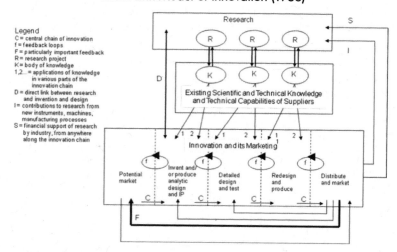

Source: modified from Stephen J. Kline and Nathan Rosenberg. 1986. "An Overview of Innovation" in *The Positive Sum Strategy: Harnessing Technology for Economic Growth*. R. Landau (ed.). Washington, DC: National Academy Press, p. 275-306.

This is the model of innovation that is widely thought to have replaced the linear model once and for all because it includes many of the important interactions.

[4] Figure 7.2 was redrawn by the author with slight changes from the version presented by Tim Padmore and Hervey Gibson (1998. "Modelling regional Innovation and Competitiveness," in *Local and Regional Systems of Innovation*. John de la Mothe and Gilles Paquet (eds.). Boston, MA: Kluwer Academic Publishers, chapter 4, p. 49) because that version was clearer than the one in the original paper of Kline and Rosenberg. It was then modified further to show explicitly the creation of IP and the capabilities of suppliers.

The internal innovation process is depicted in the form of five connected compartments in the lowest rectangular box, starting with "[assess the] potential market" and ending with "distribute and market." Each compartment is connected to the next in the so-called "central chain of innovation," and to the previous through a feedback loop. Note that design and redesign are prominent in the process. Note also the feedback from marketing into each of the upstream processes, with a particularly strong feedback into assessing the potential market. The research enterprise lies outside of the innovation chain. It interacts with the pool of existing scientific and technical knowledge (shown by the middle rectangle) through the flows of research questions generated from existing knowledge (up) and research results (down). Existing knowledge from the pool is an input into three elements: "invent and/or produce analytic design", "detailed design and test", "redesign and produce." The first of these three elements has an obvious direct two-way connection with research. The innovating firm supports research financially, and also through new instruments, machines and processes.

One important element missing from the original chain-link model is any explicit reference to creating intellectual property (IP). This belongs in the second box of the central innovation chain: "invent and/or produce analytic design." Adding the words 'and IP' there gives notice of the issue. Another missing element is the role of suppliers in the fourth box of the central chain. The chain of innovation draws on the technological capabilities of the suppliers in the design and redesign stages of the new product. Once that is recognized, it is easily fixed by adding the words 'technological capabilities of suppliers' to "existing scientific and technical knowledge" in the box above the central chain of innovation. This draws attention to the role of suppliers without making the diagram much more complicated by showing the relationship with the supply chain explicitly. The diagram shown in Figure 7.2 has been modified in both these ways.

The chain-link model explains a lot and appears widely, sometimes in a stylized form.[5] We have introduced it in

<hr />

[5] For example, in Roger A. Blais (ed.). 1997. *Technological Entrepreneurship and Engineering in Canada*. Ottawa: Canadian Academy of Engineering, p. 155.

connection with the R-E quadrant, but it can be modified to apply also to the D-E quadrant. In that case, the link (D in Figure 7.2) between research and design can be weak or missing entirely. It is also tempting to consider how the model might work for innovation in services, the subject of chapter 9. The service sectors are so heterogeneous that generalizations are dangerous, but for some technical services, a sufficient adaptation might be to replace 'produce' by 'develop education materials and train service delivery staff' in the fourth box.

## The D-E quadrant and Douglas Barber's Innovation-Commerce Cycle

The D-E quadrant represents the great bulk of industrial innovation, including product improvement, reduction in production costs and other forms of incremental innovation. We shall describe it here using Douglas Barber's Innovation-Commerce Cycle (ICC)[6] shown in Figure 7.3. This is a model of innovation in a company that already has established products and customers. In this case, the needs of the customers drive the whole innovation process, and the results are what Christensen calls sustaining innovations.[7] These needs are identified in two ways: through market intelligence by the company (left side of the figure) and through direct feedback from the customers in response to what they buy (right side). Sales and customer relations are prominent functions. Financial considerations loom large. The sustainability of the whole operation is determined by the balance between sales revenues, equity investments, debt financing and government grants on the one hand, and costs on the other. Strategic pricing of the product is given special emphasis. This model shows a company that is producing sustaining innovations to keep meeting the needs of its customers. This is innovation in response to market pull.

[6] H. Douglas Barber. 2008. "Determinants of Success in Knowledge-Based Industry," public presentation at the Telfer School of Management, University of Ottawa, January 15.

[7] Clayton M. Christensen. 1997. *Innovator's Dilemma*. Cambridge, MA: Harvard Business School Press.

## FIGURE 7.3 Douglas Barber's
## Innovation-Commerce Cycle (2008)

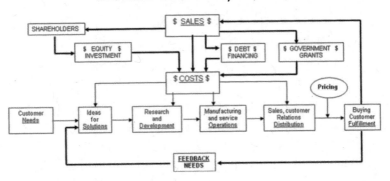

**Source:** H. Douglas Barber. 2008. "Determinants of Success in Knowledge-Based Industry," public presentation at the Telfer School of Management, University of Ottawa, January 15.

A portrayal of innovation in an established company in which commerce provides the context for innovation.

The ICC does not show any flows of knowledge into the various processes, except implicitly in R&D. We must assume, therefore, that the people involved in every process in the model of innovation have their own knowledge base and the capacity for learning to keep it up to date. We note also that the creation of intellectual property (IP) and the capabilities of suppliers do not appear explicitly in the ICC model, but could be incorporated into the three boxes labelled "ideas ...", "R&D ..." and "manufacturing ... ." If the feedback among these three boxes, and also sales and customer relations, were shown explicitly, the lower part of the ICC model would resemble the central chain of innovation in the chain-link model.

Note that design appears in both models. The chain-link model refers to design and redesign explicitly in the three central elements of the innovation chain and the ICC includes it implicitly with research and development. But neither model shows, in any detail, how complex the process is and how broad the range of influences and inputs that it must respond to in order to redesign an existing product or design an improved one. The range of these inputs and influences is suggested in Figure 7.4.

## FIGURE 7.4 Design and Redesign in Established Firms

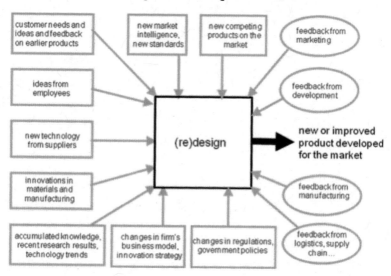

Source: Developed from Fig. 6.2 in T.A. Brzustowski. 2008. *The Way Ahead: Meeting Canada's Productivity Challenge.* Ottawa: University of Ottawa Press, p. 92.

A complicated process that requires both experience and resources.

The design process responds to ideas from customers and their feedback on the earlier products, as well as to ideas from employees for improvements. The design can incorporate new technologies from suppliers as well as new materials and manufacturing methods. The accumulating background knowledge keeps growing through research around the world, and new technology trends keep emerging. The new or improved product may be heading into a market that has changed, with new standards in place that must be met and new competing products for sale. And the whole process is shaped by the firm's business model and its innovation strategy. There may also be new government regulations and policies that affect the market and the whole business climate. And finally, for obvious reasons, the process of design must take into account several important sources of feedback: the evolution of the business model and positioning of the product in the value chain, marketing, development and beta test sites, manufacturing, logistics and supply-chain management, etc.

In the R-E quadrant, the invention underlying the innovation is research-based, namely a new use of new knowledge to do something that might not have been possible before, or to do something vastly better than it was being done before. The new product must often create its own new demand. The whole process of marketing in R-E is much more technology push than market pull, and IP issues are very important. Some parts of the information and communications technology (ICT) sector and the pharmaceutical industry provide examples of innovations in this quadrant.

In the chain-link model of innovation for the R-E quadrant, the understanding is that the link D between research and invention is very strong, that some part of the research function may be internal to the company, and that the creation of IP may prove very important. The design process would be much the same as in Figure 7.4, but assessing the potential market is uncertain, as there is no similar product on the market and, therefore, no related feedback from customers to guide the process.

The innovation-commerce cycle (Figure 7.3) could also be made to apply to R-E innovation if two modifications were made. First, the R&D process would have to be extended explicitly to include input from external research. And second, the input of customer needs would have to be expanded to include the needs of potential customers, i.e., the needs that are not being met today for which a market is expected. However, things are a little different in the pharmaceutical sector. There the research is carried on by people who are trying to develop a therapy for a condition about which much is known, and that introduces the influence of the market into the process even without an explicit feedback loop in the innovation process.

The models of R-E innovation require some additional changes to describe what happens in the pharmaceutical industry. This is a highly regulated industry in which the new product must be approved by the FDA (in the US), and by Health Canada before it can be sold in the market. It must then receive a further approval of provincial payers before it can be listed in provincial formularies, and thus be subject to government reimbursement. Approval requires the successful completion of lengthy and expensive clinical trials to demonstrate safety, effectiveness and efficacy. Once allowed in the market, the product is sold to the end customer – the patient – in a tightly controlled dispensing process that involves two sets of professionals, namely doctors and pharmacists. As a result, the chain-link model of innovation can describe what happens in pharmaceuticals if the wording in the last three links is suitably altered. The innovation-commerce cycle also applies with corresponding changes.

IP issues are very important in the R-E quadrant, but with big differences between the ICT and pharmaceutical sectors. In ICT, patent litigation is frequent, with the validity of the patents and patent infringement in intersecting technologies as the main issues. In pharmaceuticals, the issue is much more the length of patent protection, since the development of the drug and its subsequent necessary approvals can eat up half of the 20 years of protection currently provided when a new drug is patented. This has major financial implications for the innovating company because its new drug is very quickly commoditized by generic versions of it that are ready to appear on the market when the original patent expires. The original manufacturer has only about ten years of market exclusivity to recover the development costs of the drug and make a profit.

Another example of innovation in the R-E quadrant arises when companies enter into research partnerships with universities that are supported by government programs.[8] This takes place most often in the form of project research. In Figure 7.2, such public-private partnerships would be included in the K-R links between the upper two boxes. In Figure 7.3, they would lie in the box labelled research and development. The details of such university-industry research partnerships are shown in the chapter on university research.

To round out the discussion of innovation by established firms, it is important to point out that the two models are not mutually exclusive in time and space. A company may introduce a revolutionary new product by acting as described in the chain-link model, and later may settle into the innovation-commerce cycle when the product and the market for it are well established. Or one part of a company may function according to the ICC, while another is better described by the chain-link model.

---

[8] For example, the programs offered by NSERC in their RPP envelope. See www.nserc-crsng.gc.ca for details.

## A new model for the D-N quadrant

Things are different and more difficult when a new venture is set up to produce an innovation. Whatever else it might do, the new venture starts out as a small business that struggles to survive and grow and is usually short of both time and money. If its principals are inexperienced in business, they may have to learn commerce at the same time as they are commercializing their first product.

Under these circumstances commercialization is difficult. First, there is no experience in producing innovations. Everything has to be learned for the first time.[9] The chain-link model and the ICC are irrelevant because the organizational structures that they describe do not exist. There is no flow of innovations and no pipeline; a single innovation is at stake. And in the D-N quadrant there is no new research result at the root of the proposed innovation to provide some bedrock validation of the whole idea. In that sense, D-N innovation is much more a work of creativity and entrepreneurship. For that reason, the models of innovation involving new ventures are drawn in such a way as to emphasize the role of the entrepreneur.

Figure 7.5 shows a proposed model of innovation under these circumstances. It all begins with the entrepreneur who spots a need in the market or in society more broadly, gets a new idea for meeting it, and sees an opportunity for bringing it to the market as an innovation. Using market intelligence and existing knowledge in the field where the proposed idea would be implemented, the entrepreneur then develops the idea for the innovation in some detail, with the help of experienced advisors. The next step is to develop a design of the innovation, including a business model, and produce a business plan for the new venture. In the diagram, that brings us to the circle halfway up the right hand side.

The creation of the new venture and the commercialization of its product begin at that point. The vertical rectangle represents the development, both of the product and of the commercial capabilities of the company. There are feedback loops within it, but to keep the diagram as simple as possible, they are not shown. Commercialization is fed by the investment of private risk capital

---

[9] This is learning by the company, even if some of the principals are experienced. It is probably very rare for the principals to have experience in the identical set of circumstances.

in growing amounts, proceeding through the pre-seed, seed, early-stage, etc. and eventually growth. The process is continuously informed by updated market intelligence, by feedback from any failures along the way, by public response to announcements, and eventually by first sales and market feedback. Where the new venture lacks some particular capabilities that are needed in the commercialization process, these might be obtained from individuals, groups or organizations known as innovation intermediaries. Their contributions might range all the way from helping the new venture connect with the right people to providing services under contract.

## FIGURE 7.5 Design-based Innovation by a New Venture

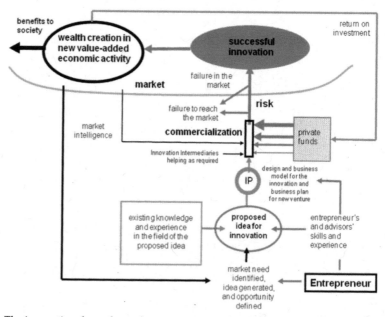

The innovation depends on the entrepreneur who works to connect a new idea (bottom) to the market (top). Many elements of this diagram will show up again in later figures.

Note that intellectual property (IP) is created in the process of defining an innovation, designing a business model, and producing a business plan for the new venture. It's not likely to be IP that can be protected by a patent, but some element of it may be protected by a trademark or copyright. However, the main point is that this aspect of business is a creative intellectual activity which needs to be recognized and treated as such. Using the terminology introduced in chapter 4, the IP generated in the D-N quadrant is mainly business IP.

The risk in commercialization is twofold. First, the product may fail to get to market for any of a number of technical or business reasons. And, second, the product may fail in the market, once again for any of a great number of reasons, including lack of customer acceptance, timing, competition, changes in the business climate, or even a single event. But if the innovation is a success, new value-added economic activity is created, there is a return on the investment, and benefits flow to society on both the supply side and the demand side of the new product.

### A new model for the R-N quadrant

The model of innovation in the R-N quadrant is very similar to Figure 7.5, but with two important differences. First, recent research results are added to the accumulated knowledge on which the underlying invention is based (square in the left lower corner). And second, an invention and new IP are created that lead from the new research results to the proposed idea for innovation. As a result, it may become possible to do something than could never have been done before, or to do something vastly better than before. And the research results on which the invention is based provide a validation of the basic idea.

The anchor position of the entrepreneur remains. That person may or may not be the inventor, but that doesn't matter. The entrepreneur is still the key person involved in proposing the idea for an innovation but, in this case, that idea incorporates or derives from the invention shown. The function of producing a design and business model for the innovation and a business plan for the new venture is still needed, and the entrepreneur and possible advisors play a key role in that.

It may happen that the researcher, the inventor, the entrepreneur and the CEO of the new venture are all the same person, but that is very rare. These four functions require different skill sets, and it is very unlikely that one individual would have them all at sufficiently high levels. A more likely possibility is that the researcher and the inventor might be one person, and the entrepreneur and CEO another.

Finally, note that we have specified nothing about the location of the research or the invention, or about the affiliation of the entrepreneur. At one extreme, the prior knowledge might be in the public realm, and the inventor and the entrepreneur might be particularly well informed and enterprising members of the public. But, at the other extreme, the prior knowledge and the invention might all be located within an established firm, where the inventor and entrepreneur are employees. If the firm decided to commercialize the proposed innovation in house, the innovation would lie in the R-E quadrant, and the entrepreneur could be called an 'intrapreneur.' However, if the parent firm decided not to pursue the innovation in house but to spin off a new company to work on it, R-N innovation would ensue. And if the parent firm decided to proceed differently and set up a 'skunk works,' namely a small, largely independent unit outside of its existing organization, specifically to pursue this innovation, this might not exactly be R-N innovation, but it would probably be close in many ways.

If the research and the invention originated in a university, it would still be R-N innovation, but the details of the process would be quite different. That case is discussed in detail in the next chapter on the role of university research in innovation.

## Griller's four modes of innovation

A different way of looking at the ways that industrial innovation happens was suggested by the work of Griller,[10] who proposed that it should be described in terms of the four very different ways, or modes, in which companies arrive at an innovation. He called them:

- science-based;
- craft-shop;
- systems integrator;
- technology purchaser.

The fact that there are four modes of innovation, just as there are four quadrants in innovation space, is a coincidence. This is not a quad taxonomy derived from two polar opposite answers for each of two independent questions. Rather, it is a proposed

[10] David Griller et al. 1994. "National Systems of Innovation: A Research Paper on Innovation and Innovation Systems in Canada," Ottawa: National Research Council of Canada, Corporate Planning and Evaluation, April. David Griller and le Groupe SECOR Inc. did the research, summarized on p. 28 of the document.

classification that captures the main differences in the ways that companies produce innovations. In Griller's work, four different ways of innovating were deemed sufficient. These four modes of innovation are very different in terms of the innovating companies' relationships with customers and suppliers, risk, cost, time scales, required skill sets and many other variables. They may characterize the business models of four different types of firms. On the other hand, they might also represent the different things that single firms have to do in pursuing their various projects, or even at different times in the work on a single project.

While the four modes of innovation are not the same as the four quadrants of the innovation, there are connections among them. Science-based innovation appears in the R-E quadrant, where the chain-link model of innovation would describe the detailed interactions, and in the R-N quad as described in the next chapter. In craft-shop innovation, the competitive advantage of the innovating firms lies in the skills and experience of their employees, their know-how, their ability to make or do things that their competitors can't. One might expect to see this at work particularly in the D-N and D-E quadrants. System integrators can operate in the same two quadrants. Their advantage derives from their ability to design and implement new systems, incorporating components already developed, by themselves or by others, to solve their clients' problems or to introduce a new product in the market.

Innovation by the purchase of new technology is, again, probably most important in the D-E and D-N quadrant. In the D-E quadrant, this is likely to be the purchase of new process technologies in order to reduce the production cost of existing products. In the D-N quad, this could be the key enabling purchase that enables the new venture to launch a new line of business.

## Standing back a bit

When we stand back a bit and look at the models of industrial innovation discussed in this chapter, we recognize that our view has been almost completely external. The internal dynamics of firms have been out of sight. We have not discussed the ways in which companies select and implement their innovation strategies within their larger business strategies. We have not looked at the different competitive environments in their different lines of business that affect their decisions. We have not looked at issues of market dynamics, of timing and phasing in the development and introduction of new products, and much more. In sum, we have not considered the many aspects of managing innovation that might mean the difference between success and failure in particular circumstances. There is a great wealth of expertise in doing this in industry, and a rich literature both in the form of business books and research papers, but the detailed discussion of the management of innovation within firms is outside the scope of the 'big picture' in this book.

The only hint of the internal structure of the innovation process in this chapter has come from the 'four modes' of innovation just discussed. They still provide only an external view, but a different view depending on the way that innovation is actually carried out within the firm. This approach has been taken further and developed in depth by Miller, Olleros and Molinié.[11] Based on a comprehensive survey of a thousand innovative established firms around the world, and some very sophisticated treatment of the data, they describe the innovation activities of these firms in terms of seven "games." Some of these games resemble Griller's four modes, but are named differently. Each game has its own place in a competitive context, its own set of strategies, its own R&D intensity (RDI), its own staff requirements and performance measures. For example, the game called "patent-driven discovery," which is close to what we have called 'research-based innovation' was found to have a research intensity RDI[12] of 29.2 percent. In contrast, the game called "cost-based search for efficiency", not quite the same as our 'design-based innovation' but close to it, had a much lower RDI of 4.4 percent. It seems that the "innovation games" approach might produce a new, fine-grained, external understanding of industrial innovation that could feed back into the internal practices of innovation management.

The corporate data discussed in chapter 12 of this book lead to a new external view – call it a new model – of industrial innovation in Canada that is generally consistent with the innovation games, but is less detailed and focused more on policy implications.

---

[11] Roger Miller, Xavier Olleros and Luis Molinié. 2008. "Innovation Games: A New Approach to the Competitive Challenge," *Long Range Planning*, 41 (4): 378-394.
[12] The ratio of R&D spending to sales revenue, expressed in % and given the symbol RDI. It is discussed in detail in chapter 12.

# CHAPTER 8

## THE ROLE OF POST-SECONDARY EDUCATION

*Students are to ideas as mosquitoes are to malaria.*

Guy Daniélou[1]

### Introduction to the system

The institutions offering post-secondary education in Canada form a landscape more than a system. There are two kinds of institutions: universities and colleges,[2] and they come in various shapes and sizes. We shall begin with a broad-brush sketch of their shapes, some numbers to get a sense of their scale, and fill in more details as we need them.[3]

### The institutions

Universities generally offer degree programs in the arts, sciences and professions. These include three-year and four-year Bachelor's degrees, as well Master's and doctoral degrees. Most universities engage in research, and their postgraduate programs are closely associated with their fields of research specialty. The universities that have medical schools also have affiliated research hospitals.

The main public universities in Canada fall into three categories: 17 with medical schools,[4] 15 without medical

---

[1] Founding President of the Université de technologie de Compiègne, France, speaking at convocation at the University of Waterloo, October 1974.
[2] Note that the Canadian usage of the terms 'universities' and 'colleges' is different than in the US. The details make the differences clear.
[3] Readers interested in a more detailed overview of education in Canada are directed to the website of the Council of Ministers of Education of Canada (CMEC) at http://www.cmec.ca.
[4] The 17 include Lakehead and Laurentian universities that share the new Northern Ontario School of Medicine.

schools but with a broad range of doctoral programs in other professional and academic areas, and 17 that specialize in first-degree programs with some graduate studies. There is also a large group of small public universities, some of them independent and some church-related[5] and affiliated with the larger institutions; and another group of private for-profit universities, some of which are exploring new formats of education, including particularly online courses. All of these institutions collect tuition fees from their students, and the public ones also receive grants from their provinces that are distributed according to a formula based on student numbers in the various program categories.[6] These grants vary significantly from province to province, from a high of about 75 percent down to a low of about 50 percent of the university operating budgets. Research funding is a separate issue. It is additional and distributed by competition, and comes mainly from the federal government, but with some provincial contribution as well.

The colleges offer a broad range of one to four-year diploma programs, many of which have a strong practical orientation. They also offer apprenticeship training in the skilled trades. Colleges are very active in continuing education, and engage in providing education on demand to meet the needs of particular groups. Some colleges have upgraded their diploma programs for transferability to universities and some now offer degrees.

There are 183 recognized public colleges and institutes in Canada,[7] including 9 polytechnics, and 48 CEGEPS – the Quebec colleges that have both a career-preparation diploma stream and a pre-university stream. The colleges generally have multiple campuses, so that altogether they have a presence in some 400 communities. Universities, on the other hand, have a much smaller number of campuses, generally a single urban main campus, with some satellite campuses in smaller cities.

---

[5] Funded by governments only for their non-denominational activities.

[6] The Government of Canada does not have a federal department of education.

[7] Council of Ministers of Education. 2011. "Education in Canada: An Overview," Council of Ministers of Education website www.cmec.ca [accessed Dec. 12, 2011].

## The students

The latest data available from Statistics Canada show university enrolment in all fields in 2008-2009 was a total of 1,112,000 of whom 828,000 were full-time students.[8] Also in 2008-2009, total college enrolment was 605,000 of whom 458,000 were full-time students. So Canada had a total post-secondary population of 1.7 million students in 2008-2009, some 5 percent of the general population of 33 million. In the same year, Canadian universities granted 244,000 degrees at all three levels, diplomas and certificates. Colleges awarded 159,000 college degrees, diplomas and certificates. That means that slightly more than 400,000 postsecondary students graduated in 2008-2009.

It is useful to estimate what the enrolments were in the subject areas that one might expect to feed the pool of highly qualified people (HQP) available for industrial R&D and production and for publicly funded research, and what the recent trend has been. We can do this by summing the numbers for the following four categories in the Statistics Canada data: (i) physical and life sciences and technologies; (ii) mathematics, computer and information sciences; (iii) architecture, engineering and related technologies; and (iv) agriculture, natural resources and conservation. We shall call these the technical categories. The results of doing this for 2004-2005 and for 2008-2009 are shown in the table below.

The first thing to notice in Table 8.1 is that enrolment in the technical categories is only a small fraction of total enrolment, and that enrolment in mathematics, computer and information sciences is again a small fraction of that fraction. More strikingly, there has been a significant decline in both university and college enrolments in mathematics, computer and information sciences over the last five years. The university numbers in this area dropped by 7,800 (i.e.: 19 percent) and the college numbers by 6,500 (25 percent). Over the same period, the total enrolment in all fields grew by 8.9 percent in the universities and declined by 0.5 percent in the colleges. This focused decline could be could be the sign of

[8] All of the data on enrolment and degrees, etc. granted were obtained from the website of Statistics Canada, www.statcan.gc.ca and from "Facts and Figures" on the NSERC website, www.nserc-crsng.gc.ca [accessed on December 12, 2011]. The enrolment numbers presented in the text and the table have been rounded. The differences were calculated before rounding.

a looming problem, since the availability of HQP with skills and knowledge in these areas has generally been considered necessary for increasing productivity. However, two emerging trends may counter that effect. First, the economic benefits of information and communications technology (ICT) are increasingly shifting from the supply side to the demand side, from people who make the equipment to people who use it in many new ways. And second, skills in using ICT are being acquired by a far broader population than just the students in mathematics, computer and information science. Students are routinely being taught the use of computers in many subject areas, and many people are learning to use them without any formal education at all. So the enrolment trends are what they are, but the jury is still out on their implications.

### TABLE 8.1 College and University Enrolment in the Technical Categories

| | | f/t + p/t enrolment in technical categories | % of total enrolment in all fields | f/t+p/t enrolment in math, CS, IS | % difference from 04-05 to 08-09 |
|---|---|---|---|---|---|
| colleges | 2008-09 | 95,400 | 16 | 19,400 | -25% |
| | 2004-05 | 104,000 | 17 | 25,900 | |
| universities | 2008-09 | 236,000 | 21 | 33,200 | -19% |
| | 2004-05 | 231,000 | 23 | 41,000 | |

This table shows the decline in mathematics, computer and information sciences.

### Research

Colleges generally do not engage in research, except for the polytechnics, since college faculty do not have the time and the institutions do not have the systems to manage research. However, colleges do engage in technical work, providing very useful services of various kinds (design, prototyping, testing, business consulting, etc.) to local businesses in the hundreds of communities where their campuses are located. And the polytechnics sometimes work downstream of universities, providing services to new ventures that are setting out to commercialize inventions emerging out of university research. In Quebec, college activity in support of innovation is arranged very systematically through the 46 College Centres for Technology Transfer.

And the college system is changing. For example, some colleges in BC have recently been granted university status. Some other colleges are starting to grant degrees and move into research, and there is new federal government support for the research they undertake. Their distinguishing label is 'applied' – so 'applied degrees', 'applied research', and even in some cases 'applied studies.' Such changes in labelling is a positive development where it reflects an upgrading of the college educational programs and of their technical activities. But it would be a less positive development if it signalled that the colleges were moving away from their current role of offering needed practical education in many vocation-oriented fields, and apprenticeship training in the skilled trades, where demographics is on the verge of creating serious shortages.

University research in Canada is top-heavy, in the sense that most of it is done by a small fraction of the universities. As a measure of this, the total research income to the top 50 Canadian universities in 2010 was $6.46 billion.[9] Of that total, 68 percent was received by the top ten universities, and 81 percent by the 16 with medical schools. The total research income for all universities for 2011 is yet to be published, but the pattern for the decade has been that the external research income in universities has been close to 54 percent of HERD.

## The faculty

The current numbers of faculty in natural sciences and engineering (NSE) give an indication of the capacity of the universities for research, since most of the faculty appointed over the last couple of decades have been expected to apply for research grants and supervise graduate students. NSERC (Natural Sciences and Engineering Research Council) data,[10] in rounded numbers, show that in 2008-2009, there were 12,000 full-time NSE faculty, made up of 3,100 in agriculture and the biological sciences, 3,700 in engineering and the applied sciences, and 5,200 in mathematics

[9] Data from Re$earch Infosource Inc. "Canada's University Innovation Leaders," distributed with the National Post, November 4, 2011.

[10] "Facts and Figures," Table 48, NSERC website, www.nserc-crsng.gc.ca [accessed December 2011].

and the physical sciences. These numbers should be compared with a total of almost 42,000 faculty in all fields. Ten years earlier, in 1999-2000, the corresponding numbers had been 33,800 total faculty in all fields, 9,600 faculty in all of NSE: 2,500 in agriculture and the biological sciences, 2,800 in engineering and applied sciences, and 4,300 in math and the physical sciences. This represents a growth of 25 percent in NSE faculty over that decade, and the possibility of a significant increase in research activity.

### Recent growth

The last decade has been a period of significant growth in Canadian university research in the NSE. This is evident both from data on HERD and from data on students in the natural sciences and engineering provided by NSERC.[11] Once again, in rounded numbers, the total full-time NSE enrolment in Canadian universities in 2008-2009 were 135,000 in Bachelor's programs, 22,600 in Master's programs, and 18,600 in doctoral programs. Ten years earlier, in 1999-2000 the numbers were 114,500 in Bachelor's programs; 14,700 in Master's; and 10,000 in doctoral. That means that the growth in that decade was: 18 percent in Bachelor's, 53 percent in Master's, and 85 percent in doctoral – with the latter two programs obviously more closely related to research. There were 33,100 Bachelor's degrees granted in 2007 as well as 8,200 Master's and 2,600 doctorates. Ten years earlier the numbers had been 26,100, 5,000 and 2,100, respectively. That means growth of 27 percent, 64 percent, and 25 percent, respectively. Finally, over the period from 1999-2000 to 2008-2009, HERD more than doubled from $5.081 billion to $10.932 billion and university research income grew from $2.433 billion to $5.872 billion, an increase of $3.439 billion, or 141 percent.

## Innovation and university research in Canada

Now that we've seen some of the dimensions of the activity, we will look at it in more detail. Canadian university research is an important subsystem of Canada's innovation system, particularly at the regional level. In turn, Figure 8.1 shows a subsystem within that, namely university research in the natural sciences

---

[11] "Facts and Figures," annual data from Stats Can extracted by NSERC in categories of particular interest for the NSE (Natural Sciences and Engineering).

and engineering (NSE) faculties. Think of this view as being imbedded in the regional innovation system shown in Figure 3.5, where it lies partly in the national and provincial and partly in the regional characteristics. However, Figure 8.1 portrays it explicitly from a different perspective as one system with its own inputs, internal structure and outputs. The interacting components of the innovation system in this case are universities, federal and provincial funding agencies, and companies that spend on R&D. The relationships among them are shown by arrows. Note that wealth creation and other aspects of commerce are not shown in this diagram.

There are three inputs to university research in science and engineering shown by the various arrows directed toward the centre: (i) the knowledge and skills of professors acting as principal investigators (PI), post-doctoral fellows (PDF), students and staff; (ii) codified new knowledge from world research and defined problems from industry, and (iii) funding. There are four outputs shown by the outward arrows: (i) highly qualified people; (ii) new codified knowledge; (iii) solutions to industrial problems; and (iv) potential intellectual property (IP) that can lead to innovations by several routes.

The research funding arrives in several ways. The direct operating costs of the research, such as student support, consumable supplies, instrument maintenance, etc. are supplied by the federal government in the form of competitive grants from the Natural Sciences and Engineering Research Council of Canada (NSERC)[12] to the professors who act as principal investigators (PI). The indirect costs, such as heat, power, light, building maintenance, insurance, financial services, etc. are supplied by the universities with significant assistance from the federal government. The remaining indirect costs and the general infrastructure for research are supplied by the universities from their operating and capital budgets.

---

[12] Research in the health sciences is supported by the federal agency, Canadian Institutes for Health Research (CIHR), in ways that are largely similar, but differ in the details of programs. Research in the social sciences and humanities is supported by the Social Sciences and Humanities Research Council of Canada (SSHRC), again in similar ways.

Specialized infrastructure and big research equipment and instruments are paid for by competitive grants from the Canada Foundation for Innovation[13] at 40 percent, generally matched by the provinces, and augmented from the universities' own resources. Private donations form an important part of these resources. An additional source of research funding that arrives with additional obligations, of course, is the partial support from industry for project research undertaken in partnership with the universities. In this case, industry means those companies that spend money on R&D, in house or externally. The industrial contribution usually includes cash and an 'in-kind' component that is likely to involve specialized equipment and facilities in the company, as well as the time of some of their experienced technical employees. In some cases, the partnership becomes so deep and long-lasting that the company employees involved form a team with the university PI and the graduate students working on the project. The contribution of NSERC to university-industry research partnerships is to exercise quality control and to pay a part of the cost, generally matching the industrial cash contribution.

---

[13] Canada Foundation for Innovation, strictly speaking, should be called the Canada Foundation for Research Infrastructure, since it has nothing to do with bringing anything to market.

## FIGURE 8.1 The Canadian University Research System in Science and Engineering

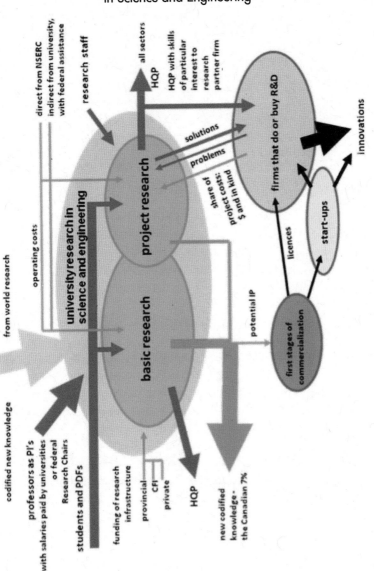

**Source:** T.A. Brzustowski. 2008. *The Way Ahead: Meeting Canada's Productivity Challenge.* Ottawa: University of Ottawa Press, p. 113.

The inward arrows indicate the inputs. In the top part: the efforts of professors, research staff, students and PDFs; funding of operating costs and research infrastructure; new knowledge from world research. In the bottom part: problems that industry can't solve with existing knowledge, and share of the costs of research projects to solve them. The outward arrows indicate the outputs; new knowledge and HQP (top), problem solutions for industry and potential IP (bottom). The potential IP may lead to innovations through start-ups or existing firms.

This listing of research costs overlooks one very significant item – the salaries of the professors who act as principal investigators. The total amount is in the billions of dollars annually. Some of these salaries are funded by the various chair programs of the federal government, but most of the money comes from university operating funds that, in turn, come from tuition fees paid by students and from provincial operating grants that, in turn, come partly from federal transfers and partly from provincial revenues – not a simple trail to follow. This cost is seldom discussed in detail as part of the research expenditure, but it does show up in the national R&D spending statistics, as part of HERD.[14]

The outputs of the research system are new knowledge and highly-qualified people. The basic research in science and engineering produces discoveries reported in published papers in archive journals, as well as highly-qualified people (HQP) with postgraduate degrees in the participating disciplines, who find employment in research in their disciplines, or in R&D more broadly, or in other functions where their technical skills are an asset. The outputs of project research done in partnership with industry are solutions to the industry's problems, some published papers, and HQP, who are familiar with the technical issues in at least one industry and ready for R&D work in it. Moreover, the experience of these graduates in working in contact with industry people within a managed research project also gives them some exposure to industrial culture which helps prepare them for employment in industry.

---

[14] See the final section of chapter 6.

## Students and two other sources of innovation

This system contributes to three sources of innovation. The first, which may be the most important in the long run but is the most difficult to predict, is the future work of the highly-qualified people emerging from the system. That includes not only the postgraduate students who earn Master's and doctoral degrees for contributing to the research, but also the undergraduate students taught by professors who lead it.

The second source of innovation lies in the solutions of industrial problems, some of which may lead to innovations commercialized by the partner companies. The third source, which can be the most exciting, is the potential intellectual property that occasionally emerges from basic research. It can lead to an invention that is then either licensed to an established firm, or commercialized by a new venture, and its impact may be marginal but it may also turn out to be huge. This is research-based innovation by a new venture is shown in the R-N quadrant of Figure 6.1. These three sources of innovation arising from university research in science and engineering are discussed in greater detail in the rest of this chapter.

Table 8.2 describes in more detail the three ways that Canadian university research is connected to industrial innovation in the system of Figure 8.1. These are: hiring up-to-date graduates who were taught by professors who do research and therefore know something about the advancing areas of science and engineering; university-industry partnerships in project research in which the government and the partner company split the cost, and the federal funding agency provides the quality control; and finally the commercialization of inventions that might arise out of basic research. The first and third of these exist in all advanced economies. The university-industry partnerships, and the networks of Centres of Excellence that take the partnerships to a multi-university national scale, are to a large degree Canadian institutional innovations in response to Canada's particular geographic and historical circumstances.

The three sources of innovation are described in terms of five attributes: (i) the nature of the work done in industry; (ii) the time scale for effectiveness; (iii) risk; (iv) the role of government in the process; and (v) the implications for IP. Readers wishing more information about any of the government programs that support these activities should consult the NSERC website at www.nserc-crsng.gc.ca.

Before we leave Table 8.2, it is useful to connect it with the quad taxonomy discussed in chapter 5. Even though the three sources of innovation arise from research in science and engineering, they are not limited to research-based innovations. The students hired by industry (top row) can be engaged in any type of innovation, as indicated. If they are hired by an established firm, they might equally likely be engaged in design-based innovation as in research-based innovation. The graduate students who had been engaged in university-industry research partnerships (middle row) are perhaps more likely to be employed in industrial R&D, but even there, they could become involved in design-based innovation. Only the third source (last row) is limited to research-based innovation.

TABLE 8.2 Three connections between Canadian University Research in Science and Engineering and Industrial Innovation

|  | nature of the work done in industry | time scale for effectiveness | risk | government role | IP implications |
|---|---|---|---|---|---|
| **hiring up-to-date graduates taught by researcher profs** | any R&D, e.g.: for market-driven product improvement, as well as productivity-driven process innovation | from almost immediate to a year or two, depending on experience of students and company training | depends on recruiting skills – least risk with students out of co-op programs in research-intensive universities | none beyond providing research funding for the professors | IP issues are in the hands of the company |
| **partnership in university-industry research projects** | planned product or process innovation requiring entirely new knowledge that can't be generated in-house | typically three to four years from defining the need to completing the project, may be longer if the company has no experience in dealing with universities | first the scientific risk in doing the required research, partly paid for by the industrial partner, and then the business risk in using the results effectively – latter can be reduced by hiring grad students who had worked on the project | funding agency controls quality through peer review of both the proposed research and the project design, and provides part of the direct research cost | government funds don't flow until the university and its industrial partner have signed an acceptable IP agreement |
| **commercialization of inventions arising out of basic research** | turning an unexpected invention coming out of basic research into a product and taking it to market where it might prove to be an important radical or disruptive innovation | several years, possibly longer if a new venture has to be created to turn the invention into a product in the market, and/or more research has to be done | generally technology push, with high risk both in developing the new products and in the business aspects of bringing them to market | funding agency controls quality through peer review of the proposed research, and provides the direct research cost | IP is owned either by the inventor or the university, according to university policy – IP may be licensed or a start-up created to commercialize it |

**Source:** T.A. Brzustowski. 2008. *The Way Ahead: Meeting Canada's Productivity Challenge.* Ottawa: University of Ottawa Press, p. 110.

## *University-industry research partnerships*

We will now move on to the university-industry research partnership and look at an example in some detail. Figure 8.2 illustrates the important features of a university-industry research partnership acting as a source of innovation. The diagram is intended to help the reader understand the written description of a complicated process.

We begin with the oval labelled university project research in the lower right corner. The origin of this activity is an industrial problem that can't be solved with existing knowledge. (If it could be, then research would not be required). The company formulates the problem and contacts the university that seems most capable of helping (first downward arrow into the oval). If there is a good fit of interest and capability, a proposal is developed to create a university-industry partnership to get the research done with some help from federal funding. The proposal includes the technical aspects of the proposed research, and also the detailed design of the project, including its objectives, budget, timelines, reporting requirements, management structure, IP agreement, etc. The proposal becomes part of an application for funding submitted to NSERC by the university.

## FIGURE 8.2 University-Industry Research Partnerships as a Source of Innovation

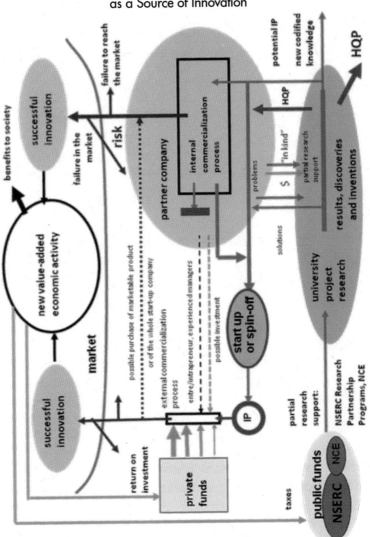

This diagram provides details of the lower right corner of Figure 8.1. It shows the partner company following four possible paths to commercialize any potential IP that comes out of the research partnership: going to market through its internal commercialization process (straight up), shelving the whole thing (dead end on the left), assigning it to a start-up or spin-off directly, and assigning it after some work on commercialization. The spin-off then acts much like a research-based new venture, but likely with the great benefit of experienced staff and investment from the parent company.

The company's contribution to the research project is generally twofold: financial, matching the cash being asked from NSERC, and 'auditable in kind' which includes the use of company equipment and facilities and the time of its employees (second and third downward arrows). If the application meets the quality standards and program rules, and succeeds in the competition for funds, it is approved and the work begins. Something very similar would occur in the NCE program, but in the broader context of a multi-company, multi-university network.

The research produces results and discoveries, and possibly also ideas for inventions. The results that contribute to the solution of the company's problem are transferred to the firm (leftmost upward arrow out of the oval). Discoveries are published in the open literature as new codified knowledge, possibly with a delay for competitive reason. The students' work may be submitted to meet thesis requirements, also with the possibility of delay that must be agreed to in advance by the university, company, professor and the students involved. When they complete their degrees, the graduate students involved in the research are available for employment by the partner company or elsewhere. All of this can occur in both the D-E and R-E quadrants of innovation space.

If the results of research suggest an invention, the potential new IP is dealt with according to the IP agreement that was part of the approved project. Most often, it is assigned to the partner company. After that, any one of four things can happen. It may enter the company's internal commercialization process and eventually be taken to market (right side of the diagram). Another possibility is that it may be taken into the commercialization process and eventually shelved. The other two possibilities are that the partner company decides to create a spin-off to commercialize the invention externally, either immediately or only after some work in its internal commercialization process. It may then be bundled with other related technologies that the partner company provides to strengthen the IP position of the spin-off. If that happens, then what follows is largely similar to the process shown in Figure 7.5. The new elements are that the partner company might invest in the spin-off and also send some experienced innovation managers to it (dashed horizontal arrows), and that it might eventually choose to buy back the spin-off if that makes sense in its own strategy.

If the public funding and university research are erased from the bottom part of Figure 8.2, what remains is a useful description of the very important process by which a large company acts as an anchor in an innovation cluster. Nortel used to work that way in Ottawa. RIM works that way in Waterloo today.

## Basic research

Now we turn to university basic research as a source of innovation, an activity lying squarely in the R-N quadrant of innovation space. We will zoom in on what happens at the bottom of Figure 8.1 when a start-up is created. This close-up view is shown in Figure 8.3 in a diagram whose general shape is undoubtedly becoming familiar to the reader by now.

Let us begin with a basic research program shown in the oval at the bottom of Figure 8.3. The inputs are as shown earlier in Figure 8.1, but now only the direct support of the research through NSERC discovery grants is shown explicitly. The research is done in the context of the related research done around the world, whose published results are available to researchers in Canada. There are three outputs: (i) new codified knowledge, communicated in internationally peer-reviewed published papers; (ii) HQP who earned advanced degrees by contributing to the research results, and (iii) occasionally, a proposed invention or potential IP that has to be disclosed to the university.

## FIGURE 8.3 University Basic Research as a Source of Innovation

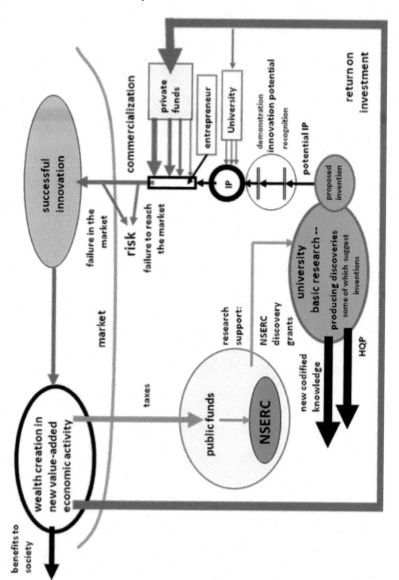

**Source:** T.A. Brzustowski. 2008. *The Way Ahead: Meeting Canada's Productivity Challenge*. Ottawa: University of Ottawa Press, p.116, with slight modifications.

This diagram illustrates a new venture based on university research. It provides details of the bottom centre part of Figure 8.1, and it has much in common with Figure 7.5. The big differences are the research as the source of the proposed invention and potential IP, and the role of the entrepreneur further downstream in the commercialization process. The bottleneck is recognizing that a research result might lead to an invention that has innovation potential, and then demonstrating it to potential investors. The involvement of the university in the first stages of commercialization depends on the institution's IP policy.

At this point, we must take time out to fill in a very important element that does not appear explicitly in Figure 8.3, namely the process of invention which translates the research results into a practical idea. Figure 8.4 shows it in detail. Think of this diagram as the detail of the oval at the lower right of Figure 8.1.

Inventions don't pop out of research results. First, somebody has to recognize that there is something in the results that might lead to an invention. But recognizing a potential invention may not always be the top-of-mind issue for researchers, since their reputation depends on the priority of discovery which is established by the first publication of results. An understanding of what might be needed in the market and the ability to imagine how it might be provided in light of the new research results are essential requirements for invention. After that, the design of the proposed invention requires a thorough knowledge of prior art and high skills. Experience helps. When researchers are exhorted to "commercialize their research," that is code for "commercialize the inventions that might be suggested by the results of their research," and Figure 8.4 suggests most individuals need specialized help to do that.

## FIGURE 8.4 How an Invention might arise from the Results of Basic Research

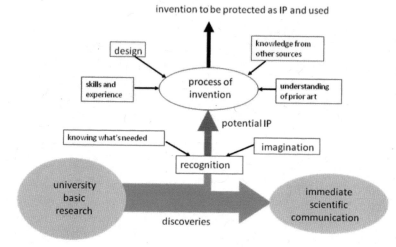

Research results seldom point the way directly to invention, but the complex process shown in this diagram is seldom discussed explicitly. It is often assumed that good researchers are able to do all this themselves, but it is more likely that only very few can.

The challenge with a possible invention arising out of basic research is to determine realistically whether it might have some potential to lead to an innovation in the market, and if so to demonstrate that to those who might invest in its commercialization. This task is made more difficult by the fact that the marketing of any such invention would be much more 'technology push' than a response to 'market pull.' It would be much more like shouting "I've got a great thing for you to buy!" than responding to someone saying "Sell me your solution to my problem."

Anyway, if the innovation potential has been recognized and demonstrated successfully, the next step is to improve and protect the IP. This involves proving the concept of the invention, testing its robustness and scalability, writing and filing a patent application, and perhaps starting on developing a prototype. If the university owns the IP, or if the owner requests it,[15] then the university's technology transfer office[16] provides the knowledge, business skills and some funding to start on this (shown by the three little arrows pointing to the IP circle from the university). At this point, an entrepreneur may be attracted to the invention and a new venture created to commercialize it. In some cases, an entrepreneur experienced in the sector might be involved in defining the invention and the IP, and developing a business model for taking it to market. In other cases, as shown in Figure 8.3, the entrepreneur might become involved only at the beginning of the commercialization process. The entrepreneur could, of course, be the professor who led the research, but this is rare because the successful commercialization of a research-based invention requires great skill and much experience in business, and those attributes are not often found among leading academic researchers.

What follows after that is the same process that was described in Figure 7.6, namely growing a new venture fed by investment of risk capital in successive stages, from pre-seed through seed, first-stage, across the 'valley of death,' etc. Conventional wisdom has it that the private funds required to bring a new product to market usually amount to much more than the cost of the research. Moreover, the private funds are exposed to commercial risk, whereas the research funds are exposed only to scientific risk that is well understood and managed through peer review. The cost multiplier may be in the single digits in some sectors, and several hundred in others. As already pointed out in chapter 6, such data are notoriously difficult to get. However, the conventional wisdom on costs and the obvious difference in risk levels serve to defuse the argument that this process somehow makes an undeserved gift of a publicly funded invention to private enterprise that will profit from it. The private investors must risk far more in commercializing that invention than the public did in supporting the research that led up to it.

---

[15] Canadian universities have different policies on the ownership of any IP generated from research on campus. Some give ownership to the inventor (e.g., Waterloo), while others retain ownership for the university, and still others have various blended or partial ownership arrangements.

[16] Technology Transfer Office is also called by other names, such as Industrial Liaison Office, or Enterprise Development Office, etc.

---

If the innovation finally makes it to market and succeeds in attracting sales, new value-added economic activity arises and new wealth is created. New wages are paid, new revenues flow back to the government, and the investors earn a return. One of those investors, of course, is the university where the research was done. Some university benefits are in the form of equity positions in new ventures; others may be royalties from IP that has been licensed. The Canadian experience is that, with the odd exception, the university's direct financial benefit is generally very small. A much greater source of benefit to the university, and to the community beyond it, is philanthropy by local entrepreneurs who become rich.

In 2003, all Canadian universities together received about $55 million in fees for licensing their IP to industry. However, their cost of managing the IP added up to $46 million.[17] The total net income to all Canadian universities was, therefore, only $9 million, or about a fifth of one percent of HERD. However, the total of licence fees is much more important than the net income to the universities, because it reflects the sales of products based on university-generated IP. A study of the Communications Research Centre, a federal agency not unlike a collection of university research labs, by D. Doyle showed that the licence income to the source of research-based IP was about 2.5 percent of the related sales revenue earned by the producers of products incorporating it.[18] This means a multiplier of 40 between licence revenue and sales of products involving that IP. If the same relationship held for IP licensed by universities, that suggests that the university IP was involved in sales of $2.2 billion in 2003. That is an important amount in the Canadian economy.

## What can be done in a system designed for something else

Finally, consider the whole system in which innovations might arise out of basic research. It is a system that was designed to achieve something else, namely to generate new knowledge that

[17] Numbers published by the Association of Universities and Colleges of Canada (AUCC) in a report entitled "Momentum – the 2005 report on university research and knowledge transfer," Ottawa: Association of Universities and Colleges of Canada, 2005.

[18] Denzil Doyle. 2007. "Cost recovery from publicly funded research," Opinion Leader, Re$earch Money, 21 (1): 8.

answers important questions about nature and humans. NSERC makes funding decisions in the Discovery Grants program on the basis of the applicants' record of publishing papers in the international, peer-reviewed literature and of supervising postgraduate students. Any potential IP generated in the research is incidental and unexpected with respect to these funding criteria, but it is central in government's expectations of economic benefits. One often hears that our problems would be solved if "Canadian business had a receptor capacity for research," or if "researchers were better at commercializing their research." In fact, that receptor capacity does exist and shows up in the many successful university-industry research projects in all sectors. This is a much more predictable and realistic arrangement than looking for industry to embrace and invest in unexpected and often isolated inventions that might result from basic research.

But even if the programs of university-industry research partnerships work very well, their goals are relatively short term, and they don't produce the revolutionary, long-term, game-changing innovations that one hopes for from basic research. Any program, no matter how enlightened in substance and convenient in format, that is designed to support research to meet today's needs will produce results constrained by today's perception of those needs. But basic research, supported with maximum flexibility gives free reign to imagination and surprise.

So, back to 'researchers commercializing their research.' This expression is short-hand for commercializing an invention suggested by the results of research. And in the absence of the participation by established firms, it takes the form of the research-based new venture that we have been discussing. Its success requires the commitment of an entrepreneur, the investment of private risk capital in the right amounts, under the right conditions and at the right times, and business skills of high order. But all of that can begin only if there is someone near the research who is very familiar with both the research and the market in related sectors. Such a person might first recognize and then demonstrate any innovation potential of inventions suggested by the research results. Unfortunately, there aren't enough such people in Canadian universities or in our venture capital industry – contrary to the US where there are many – and that creates a bottleneck.

What can be done to make a better connection between basic research and innovation? Tearing down the present system of support for basic research in some fit of Schumpeterian destruction wouldn't work, because there is no proven model for rebuilding it better.

Nevertheless, I believe that it is possible to improve the system of support for basic research so that an invention suggested by research results might have a better chance of becoming an innovation in the market. The momentum to excellence must be maintained, but the criteria for funding and the measures of success could be more discerning. The idea of Stokes[19] that there is a quad taxonomy of the goals of research (see Figure 8.5) suggests a possible approach.

The two independent dimensions in Stokes' taxonomy are new use and new understanding. Was the research undertaken to develop a new understanding – yes or no? Was it undertaken to develop a new use – yes or no? The yes-yes quadrant was named after Louis Pasteur, the chemist who became one of the founders of microbiology. He conducted research to develop a new understanding of the various biological processes active in disease, in rabies and milk-borne diseases among others, and to put the discoveries to use to prevent disease. The yes-no quadrant was named after Niels Bohr, whose research goal was to understand atomic structure, with no concern for its use. The no-yes quadrant was named for Thomas Edison, whose goal was to find new uses for what was already understood. Stokes did not give a name to the no-no quadrant, where neither a new understanding nor a new use was pursued.[20]

---

[19] Donald Stokes. 1997. *Pasteur's Quadrant*. New York: Brookings.

[20] Perhaps to avoid insulting anyone. However, interesting and important work can be placed in the no-no quadrant, e.g., improving the values of the fundamental constants of physics, classical taxonomy, and probably others.

## FIGURE 8.5 The Pasteur's Quadrant Taxonomy of the Goals of Research

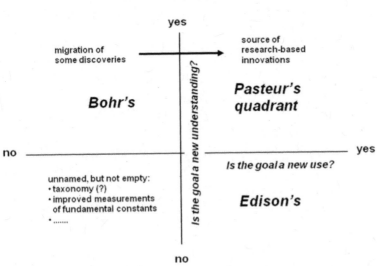

**Source:** Drawn by the author on the basis of the ideas in the book by Donald Stokes. 1997. *Pasteur's Quadrant.* New York: Brookings.

This diagram illustrates the quad taxonomy of the motivations for doing research, as proposed by Stokes and adapted by the author to the discussion of innovation.

Research undertaken to produce only a new understanding, located in Bohr's Quadrant, is the realm of the natural sciences. Biomedical and engineering research that aims for both new understanding and new use lies largely in Pasteur's Quadrant. Research excellence can, of course, be achieved in either. And movement between the quadrants might often make sense. For example, research in Bohr's Quadrant might suggest the principles of a new scientific instrument. The next phase of that work might move to Pasteur's to find out if an instrument based on those principles might be feasible. And if that succeeds and a new instrument becomes available, the work might move back to Bohr's and be used in making new discoveries.

If Stokes' distinctions were implemented in research funding, the criteria, the expectations and the measures would be somewhat different for the researchers who chose to work in Pasteur's Quadrant than for those who chose to work in Bohr's.

In particular, researchers in Pasteur's Quadrant who have disclosed some potential IP on the basis of their research results should be eligible for modest but prompt support for creating that invention and for the first steps in its commercialization, with just a simple follow-on application at any time during their grant cycle.

The recognition/demonstration bottleneck in the universities needs to be addressed promptly. In the United States, the venture capital industry has many people with enough technical depth to help in this role. Many of them have degrees in science or engineering as well as in finance or IP law, and many have experience in running companies. In Canada, the venture capital industry is small and relatively inexperienced, and less able to help, so it will be up to the universities to address this issue. The recognition/demonstration function is not a post-retirement job for a professor, nor is it an entry-level job for a budding research administrator. It is a very specialized position, requiring both a technical education and business experience, and it needs to be the subject of careful recruiting, adequate remuneration and imaginative incentives. And for the longer term, universities need to develop multidisciplinary programs to educate such people, both within the university and through internships in innovative firms.

# CHAPTER 9

## INNOVATION IN SERVICES

*Goods are objects; services are actions.*

### Introduction

In the earlier chapters, we noted several times that product innovation includes both goods and services, but the models and examples discussed so far have largely dealt with industrial innovation in goods. In this chapter, we shall discuss innovation in services explicitly.

The service sectors are a major part of today's Canadian economy, with 71.2 percent of gross domestic product (GDP)[1] derived from the service sectors, and 78.4 percent of the workforce[2] employed by them. The goods-producing sectors contributed the remaining 28.8 percent of GDP and 21.6 percent of employment. Employment in agriculture was 1.8 percent, so just under 20 percent was in the remaining goods-producing sectors, mainly manufacturing and construction. These numbers are part of a trend. The proportions of people employed in agriculture and in the goods sectors in Canada

---

[1] Statistics Canada. 2011. "Gross domestic product at basic prices, by industry (monthly)," Catalogue No. 15-001-X, updated November 30 [accessed December 22, 2011]. The number quoted is calculated from the data for September 2011. The text uses the industry classifications as in the Statistics Canada tables.

[2] Statistics Canada. 2011. "Table 2, Employment by class of worker and industry (based on NAICS) – seasonally adjusted," Latest Release from the Labour Force Survey, updated December 2011 [accessed on December 22, 2012]. The number quoted is calculated from the data for October 2011.

have been declining steadily for most of the last century,[3] and employment in the service sectors has been rising. For example, employment in services was about 53.7 percent of the workforce in 1971, and it had risen to 65.3 percent in 1984. Agriculture had employed 5.9 percent in 1971 and only 4.7 percent in 1984.

This situation is not unique to Canada, but is typical of the older, industrialized economies. A century ago, a much larger portion of the Canadian population worked in agriculture and in the manufacturing industries. So what has happened since then? We haven't stopped eating. And we haven't lost interest in manufactured goods, either. In fact, we buy a growing profusion of goods of all descriptions. Clearly, an important part of the answer is that the productivity of agriculture and of manufacturing has grown so much that we are now fed and equipped by the efforts of a much smaller workforce. Farm machinery, new fertilizers, new crops and new practices have driven the productivity increase in agriculture; production machinery, new materials, new processes and tools, and new information technologies have done it in manufacturing. In other words, innovation has freed up agricultural and industrial workers to do something else. And that something else turns out to be a growing volume of work in the service sectors. So what are these people doing?

This question is made more interesting by the fact that while service employment has grown significantly during the 20th century, many familiar services have disappeared. For example, at one time mail was delivered to the door twice daily and on Saturdays, but now it is delivered once a day on weekdays or picked up at neighbourhood boxes. Domestic servants in middle-class homes have all but vanished. Many bank branches and local post offices have been closed. Most ticket agents at airports have been replaced by check-in machines. Salespeople in department stores are becoming a vanishing breed. The do-it-yourself (DYI) movement in home maintenance has just about eliminated the professional handyman, and there are many other examples. So if employment in the service sectors has been growing

[3] Except for a surge of employment in the manufacturing of armaments during World War II. In 1945, at the end of WWII, 25% of the workforce was employed in manufacturing, a temporary increase from 17% in 1920. Data from Roy A. Phillips. 1985. "Manufacturing," *Canadian Encyclopedia*. Edmonton: Hurtig Publishers Ltd., p. 1086.

while many familiar services have been disappearing, a lot of innovation in services must have been going on in areas that we don't see so readily.

Three drivers of that innovation come to mind very quickly. One is the explosive development of modern information and communications technologies (ICT) that has made possible a profusion of new knowledge-intensive business services (KIBS), explosive growth in financial services (e.g., the credit-card industry), and whole new service industries (e.g., online sales) whose workers are in back offices out of contact with the public. Users of ICT have also taken established industrial services to a new scale and promoted them to a new importance (e.g., logistics), created entirely new business models (e.g., Amazon, iTunes), and much more. Another obvious driver of service innovation has been cheap jet travel that has caused a global boom in tourist services of all kinds. And a third driver has been the institutional innovation in many western countries that has led to a massive growth in government and other public services to their citizens.

## The importance of services in the Canadian economy

It is instructive to look at the various service sectors as they appear in the national accounts of Canada. The sectors in the whole economy are divided into goods-producing and service-producing sectors. This is a macro division. It does not capture some details at the micro level, such as customer services provided by manufacturers and business services internal to firms in all goods sectors.

The number of people working in Canada in all sectors is just under 17.35 million.[4] Of that number, 3.75 million, or 21.6 percent are employed in the goods-producing sectors that are listed in the Statistics Canada tables as: (i) agriculture; (ii) natural resources (forestry, fishing, mining, quarrying, oil and gas); (iii) utilities; (iv) construction; and (v) manufacturing. Manufacturing is by far the biggest employer in the goods sectors with 1.7 million employees or 9.8 percent of total employment in the economy, and the biggest contributor to the GDP, at $162.6 billion, or 12.75 percent of the total GDP.

---

[4] By coincidence, this number is close to one half of the Canadian population, and that approximate relationship has held for some years.

The other 13.6 million people, or 78.4 percent, work in services. The service-producing sectors listed are: (i) trade – wholesale and retail; (ii) transportation and warehousing; (iii) finance, insurance, real estate (FIRE) and leasing; (iv) professional, scientific and technical services; (v) business, building and other support services; (vi) educational services; (vii) health care and social assistance; (viii) information, culture and recreation; (ix) accommodation and food services; (x) other services; and (xi) public administration. Of these, (i) through (v) and (viii) and (ix) are in the private sector, while (vi) and (vii) are mostly in the public sector, and (xi) is totally public.

In terms of employment, (i) trade is the largest private service sector, employing about 2.7 million people, or 15.5 percent of the employment in the whole economy, and more than twice as many as (iv) professional, scientific and technical services, which is second. In terms of contributions to GDP, (iii) finance, insurance, real estate (FIRE) and leasing is the single largest sector, contributing $265.4 billion, or 20.8 percent of the total GDP.[5]

Without examining the details of what is included under the various sector labels, it is difficult to pin down accurately which ones serve mainly individuals and which ones serve mainly corporations. Suffice it to say, that service sectors (i), (ii), (iii), (iv), (viii), (ix) and (xi) most likely offer some services to individuals and some to corporations. Sectors (vi), (vii) serve individuals, and sector (v) mainly corporations.

## The definition of services

When we begin to examine how innovation in services actually happens, it quickly becomes evident that this is very different from industrial innovation in goods. Many of the differences are pointed out in the excellent survey by Miles.[6] Many authors have pointed out that the models of innovation in industry don't apply to the services sectors, and that policies designed to promote industrial innovation don't work for services.

[5] Note, however, that the description of the FIRE sector in the GDP table includes the management of companies and enterprises, an activity that is not included in the employment table.

[6] Ian Miles. 2005. "Innovation in Services," in *Oxford Encyclopedia of Innovation.* Jan Fagerberg, David C. Mowery, and Richard R. Nelson (eds.). Oxford, UK: Oxford University Press, 433-458.

'Services' is another one of those words 'that everybody knows,' but services, as such, are rarely defined in the innovation literature. In the words of Ettlie,[7] "Although services are difficult to define and quantify, they have sometimes been called anything that can be bought or traded that cannot be dropped on your foot ..." The academic literature treats services as economic goods that are produced, exchanged and consumed. But they are economic goods with various special properties that require special labels. Some services must be used at the time they are produced, and they are called perishable or unstorable. Others still must be consumed where they are produced; these are called untransportable. And some services are produced and consumed at the same time and the same place, like restaurant meals. They are called coterminous. In turn, some of those are called interactive if they are shaped by the interaction between consumer and producer. Those services that are the same for all customers and available everywhere are called commodity services, such as fast-food meals and dry cleaning, and their opposites are custom services, such as making a suit to measure for an individual customer. Services offered to individuals are called personal services; those offered to corporations are called business services. There are physical services, like having snow cleared from your driveway, and knowledge-intensive services, like having your income tax return prepared. And many knowledge-intensive services are intangible.[8] There are many other modifiers for services and much variety in the language used to describe them. In general, services are described as heterogeneous because of their great variety.

However, in what follows, we will look at services from a different perspective. We shall take a simpler approach and focus on a much smaller number of distinctions. Instead of treating services as economic goods with a great variety of characteristics, we shall make an explicit distinction between goods and services. Briefly put, goods are objects and services are actions. Many characteristics of services are more simply described as routine aspects of familiar actions than as some special requirements

---

[7] John E. Ettlie. 2006. *Managing Innovation*, 2nd edition. New York: Elsevier Butterworth-Heinemann, p. 21.

[8] Many knowledge-intensive services are intangible with obvious exceptions that can be felt, such as a root-canal procedure in a dental office.

of economic goods. And many differences in detail between innovation in goods and innovation in services follow from that difference in their basic nature.

For example, one important difference between goods and services shows up clearly in the use of knowledge. In the case of knowledge-intensive goods, customers purchase the knowledge that has been embodied in artifacts through R&D. In the case of knowledge-intensive services, customers buy the actions of the service providers that are made possible by the personal knowledge they acquire through education, training and experience, and by the knowledge embodied in the tools that they use. This means that innovation in knowledge-intensive services involves not only developing the substance of a new service, but also training and equipping the service providers who offer it to customers. In contrast, innovation in knowledge-intensive goods stresses more the developing of a new product and demonstrating to customers what they might do with it.

We now propose a definition of services that will open the door for some useful discussion of the various types of services and innovation in them. We begin with the very first definition of service given in the *Concise Oxford Dictionary* "the act of helping or doing work for another ..."[9] and then add an element of motivation, so that:

> **Services** *are actions that meet the needs of persons who cannot or choose not to do so themselves.*

The persons receiving the service may be individuals or they may be corporations. The services may be provided by firms in the private sector, or by organizations in the public sector. Some services are bought by choice; others are required by law. For example, I can choose when to get my hair cut and where, but I must get my driver's licence renewed at a government service office or kiosk before a particular expiry date. Some services may meet the needs of customers individually, that is a cab ride to the airport; others may meet the same need for many people at once, such as a bus route to the airport. There is no need to find complicated new ways of labelling economic goods to describe such obvious differences in actions.

[9] *The Concise Oxford Dictionary of Current English*, 8th edition. Oxford, UK: Oxford University Press, 1990.

In discussing many of the features of services, it is useful to break services down into two phases of action: diagnosis and execution. So, following the pattern introduced in chapter 4, we will use an equation-like relationship between a service and its two phases:

- service = diagnosis + execution　　　　　　　(9.1)

In the diagnosis phase, the service provider analyzes the customer's need and identifies possible solutions. In the execution phase, a solution is implemented. The relative proportions of diagnosis and execution can differ, of course. At one extreme, for example, the emergency roadside service of replacing a flat tire is almost all execution with very little diagnosis, whereas at the other extreme fixing a bug in a data processing program may be almost all diagnosis followed by a minimal execution phase consisting of changing a few lines of code. The latter is, of course, knowledge-intensive, and effective knowledge-intensive services must start with accurate diagnosis. The important point is that services vary in the relative importance of diagnosis and execution, and that has implications for the location, timing, cost and other aspects of how services are offered to clients.

## Competition in services

The simple definition of services given above says that there are two kinds of competition in services in the private sector. First, the service providers must compete for their customers' business in the market with other firms providing the same services. And, secondly, in those cases where the customers have the potential to meet their own needs – to serve themselves – the service providers must, in effect, compete with their potential customers. In the case of individual customers, the competition is with the 'do it yourself' (DIY) option, and in the case of corporations with the 'make' option in the 'make or buy' (MOB) decision.

In contrast, the service providers in the public sector face competition of just one kind. For example, an urban public transit system does not compete with another transit system that serves the same area in the same way, but it does have to compete with DIY. Its competition comes from people who might choose to meet their own needs for transportation by driving (or biking or walking, or even taking cabs). Even though it offers a monopoly service, a public transit system must compete with DIY to attract the ridership that will justify the continuing public investment in it.[10]

This is important because competition is a very important driver of innovation, and the form of competition affects the form of innovation. For example, restaurant chains compete against one another, but they must also remember DIY and work to make it attractive for people to go out for meals rather than eat at home. Depending on their specialty, their innovations and their advertising will emphasize one or another of the taste of their food, the price, the selection, the convenience, the quality, or some specialty of their cuisine. Airlines compete among themselves on the quality of their service, railways compete with air travel as a whole, and in short-distance travel they both compete against driving. The airlines innovate to improve on-time performance, to increase passenger comfort in the terminal and in the cabin, to reduce the impact of their own costs (e.g., fuel) on ticket prices by introducing more fuel-efficient new planes, and to improve convenience through scheduling, code-sharing, etc. The railways (strictly speaking, VIA Rail) innovate in scheduling city centre-to-city centre service to increase the relative convenience of rail over flying or driving, and in amenities (such as Wi-Fi on trains) to make the experience more enjoyable and the travel time more productive.

It seems quite reasonable to conclude that service providers innovate in those areas where they must compete, and they do it in ways that enhance their competitive advantage.

### Services in the quad taxonomy of innovation

To pursue the discussion of private-sector services further, it is useful to look at them from the perspective of the quad taxonomy of innovation. We begin with the D-N quadrant, the design-based service innovations commercialized by new ventures.

---

[10] The word 'ridership' to describe transit riders as a group is attributed to William G. Davis, Premier of Ontario in the 1970s and early 1980s, who was a strong advocate of public transit.

## Design-based, new venture (D-N)

The service sectors lying in this quadrant are (i) trade, (viii) information, culture and recreation services – including entertainment, of course, (ix) accommodation and food services. Most of these include obvious services to both individuals and corporations. Services offered mainly to corporations might include design, advertising, office cleaning, translation services, etc. lying in service sectors (iv) and (v). In the D-N quadrant, innovation in services consists of creating a new venture to offer some service that makes use of prior knowledge, but is different from what had been available before. Opening a new convenience store wouldn't count, but opening a new restaurant that offers new cuisine would. If new intellectual property (IP) is created, it is more likely to be protected by copyright or trademark than by a patent. The whole process is shown in Figure 7.5, which applies equally well to goods and services.

Entrepreneurs in the D-N quadrant must understand current customer needs and be able to design attractive new services to meet those needs. New technologies that enable the new services would be considered prior knowledge; they would be purchased rather than developed. Success in these services would probably depend much more on excellence in execution than on diagnosis. However, in setting up the new venture, good market intelligence is crucial. Entrepreneurs contemplating D-N have to know what the competition is doing, what market needs aren't being met, and what new tools and methods are becoming available for developing their own new services. The best entrepreneurs will understand social trends and developing tastes well enough to foresee new needs or wants, and respond to them with new services that 'catch the wave' and create their own new demand.

## Research-based, new venture (R-N)

The R-N quadrant, where research-based service innovations are commercialized by new ventures has many business challenges similar to those in D-N, but differs substantially in how knowledge is used.

Research-based innovations in services will be knowledge-intensive, almost by definition. Research in the natural sciences and engineering tends to suggest inventions that are new goods or new processes for the goods-producing industry. Inventions that lead to new knowledge-intensive services are more likely to be suggested by research in mathematics, in computer science, in the health sciences and in the social sciences. Many such inventions might take the form of software.[11] R-N innovation occurs when a new venture is set up to commercialize such a new service. Examples of new proprietary knowledge-intensive services created this way have included new encryption software that makes online financial transactions more secure, arising from research in pure mathematics, new polling approaches suggested by research in sociology and statistics, new business methods suggested by results in management science research, new tools for logistics derived from computer science research in algorithms, and a fast and cheap personal gene-sequencing service emerging from research in genomics and instrumentation. An important feature of services in this sector is that many of them are likely to emphasize diagnosis over execution, leaving it to the clients to implement the advice or use the results produced. That means that they might not require much capital investment to launch the new service business, and might be able to stay small and flexible. But early in the life of such small new ventures, learning how to do business will compete for time with learning how to develop the new service products.

### Research-based, established firm (R-E)

Things are different in the established firms. On the one hand, they have the organizational structure to support innovation, and that should make innovation easier to achieve. But at the same time, they are likely to be less nimble, more unwieldy and hierarchical, and more resistant to new ideas than the new ventures.

Research-based innovation in services offered by established firms might in many ways be similar to (R-E) innovation in the goods-producing sectors. This was hinted at in chapter 7 where only a slight change in the chain-link model of innovation was suggested for services. The firms in this quadrant are connected to university and government research, the natural sciences, engineering, as well as the health and social sciences. Some

---

[11] Note that software is treated here as a knowledge-intensive good. In the literature, it is sometimes treated as a knowledge-intensive service.

firms buy or conduct R&D to develop new products and tools for their own business. For example, telecommunications carriers do research in mathematics as well as electrical and systems engineering to manage and upgrade their networks; insurance companies do research in actuarial science to study new kinds of risk under emerging circumstances, discover new relationships, and use them to develop new insurance products for individual customers; financial institutions do research to develop new investment vehicles and trading algorithms for their clients and for themselves. A feature of some of this R&D is the use of historical data to test the performance of the proposed new products in a 'backcasting' mode, not something that is common in R&D on new goods. The internal education and training of employees in depth in the new products is important and, because the firms are already established, it does not have to compete for time or attention with learning how to run a business.

However, there is another way that R&D contributes to innovation in the R-E service quadrant. There are established firms whose business it is to sell R&D as a service to other firms. They have the capabilities to carry out many of the tasks involved in preparing a new product for the market under contract to the owners of the IP. Such firms are examples of innovation intermediaries. The owners of the IP may arrive with a proven concept and leave with a product ready for the market. In the meantime, their own resources are focused on all the other aspects of commercialization. Such work may be routine for the R&D service firm, but it produces new knowledge for its client and leads to an innovation in the market. That innovation itself may be a good, but it is the result of a service provided by the innovation intermediary.

## Design-based, established firm (D-E)

The designation of this quadrant as 'design-based innovation in services by established firms' requires some interpretation because it can be approached from two sides. First, we consider established service providers that sell services to help their clients solve their problems and meet their needs. Many of those needs have to do with innovation by the clients, but the services they buy may be routine for the service-providers. The advertising campaigns designed by established advertising agencies for the clients' new products are a good example. They may be innovations for the client, but we would not consider such cases to be D-E innovations for the ad agencies. They would be classified according to client's circumstances. A different example is the work of a structural engineering consulting firm on a building of novel design. The building may be an innovation for the client, but the structural engineering service is routine. The properties of materials are known, and proven tools are used, so if a routine design was produced then no D-E innovation has occurred. (Note the nuanced difference between this example and the discussion of R-E innovation in the previous paragraph). However, if the structural engineer had to develop some new structural design approach to make the building design work, then a D-E innovation has occurred. This sounds paradoxical at first. We limit this quadrant to the established service providers who develop some new service using prior knowledge. Research is not involved. However, industry-wide experience and the lessons learned in their own prior projects contribute to the prior knowledge from which their service innovations arise.

But design-based innovation in services can also start from a different direction within a different business model. Some innovations in knowledge-intensive goods have a long 'service tail.' For example, the BlackBerry smart phone is manufactured by RIM and is offered by various telecommunications carriers (telcos) around the world. But the telcos have not had to master the technical aspects of providing BlackBerry service. That is done by RIM. As a result, a substantial part of RIM's revenues consists of service fees collected through the local telcos. That means that a handset manufacturer selling to consumers has become also a service provider to the telcos. This is a big service innovation. It required great business skill, but no new knowledge beyond what RIM had already learned as it developed the BlackBerry. There are other examples of recent service innovations of this kind. Perhaps the best known of all is the move by Rolls-Royce from selling aircraft engines to selling engine running hours. Rolls-Royce supplies the engines, keeps a continuous real-time record of the performance of each one around the world, and services, maintains, repairs and replaces the engines as required. The

Rolls-Royce employees who used to build the engines still build them, but the company now also has employees who deliver a service to the airlines. Once again, a traditional manufacturer has become also a service provider, using a new business model.

## Innovation in public sector and government services

We now consider innovation in the services offered to the public by government and the broader public sector, specifically service sectors (vi) education services, (vii) health care and social assistance, and (xi) public administration. In general, these services are driven by supply-side considerations, and they face very little market competition, or none at all. For example, in health care local competition occurs only in dentistry and a handful of specialty treatments, which operate as private services. In public education, universities compete for students among themselves, and so do colleges, but that competition is among institutions that operate under system-wide provincial government controls and are largely similar. Of course, patients who can afford it may choose to seek treatment outside of Canada, and students who have the means may enrol in private schools or seek an education abroad, but that is not enough competition to affect these sectors at home. Perhaps the only real competition in the broader public sector in Canada is the competition among universities for research funding from the federal government.

Most government services are delivered through programs. Innovation in creating or eliminating government service programs is usually driven from the centre of government in response to political pressures, election promises of the governing party, etc. Innovations that only change existing services may be a local departmental or ministry initiative, but it must still be approved at the centre to be announced and proceed. Some government innovations may require new legislation and Parliamentary approval, but some may fall within existing legislation. Innovation takes the form of initiatives for changes in policies, regulations, programs and procedures, etc. that may occasionally also involve changes in the structure and organization of government agencies or of government itself. But government innovation is not driven by market competition. Governments offer monopoly services; there is no choice among service providers. And many of the services, such as taxation, are obligatory; there is no choice but to use them. In fact, the culture of government fundamentally opposes competition. Any significant overlapping of mandates between departments or agencies is not seen as worthwhile potential competition that might lead to improvements, but rather as 'wasteful duplication' that needs to be eliminated. From the point of view of the efficient use of public resources in the short term, this is entirely sensible, but it probably closes the door to much innovation.

However, the potential for improvements in efficiency and the possibility of cost reductions will always offer a motivation for innovation in the delivery of government services. Such operational innovations often take the form of reorganization and perhaps the implementation of new information technology, but outsourcing the delivery of some services to the private sector may sometimes also be an option. That last possibility comes close to introducing an element of market competition into consideration.

The knowledge base for innovations in government services is quite heterogeneous. It includes national statistics, research results from government's own laboratories, results of academic research mainly in the social sciences, and reports by Royal Commissions, by expert panels, by various domestic and international think tanks, by numerous internal advisory councils, by private consultants, etc. It also includes analyses of precedents by the public service, polling results, experiences in other countries, the occasional influential book, briefs submitted by lobbies, media reports, the results of consultations, and more. But it does not include controlled experiments and, as a result, the links between cause and effect are more hoped for than proven. The reason is that experiments in what governments do would have to involve very large numbers of people and take a very long time, and governments' time horizons rarely reach beyond the end of their immediate mandates. Occasionally, in the absence of any great urgency or contention, a pilot project might be mounted to test a program or institutional design. That is useful, of course, but it is not an experiment. The idea is only to see if the thing works as expected, not to test competing hypotheses.

The momentum of a huge government bureaucracy – some might say inertia – makes change very difficult. The culture of government is not conducive to risk-taking and innovation.

Programs are always difficult to stop. When they are cut, it is usually for financial reasons in a fit of budget-driven belt-tightening, and not in any Schumpeterian prelude to major innovation. It is clear to individual civil servants in the lower ranks that taking chances is a no-no. At the same time, those in the executive ranks find themselves acting as the rope in a tug of war between exhortations for excellence and innovation from on high, and a relentless insistence on increasingly detailed accountability from only slightly lower down. This leaves little room for trying out new ideas. But in spite of all that, some innovation takes place. For example, there have been some extraordinary innovations by the federal government in the last decade and a half in the area of support for university research – particularly the Networks of Centres of Excellence (NCE), the Canada Foundation for Innovation (CFI), the Canada Research Chairs (CRC) and Canada Excellence Research Chairs (CERC), and the Centres of Excellence in Commercialization of Research (CECR). The fact that they were created, and sustained, when the cards are stacked against innovation in government underlines their importance and is an eloquent tribute to the leadership of the officials involved.

All of that is to say that if there is to be more innovation in services provided or paid for by government, it will have to be driven by political leaders who are prepared to take the long view, make difficult decisions, and act consistently and persistently to achieve the goals.

One area where this has become very urgent is health care. Innovation is desperately needed in Canada's health care system. The system was designed decades ago to provide acute care to a young population, but it is now expected to provide chronic care to an aging population. There is no competition to drive innovation, and the political rhetoric describing the health care system as a 'sacred trust' does much to freeze the status quo, even though this emotive label refers to equal access to health care rather than to the design of the health care system. There is discussion about innovation in health care, but it is mostly about innovations arising out of research in universities and research hospitals. Some excellent work is being done, important discoveries are being made, and new diagnostics and therapies are being developed. This is detailed research-based innovation and it involves both established firms and new ventures. But one doesn't hear much about design-based innovation at the level of the health care system as a whole – innovation based on existing management knowledge to redesign the system in light of the demands that are actually being made on it today. And there is no shortage of ready indicators. Waiting times might be the best known to the public, but others such as the relative numbers of acute-care beds and chronic-care beds available in the system might be more significant. Innovation in health care awaits the high-level leadership that will cut through the web of barriers that inhibit it today.

Innovation in the other major area of public expenditure, education, varies with the level. Elementary and secondary education, like government, suffer from a lack of controlled experiments. Innovations do take place, but not all are evidence-based. Mathematics is introduced to children in new ways. That may lead to better understanding in the long term, but nobody can tell yet. In the meantime, parents complain that they can no longer help their children with math homework. Changes are made in high schools, programs are shortened, cohorts are doubled for a while. A shorter high-school stay is supposed to make things better in the long term, but for now some students stay longer to repeat some courses and get the higher grades that might get them into university. As pointed out in the example discussed in chapter 3, there are fundamental difficulties in assessing the impact of changes in education because of the long time scales involved and the range of confounding influences. These are not problems of funding. Their solution will require innovation based on evidence that includes a deep understanding of the conditions for success in a society's educational system, and the ability to see education as more than schooling. After all, while the schooling of children is a service provided by government with massive resources, we continue to see that success in education is also strongly dependent on the children's experience of a culture of learning within the family at home.

In post-secondary education, the students are more mature and they stay in the system for a much shorter time. In both colleges and universities, there is a profusion of detailed innovations in curricula, in programs, in teaching methods. But there are few innovations at a higher, more general, level.

In colleges, the most visible recent innovation has been an 'upmarket' movement. Some colleges in BC have recently become universities; colleges across the country are starting to offer 'applied degrees' instead of just diplomas, and some colleges – including, particularly, the nine that are now called polytechnics – have begun to engage in research. All of this is to the good if it raises the prestige of colleges and makes them more attractive to potential students and their families. But it will have a serious downside for Canada's technological capabilities if, in the process, the colleges move away from their practical orientation. It is very important for the colleges to expand and upgrade their apprenticeship training in the skilled trades to deal with the looming worker shortages as demographics work their inexorable effect. It is important that colleges should continue to offer practical technical assistance to SMEs in their communities, and not abandon it to take up research instead. It is also very important that colleges should maintain their demand-driven educational activities in which they respond to the specific training needs of local employers by mounting targeted courses where needed, when needed, and with the needed content.

In universities, there have been many recent innovations associated with the conduct and organization of research, and a flood of research achievements as a result. On the teaching side, there have been new programs created and new departments set up, and new teaching methods tried. There has been a great deal of innovation within the established context, but little change in the context. University faculty are very innovative in their own teaching and even more in research, but at the same time, they can be very conservative in dealing with the context in which they do their academic work. This conservatism reflects the strong external influence of the disciplines in the hiring, teaching and promotion of faculty, and in the peer review of research grant applications and scholarly papers. It is reinforced by the program approval requirements of the various provincial governments. One can point to the NCE, the CFI and the Canada Research Chairs, etc. as great innovations in Canadian universities, but they were innovations of the federal government, not of the universities themselves. There are perhaps only two major innovations in Canadian universities in the last half-century that have substantially changed the services they offer to students: co-operative education pioneered in Canada by Waterloo and online degree programs pioneered in Canada by Athabasca.

We will give the final word on innovation in Canadian post-secondary education to the thousands of students who have produced a perfect example of user-driven innovation in this sector. These are the people who went from high school to university, graduated with a general degree in arts or sciences, and then enrolled in a diploma program in a community college. They acquired general knowledge and self-awareness at the university, and on that basis then went on to develop job-related skills at a college. The many 'articulation agreements' signed between universities and colleges to make such arrangements easier in both directions might now be considered a service innovation of the colleges and universities together.

# CHAPTER 10

## INTERACTIONS FOR INNOVATION

*Innovation is a body-contact team sport.*

Innovation is too difficult for any one person to succeed alone. There is too much to do, too many things to consider. And even if it originates with a skilled and experienced team, an innovation still requires the additional contributions of many others to succeed in the market. This is basic. Innovators must interact with many people in many different ways to achieve success, because what may start as a single idea on the supply side must eventually earn the acceptance of very many on the demand side. New ventures commercializing inventions must interact with many people to develop the new products, to learn commerce and to become known and trusted; established firms need to interact with outsiders to acquire new perspectives, broaden the range of possibilities, and find new ways to build on their successes. And both must interact with customers whom they need to attract, satisfy and keep.

This chapter deals with some of the interactions that are necessary for success in innovation. It begins with person-to-person contacts at the creative level, and then moves on to innovation clusters, innovation intermediaries, and partnerships. Culture at various levels turns out to be very important in all of them.

### People working with people

Steve Jobs, the innovation genius behind the success of Apple, attached great value to informal encounters among his employees, and actively created opportunities for that to happen in the design of the buildings where they worked. "If a building doesn't encourage that, you'll lose a lot of innovation and the magic that's sparked by serendipity. So we designed the building to make people get out of their offices and mingle in the central atrium with people they might not otherwise see."[1] This culture of informal interactions among people who play related but different roles in a company helps bring a diversity of perspectives, insights and skills to bear on their work. Jobs paid special attention to the interactions among his most creative employees, the ones he called "A players." His three decades of experience had taught him that "... A players like to work only with other A players."[2] Very good creative people like to work with other very good creative people because they stimulate one another. What they don't like is working with "B players" (or "Bozos") who can't see what they're trying to do and slow them down. So for their A players to achieve the most, a high-performance innovative company must recruit other A players, and weed out those who turn out to be Bs. And then it must make it easy for the A players to interact, informally as well as formally. In this sense, innovation is a body-contact team sport. This simple language describes a complicated cultural challenge to an innovative company, but one that Jobs and Apple met and kept meeting with resounding success.

Looking at innovation within the framework of the quad taxonomy (chapter 6), it is pretty clear that innovative new ventures need a lot of help, whether the inventions that they are commercializing are research-based or design-based. They just don't have all the capabilities they need to get a new business going and to take a new product to market. Even if they can handle all the technical issues themselves, they still have much to learn about doing business in a particular place, and at a particular time. They need advice on the strengths and weaknesses of the local business community, on what services are available locally to help them get established in it, on local sources of risk finance, on legal expertise in intellectual property (IP), on possible customers and suppliers, on channels to market, on sources of skilled people, on government support programs, and much more. They need to meet the people who offer these services locally, as well as those who have been their clients.

[1] Walter Isaacson. 2011. *Steve Jobs*. New York: Simon & Schuster, p. 431.
[2] Ibid., p. 181.

They need to become connected, to get to know the local business leaders, and to become known and trusted themselves. They need information, they need referrals, and they need help with using what they find. They need to meet angel investors and other experienced business people in the community who will take the time to listen to their ambitions and offer reactions and advice. They need to test their initial business model with them, and to hear suggestions for improvement. Dozens of testimonials by entrepreneurs in two of Canada's technology centres – Ottawa and Waterloo – collected in the two books on entrepreneurship by James Bowen describe how interactions of all these kinds have been important in their own success.[3]

The established firms need interactions as well, but of a different sort. They may have the organizational structure to support their innovation, whether design-based or research-based. And they may have established procedures and budgets for innovation, in-house expertise in IP, an established line of profitable products, and satisfied customers – in short, all the makings of business success. But they may also believe that everything they're doing is just right and they don't need to change, that their procedures are very systematic and not at all bureaucratic, that they have some of the smartest people in the business as employees, that they measure their employees' performance appropriately and reward it in ways that provide the right incentives, that their business model is the perfect one for them, that they have nothing to learn from anyone else, and that they just need to carry on carrying on. In such cases, what they really need are interactions with people who will question them.

This is where culture comes in. Recall that culture is what people consider important, what they believe, what language and metaphor they use to express it, what they're used to, and how they act as a result. If a firm is inward-looking and confident that it can generate all the ideas it needs, because it may have done so in the past, then the interactions of its people with other knowledgeable people will be limited. It will forgo the possibility of acquiring better new ideas in order to protect the ones it has. It takes a receptive internal culture and secure management for a

[3] James Bowen. 2009. *The Entrepreneurial Effect*. Ottawa: Invenire Books, and James Bowen. 2011. *The Entrepreneurial Effect: Waterloo*. Ottawa: Invenire Books.

firm to be open to learning from outsiders, without implying any lack of confidence in the abilities of the people inside the firm. For such a firm, striking a balance between disclosing enough to others to get useful feedback and disclosing too much and giving away one's competitive advantage is a manageable issue, and it begins with the individual employees who are trusted to manage it well.

The culture of the firm is one thing; the culture of the community where it is located is another. Opportunities for informal interactions among the employees of local firms are very limited if they are mostly commuters who disperse to their various remote bedroom communities at the end of the working day. On the other hand, people who live where they work and participate in grass-roots community activities see many more opportunities for informal interactions with the employees of other local companies in the same sector, whether at their kids' hockey rink, at a concert, at a school meeting, at worship, or even in a pub. They are able to participate more in the diffusion of tacit knowledge than the commuters are.

The importance of such considerations emerged from the seminal work of Saxenian comparing the performance of information and communications technology (ICT) companies in Silicon Valley in California with those in the Route 128 area near Boston.[4] Silicon Valley did better for many reasons, some of them cultural. The Silicon Valley companies were staffed by many newcomers from elsewhere, some of whom were former rebels, ready to question any established order. They really liked to do 'neat things' with technology, talked shop at every opportunity, changed jobs among established firms and new ventures, and in the process created not only new technology but also new firms and new traditions. In contrast, the Route 128 companies were more traditional. They were staffed by people whose loyalty was more to the firm than to the technology, who had established roots in the bedroom communities where they lived, and who were committed to activities that had little or nothing to do with their work. Long-term employment with one firm was a mark of stability, even respectability. Informal meetings with employees of other firms in the Route 128 area were rare compared to Silicon

---

[4] AnnaLee Saxenian. 1994. *Regional Advantage: Culture and Competition in Silicon Valley and Route 128.* Cambridge MA: Harvard University Press.

Valley. In the end, Silicon Valley became the boiling pot of new ideas in ICT, eclipsing Route 128.

Which brings us to clusters.

## Clusters

In 1990, Michael Porter published an important book on the competitiveness of nations.[5] His main point was that it was companies that made a nation competitive, and they were most competitive when they were part of a cluster of interacting companies that included all the services that they needed in their business, as well as competing companies in the sector. Porter identified four interacting characteristics of such a sector as: (i) firm strategy, structure and rivalry; (ii) related and supporting industries; (iii) factor conditions; and (iv) demand conditions, all of them affected by (v) government and by (vi) chance and events. A focus on one sector and a certain geographical concentration of the firms are implicit. The prominence of the four characteristics led to this model being called Porter's Diamond.

Companies are competitive when they maintain their market share and value-added in the face of competition. According to Porter, this happens when all four determinants (i) to (iv) above are favourable, government is supportive, and the probability of destructive events is low. This means that a cluster of firms in a particular sector is competitive when (i) the firms are well organized and managed, and they compete among themselves, thus prompting each other to get better at what they do; (ii) they can find their suppliers and build their supply chain locally; (iii) skilled labour, sources of needed knowledge, financing and the necessary infrastructure (electric power, transportation links, etc.) are readily available; (iv) demanding customers provide a stimulus for company learning and innovation; (v) government policies and regulations are supportive and government is prepared to make key enabling investments; and (vi) there is a record of political and economic stability as well as an absence of natural disasters. (It may be useful to refer to Figure 3.4 at this point to recall the features of a regional system of innovation which are closely related).

[5] Michael E. Porter. 1990. *The Competitive Advantage of Nations*. New York: The Free Press, New York, republished with a new introduction in 1998.

Today, more than two decades after the publication of Porter's book, 'cluster' is one of those words 'that everybody knows.' Clusters are labelled by location and the dominant industry. So, for example, Hollywood is called an entertainment cluster, the City of London (UK) a financial cluster, Detroit an automotive cluster, etc.

Innovation systems and clusters have been the subject of an extensive program of research projects at the Innovation Systems Research Network (ISRN) since 1997, and a review of lessons learned has been a helpful guide to the discussion of clusters in this section.[6]

Connecting a cluster with innovation, we get an 'innovation cluster.'

- **innovation cluster**: a grouping of interacting, innovating companies that is concentrated geographically and focused on one sector of business or industry.

In what follows, Porter's Diamond model will be used as a framework to guide the assessment of a small sample of six innovation clusters in Canada that are chosen to illustrate different features.

Many of the factors that contribute to creating a cluster also appear in the description of the regional or local innovation system. The two are clearly related, but they are distinct. The regional innovation system is the ensemble of factors that might enable local innovation in general. The innovation cluster is a particular case of companies in one sector taking advantage of these factors. This means that there can be multiple innovation clusters in different sectors within one regional innovation system.

The world's best known innovative cluster is, of course, the ICT cluster in Silicon Valley, but there are many others working in many sectors in many countries. The reasons for them are clear, and they can be thought of as the details behind the labels of Porter's determinants. Companies in the same sector clustered in close proximity to one another in a strategic location enjoy

---

[6] David A. Wolfe and Meric S. Gertler. 2003. "Clusters Old and New: Lessons from the ISRN Study of Cluster Development" in *Clusters Old and New – The Transition to a Knowledge Economy in Canada's Regions*. David A. Wolfe (ed.). Kingston, ON: School of Policy Studies, Queen's University, McGill-Queen's University Press, chapter 1.

substantial benefits. The location may be strategic because of a nearby university, government laboratory or anchor firm(s), and these may provide new knowledge, highly qualified people (HQP), expert advice, spin-off new ventures etc. But beyond that, if the culture is right there is a whole list of additional benefits. First, the companies in the cluster find their competitors close at hand. Their employees encounter each other within industry organizations, in the course of doing business, and in many casual ways. They get to know one another and that helps develop mutual trust and promotes the diffusion of tacit knowledge. It also means that the competing companies might be able to take more formal local cooperative measures, such as supporting apprenticeship training or programs of continuing education, that benefit them all. Second, their concentration creates a demand that attracts a range of dynamic services, such as venture capital firms, IP law firms, various innovation intermediaries, specialized business consultants, etc. to set up local operations. Third, the companies are likely to help one another and become one another's suppliers and customers as supply chains are developed. Fourth, because employees of the clustered companies can communicate easily and frequently, often in the context of local social activities, they may also frequently change jobs among the companies. This aids in the diffusion of new technology and in collaboration on projects, and creates a natural environment for open innovation. Fifth, the IP and employees of failing companies are known and therefore more readily available for redeployment in the winning efforts of others. And there are probably many more benefits of this kind of concentration.

Many innovation clusters have emerged close to strong research universities because students or faculty started some of the early companies. Once again, Silicon Valley is a great example, with Stanford as the key university and Hewlett-Packard as the lead company. A government laboratory can be a seed as well. The obvious Canadian example is the high-tech cluster in Ottawa that grew up around the laboratories of the National Research Council of Canada (NRC) and later Nortel Networks (and its predecessor companies). Nortel is gone, but that cluster still benefits from the presence of two universities and the concentration of national laboratories.

And innovation clusters don't appear quickly. For example, the Waterloo high-tech cluster took about 50 years to emerge, the aerospace cluster in Montreal took about 80 years, and plant biotechnology has been a focus in Saskatoon since before World War II. Nevertheless, the local and national economic advantages of successful clusters are so attractive that governments try to give them a quick start. Placing a government laboratory near an existing university that has strengths in the same field, in an area where there is already some related industrial activity, and adding some financial support programs for new ventures seems to be the standard approach to creating a nascent cluster.[7] That is about all one can do in terms of structure to get started; the rest will depend on what people manage to do with it. It probably requires the visible emergence of an active supportive culture in the institutions and in the community, as well as some notable commercial successes, for the cluster to reach a critical mass and begin attracting the operations of established firms. However, we don't know if this would suffice to achieve long-term success, or whether something else is needed as well – some favourable combination of local historical, cultural, sociological and political factors that is easier to see in hindsight than to predict.

## Six examples of clusters in Canada

Canada has many nascent innovation clusters, and numerous mature ones. We shall briefly describe a small sample of six self-identified clusters, selected here to illustrate some important differences and similarities: aerospace in Montreal, photonics in Ottawa, medical biotechnology in Toronto, information and communications technology in Waterloo, plant biotechnology in Saskatoon and biotechnology in BC. There are clusters in other regions as well, of course, and there are more clusters than the ones cited in the six regions chosen, but we will leave it up to the reader to learn about them.

[7] For example, NRC lists 11 'cluster initiatives' where precisely this has been done. These are (from west to east): fuel cell and hydrogen technologies in Vancouver, nanotechnology in Edmonton, plants for health and wellness in Saskatoon, sustainable infrastructure in Regina, biomedical technologies in Winnipeg, photonics in Ottawa, aluminum transformation in the Saguenay, IT and e-business in Fredericton and Moncton, life sciences in Halifax, nutrisciences and health in Charlottetown, and ocean technology in St. John's.

## Aerospace in Montreal

Aerospace in Montreal is a very large manufacturing cluster, and fundamentally different from most others. The following information about it comes from two sources: a study of the aerospace cluster by the Montreal municipal government,[8] and a study of knowledge spillovers in aerospace clusters by Niosi and Zhegu.[9] The scale is impressive: some 260 firms, including two dominant prime contractors (Bombardier and Bell Helicopter), four equipment manufacturers in engines, electronics and landing gear, several system integrators and more than 200 suppliers, all told employing more than 28,000 (about 50 percent of Canada's national total employment in aerospace), with $13 billion in sales (2003). The cluster took some 80 years to attain the present size, and is generally considered to be the world's third largest centre of the civilian aerospace industry.

Montreal has four large engineering schools easily accessible on the subway system (Concordia, École polytechnique, ÉTS and McGill) and all four participate in a master's program designed for the aerospace industry. Their undergraduate students can specialize in various aspects of aerospace technology. Graduate study and research on many aspects of aerospace engineering is being carried on at all four. The essential area of manufacturing processes is the focus of the Aerospace Manufacturing Technology Centre of the NRC, located on the campus of the University of Montreal, where small and medium-sized supplier firms can learn about the most modern manufacturing techniques in the industry. This centre also enables government and university researchers to contribute to solving manufacturing problems on an industrial scale.

The aerospace sector in Montreal is very well organized, with numerous active businesses and technical associations. It receives strong and active support from the civic, provincial and federal governments, as well as from labour unions. The dynamic services needed by the industry are well established in Montreal.

[8] Communauté métropolitaine de Montréal. 2004. "Aerospace Cluster," 50 pp. ISBN 2-923013-25-5, http://cmm.qc.ca [accessed at on January 10, 2012]. This is a background study for an 'integrated economic development and innovation strategy' for Montreal.
[9] Jorge Niosi and Majlinda Zhegu. 2005. "Aerospace Clusters: Local or Global Knowledge Spillovers?" *Industry and Innovation*, 12 (1): 1-25.

And there is an active calendar of events and meetings at which people in the sector can meet each other.

It is often said about Montreal that it is the only place in the world where all components of an aircraft are made: airframe, engines, landing gear, avionics, and even the flight simulator for pilot training. This is both accurate and impressive, but it can be misinterpreted.

There is, in fact, no single aircraft that is assembled in Montreal entirely from components that are made locally. Components from other countries are included in aircraft built in Montreal, and components from Montreal are included in aircraft built in other countries. The two airframe manufacturers, Bombardier and Bell Helicopter, engage in design-based innovation.[10] They assemble the latest information about aerodynamics, engines, and lightweight materials and structures, create a design, and test it both as a physical model in the wind tunnel and a numerical model on the computer. Once they have produced an optimal design that might meet the needs of their potential customers better than competing products, they function very much as system integrators, assembling complex components from suppliers around the world who share the risk in R&D.[11] Some of their Tier 2 suppliers also function as system integrators, providing complex components that, in turn, are systems that integrate the products of suppliers in Tier 3. On the other hand, the local engine manufacturer, Pratt & Whitney Canada follows a different business model and ships complete products from their plant to aircraft manufacturers around the world.

If one looks at this pattern of activity from the perspective of the Porter Diamond model, it becomes clear that it doesn't fit perfectly. There is no local competition for Bombardier or Bell, no firms competing in making similar goods. The competition is fierce and the customers very demanding, but they're all over the world, and not part of the local cluster. Firm strategy is very important, since the development of a new aircraft is so expensive that in a very real sense the aircraft manufacturer 'bets the company on

---

[10] Sometimes also referred to as Tier 1 contractors or as original equipment manufacturers (OEM).

[11] Today that need stresses lower fuel consumption per seat-mile travelled, in the evolving airline route patterns.

the next project.' The forthcoming Bombardier C-Series jet will have to compete in the 100-seat-plus market segment with Boeing, Airbus, Embraer and possibly also with Russian and Chinese manufacturers. In the case of related and supporting industry, it is essential for Bombardier to find suppliers anywhere in the world who will develop complex components, and thus share in both the cost and risk of the R&D; this is much more important than simply the convenience of having suppliers across town. Once again, in terms of the model, it means that many important knowledge flows in the cluster actually originate in many places around the world.

The factor conditions in Montreal are good; the business infrastructure is well developed. There is an adequate supply of HQP, with a tighter situation in the skilled trades. Aerospace engineering research in Montreal universities is very good, indeed some of it is quite outstanding (e.g., the work on aircraft icing in flight), but it is work that could be done anywhere. The particular advantage to the cluster of it being in Montreal is the easy availability of the research experts as consultants to the companies.

The role of the municipal, provincial and federal governments in the Montreal aerospace cluster is supportive and internationally competitive. It has to be. Governments all around the world support their aerospace industries, so if sufficient government support in Montreal wasn't there, the sector would probably not be there either.

It is interesting to conclude the discussion of Canada's largest cluster with the assessment by Niosi and Zhegu of why the sector grew where it did: "The attractors are large system integrators, not universities, government laboratories or other institutions."[12] The other five clusters in our sample are different in that regard.

### Photonics in Ottawa

The photonics cluster in Ottawa is relatively small and very new (first event staged in 2005). The much broader Ottawa Technology Cluster (OTC) is deemed to have been born in

---

[12] Jorge Niosi and Majlinda Zhegu. 2002. "Montreal Aerospace Cluster – Attractor and Dynamics," paper presented at the Innovation System Research Network, Quebec City, May 9-10.

1948 when Computing Devices of Canada Ltd. was launched.[13] For more than two decades, OCRI, a member-based economic development corporation,[14] was the industry organization that connected firms in the OTC, worked to enhance their capabilities in many ways, and marketed the region to the world. The scale of OTC is revealed by the membership numbers of OCRI: 700 plus companies, 120,000 people in clusters dealing with life sciences, digital media, e-business, cleantech, wireless, software, security and now photonics.

Within that large tech community or regional innovation system, photonics is a small cluster of some 70 companies. That number had been as little as 30 at the bottom of the telecom downturn, but since then the applications of photonics pursued by member companies have expanded from fibre optics in telecom to include health care, life sciences, environmental monitoring, and defence.

A key resource for Ottawa's photonics sector is the Canadian Photonics Fabrication Centre operated by the NRC. It provides "world-class engineering and manufacturing assistance, and commercial grade prototype and pilot-run production facilities."[15] It also plays a significant connecting function, since access to such facilities enables companies in the cluster to 'demonstrate the value of their technology and secure venture capital funding.' Services of this kind had been available from Nortel, but the facility was sold off when Nortel was dismantled.

Part of the knowledge base of the sector has been the research in photonics at NRC, and some of the companies in the photonics sector had been spun off from the NRC. Research in various aspects of photonics is also strong at the two local universities, University of Ottawa and Carleton University, and graduates from both are available as employees to companies in the cluster.

---

[13] Doyletech Corporation. 2005. "The Ottawa Technology Cluster – Past, Present and Future," paper presented to the OCRI Showcase, March 31.

[14] Most recently, OCRI stood for The Ottawa Centre for Regional Innovation. In earlier incarnations, it had two different names with the same acronym: first, Ottawa-Carleton Research Institute, and then later Ottawa Centre for Research and Innovation. Today, its name has been changed to Invest Ottawa and its role is evolving.

[15] National Research Council of Canada. 2009. "Ottawa, Ontario – Photonics Cluster" and "Ottawa – Photonics Cluster Fact Sheet," http://www.nrc-cnrc.gc.ca [accessed January 13, 2012].

This cluster is very different from aerospace in Montreal. Photonics in Ottawa once had two large anchor companies in telecom applications (Nortel Networks and JDS Uniphase), but they no longer play a role. Instead the cluster is growing by the agglomeration of SMEs developing photonic devices for a diverse range of applications. In fact, what attracts companies to join the cluster seems to be the NRC's Canadian Photonics Fabrication Centre.

### Life sciences in Toronto

The life sciences cluster in the Toronto region[16] is Canada's largest biotechnology cluster, comprising a high concentration of industry, research and educational institutions.[17] The greatest concentration of resources is in the Discovery District (DD) in downtown Toronto, which includes the University of Toronto, its affiliated teaching and research hospitals, various medical research centres, and some biomedical companies. A key player is the MaRS Centre which provides facilities and a broad range of services dedicated to cluster activities.[18] Another important player located close to the DD but reaching beyond it is the CCR-OCE.[19] This innovation intermediary helps new ventures arising out of university research get their products to market more quickly by providing the services of embedded experienced executives, and by making small but key investments from their own resources that leverage much larger private investments.

In the broader Toronto region, the resources listed include: 200+ pharmaceutical and medical device companies (that's more than ½ of the national number) with 37,000 employees (i.e., 30 percent of the total life sciences employment in Canada); 80+ contract research and manufacturing companies; 100+

---

[16] Comprising the City of Toronto, as well as surrounding regions including Hamilton, Guelph, Kitchener and Waterloo.

[17] Information taken from Toronto Region Research Alliance (TRRA). 2011. "Regional Innovation Cluster – Life Sciences in the Toronto Region," Toronto: Toronto Region Research Alliance, December.

[18] Initially construed as medical and related sciences, MaRS now has a broader meaning, embracing various innovation intermediary functions as well as entrepreneurship education.

[19] CCR-OCE is the Centre for the Commercialization of Research, operated by the Ontario Centres of Excellence and supported under the federal program of Centres of Excellence for the Commercialization of Research.

supporting service firms; 63,000 health care professionals; 12 research hospitals; 17 universities and colleges. The last category includes the University of Toronto and McMaster University in Hamilton, both of which have medical schools, seven other universities that are active in related research, and eight of the largest colleges in the country.[20] In 2009, the universities had 38,000 undergraduates and 8,300 graduate students enrolled in programs related to the life sciences, and granted 7,600 Bachelor's and 3,200 graduate degrees.

As a measure of success in innovation, the TRRA report lists a sample of 14 start-up companies emerging from local research and specializing in the diagnosis or treatment of some challenging conditions and in the related tools. A second table under the title "Examples of international recognition for locally-developed technologies" lists 13 transactions between multinational enterprises and Toronto companies. In seven cases, the multinational enterprise (MNE) acquired the Toronto company. In four, the Toronto technology was licensed to the MNE, and there was also one joint venture formed, and one research collaboration.

A number of pharmaceutical and biotechnology MNEs have their Canadian head offices in the Toronto region, and several also have R&D and manufacturing facilities. Canada's largest generic drug manufacturing firm, which is one of the largest R&D spenders in the sector, is also located here. The region includes dozens of contract research organizations, some of them specializing in specific diseases, and others in specific functions, such as managing clinical trials. It also has some contract manufacturing organizations. Supporting services include firms that help with regulatory affairs and logistics.

The educational needs of the cluster are provided by universities, colleges, teaching hospitals and research institutes. Together, in the words of the TRRA report, "This integrated network of scientific researchers, engineers, academic faculty and healthcare professionals generates a continuous supply of qualified life sciences talent." The colleges offer programs leading to chemical, biomedical and biotechnology technician

[20] Universities: Ontario College of Art and Design University (OCAD), Ryerson, Guelph, UOIT, Waterloo, WLU, and York; and colleges: Centennial, Conestoga, Durham, George Brown, Humber, Mohawk, Seneca, and Sheridan.

and technologist diplomas, and additional programs in clinical research and regulatory affairs that are designed to meet industrial needs and taught by experts from industry. In addition, MaRS offers a hugely popular free non-credit introductory course entitled Entrepreneurship 101. This course is free and open to graduate students and other researcher workers from all fields. It provides an introduction to the nuts and bolts of starting a business, IP protection, sources of financing, etc.

The quality of research in the cluster is very high by both input and output measures. For example, in terms of total research funding, much of it won in competitions, the cluster houses four of the top five hospitals in Canada. Together, they received almost $750 million in 2010. The universities in the Toronto region are very strong as well, as indicated by the fraction of the national grants awarded to them for Life Sciences research in the decade 2001-2010.[21] Of the total amount of $6.6 billion, Toronto region institutions got 28 percent, vs. 40 percent for all of Ontario. Another indicator is the number of Canada Research Chairs in the life sciences for which they competed successfully: of 880 CRCs in place across Canada in 2010, Toronto region had 256, or 29 percent, compared with 43 percent for Ontario in total.

On the output side of research, the number of publications in the life sciences by researchers in the Toronto region in 2010 was 5,000, or 35 percent of the Canadian total, and even more significantly 1.72 percent of the world total. Ten years earlier, the numbers had been 2,400 publications, 32 percent of the Canadian total and 1.36 percent of the world total, indicating a Toronto region growth rate significantly ahead of the world. Finally, in terms of patents, inventors in the Toronto region were granted 310 patents in 2010, or 31 percent of the Canadian total and 0.9 percent of the world total. In 2001, those numbers had been almost the same: 303, 32 percent and 0.9 percent. In between, the world total dipped by about a third in mid-decade, but the local percentages held.

Another indicator of the relative strength of the Toronto region life sciences cluster comes from information about the numbers of jobs and establishments related to the Life Sciences.

---

[21] Grants awarded in competition by the Canadian Institutes of Health Research (CIHR), by the Natural Sciences and Engineering Research Council (NSERC) and by the Canada Foundation for Innovation (CFI).

The US data are for 2008 and the Canadian data are from 2006, but they show the relative scale of the Toronto region cluster. In terms of jobs, at 37,000 the Toronto region was in sixth place after the regions of New York, Los Angeles, Boston, Philadelphia and San Francisco and ahead of Chicago and San Diego. In terms of the number of establishments, the region was tied with New York at 1,800 ahead of the other six US regions.

Finally, a bottom line indicator. In terms of net profit as percent of sales in four areas: clinical trials, biotechnology, pharmaceuticals and medical devices, the companies in the Toronto region were more profitable than those in the seven US regions cited above. The margin was huge in clinical trials, big in pharmaceuticals, and substantial in the other two. In turn, the business cost index was consistently lower in the Toronto region than in the rest, but by a much smaller margin.

The numbers clearly show that the life sciences cluster in the Toronto region is competitive in terms of both quality and scale, and is well connected internationally. There is no NRC or other federal research lab in the area, but research flourishes anyway. The supportive factors in Porter's Diamond are all there, and it is hard to imagine a better conjunction of circumstances for success in a knowledge-intensive field. But the numbers also show some disturbing features of the Canadian scene. First, compared with the competing US regions, the data on employment and the number of establishments show that the Toronto region has many more small companies. The listing of firms reveals that few are engaged in manufacturing. Second, the data on the transactions that are described as 'international recognition' suggest that in at least eleven of the thirteen cases cited (acquisitions and licences) the IP generated in the region might be used to create wealth elsewhere. And, third, the Toronto region's percentage of world publications is well ahead of its percentage of patents. The research is great, but invention is lagging. Taken together, these three comparisons offer an example of excellence in science and engineering not being as strongly connected to wealth creation in Canada as it is in other economies, even though business costs here are low and profits can be high.

## Digital media and ICT in Waterloo

The digital media and information and communications technology (ICT) cluster represents almost precisely one half of the more than 700 technology companies in Waterloo region.[22] The region also includes more than 200 start-ups in various stages. Employment in the tech sector counts about 30,000 and there are a couple of thousand unfilled jobs. Kitchener has traditionally been a manufacturing centre, at one time 'Canada's shirt and shoe capital,' and also important in rubber, tire, furniture and home electronics products, as well as general metal fabrication. Waterloo has been home to several insurance companies. Cambridge was the home of textile mills and boiler manufacturing. Many of the old industries have now gone, and Waterloo region is best known for its post-secondary education, its insurance companies, its tech sector, and its manufacturing base that still remains strong. In 2007, the share of employment in manufacturing in the area was 23.4 percent, two thirds more than the Ontario average, and almost twice the Canadian value. In services, the proportion of employment in the FIRE sector and educational services was also well above the average for both Ontario and Canada.[23]

Waterloo region is well served in post-secondary education. University of Waterloo (UW), Wilfrid Laurier University (WLU) and Conestoga College together with the University of Guelph (U of G) have an enrolment of some 88,000 students, of whom 26,000 are in co-operative education programs. UW is

[22] The names are sometimes confusing. Waterloo Region is the informal name of an area of south-western Ontario about 100 km west of Toronto that includes the cities of Kitchener, Waterloo, Cambridge and surrounding counties. Canada's Technology Triangle Inc. is an incorporated regional economic development organization promoting industry in the Waterloo region. Communitech is an industrial association of some 400 member companies running a full program of business activities to help its members connect and grow, as well as promoting commercialization and the development of new tech companies in the Waterloo region. Waterloo-Guelph is Waterloo region plus the City of Guelph, and has a total population of about 655,000. Guelph is often lumped together with Waterloo region in statistics because of the strong interactions among the industries and institutions of the four cities. Waterloo-Guelph is included among the members of the Toronto Region Research Alliance (TRRA).

[23] Bank of Montreal. 2008. "Canada's Technology Triangle," economic research paper. Toronto, ON: Bank of Montreal Capital Markets, February.

particularly strong in both teaching and research in engineering, mathematics, science and computer science, and has produced both a steady stream of very well qualified graduates in these fields and a number of start-up firms. The IP policy of UW is that the inventor owns the IP for any invention arising out of research done on campus. Many local entrepreneurs claim that this policy has been a spur to the formation of research-based new ventures. Open Text, DALSA, Maplesoft and other companies have grown from such roots.[24]

And today's start-ups benefit from new sources of support. The Accelerator Centre (AC) is located in the Research and Technology Park on the North Campus of UW. The AC's mission is to accelerate the growth and success of start-ups in a variety of technology sectors. It provides support services and education programs to help client firms move products to market faster. It is also a partner with Communitech in a broader effort to make it easy for start-ups, entrepreneurs, and investors in the Waterloo region to find the needed resources for commercialization.

Companies in the Waterloo region export much of their production. The label 'The 5/95s' originated here. It means that the companies do only 5 percent of their business in Canada, and export 95 percent. But there's another international connection as well. Some major international companies have acquired UW start-ups in the last few years, including Agfa, Electronic Arts, Google, Intel, 3M and Oracle. Some of them set up local offices, and one brought its world centre of R&D in a new product line to the UW's Research and Technology Park.

There is no government research laboratory in the Waterloo region, but the two local universities, UW and WLU and the nearby U of G are actively engaged in a broad range of federally funded research projects, house a number of expert research institutes, operate some specialized research facilities, and have earned the reputation for excellence in many areas. Knowledge flow between these institutions and local industry occurs in all three of the forms shown in Table 8.2, namely the hiring of graduates, university-industry research partnerships, and

---

[24] Research in Motion (RIM) was started by Mike Lazaridis, a Waterloo undergraduate student of electrical engineering, but it did not arise from research done on campus.

research-based innovation arising from basic research. Within the local industry, the companies do a lot of their own R&D of course, and also acquire start-ups with their new technologies. In terms of Porter's Diamond, most of the conditions for success are in place. There are four anchor companies: RIM (the maker of BlackBerry), Open Text (Canada's largest software company), Christie Digital (world leader in projection technology) and COM DEV (Canada's leader in electronics for communications satellites). They are well managed and successful. They serve completely separate markets, so if they compete among themselves locally, it is probably for skilled people. Their customers are demanding, but they are mostly not local. Specialty services, qualified people, financing and infrastructure are readily available, and there seem to be no particular problems with developing supply chains.

And there is one more thing. It's the culture. The Waterloo region has a strong culture of self-sufficiency on the one hand and community collaboration on the other. People start out to do things for themselves, and others join in to help. This derives from the culture of the Mennonite and other immigrant communities. The University of Waterloo was founded by three local business leaders who wanted to make sure that there would always be sufficient skilled labour in the community for their companies, and 'town and gown' issues have never been much of a problem. The cooperative format of engineering education was adopted to give students some industrial experience throughout their period of study. Ultimately the university founders' companies didn't survive, but the concept thrived.

## Plant biotech in Saskatoon

The Saskatoon plant biotechnology cluster is a small cluster in a small city of about 250 thousand people. The city has long been known for its business in POW – potash, oil and wheat – but in the world of innovation it is best known for its connection with Canola.

For a small city, Saskatoon is well endowed with research organizations and facilities. The anchor institution is the University of Saskatchewan (U of S), and most of the specialized research facilities are located on or adjacent to the U of S campus. These include the Saskatoon Research Centre of Agriculture and

Agrifood Canada (AAFC); the Plant Biotechnology Institute of the NRC, the Canadian Light Source which is the nation's only synchrotron, and VIDO-InterVac, a laboratory that carries out research and develops vaccines against infectious diseases in humans and animals.

On the business side, Saskatoon is the home of both the potash and uranium industries, with the world headquarters of Potash Corp. and of Cameco Inc. located there. The city also provides close links between business and research at Innovation Place, a research/technology park operated by a Crown corporation of the Government of Saskatchewan next to the U of S campus. Innovation Place houses some 150 firms in biotechnology and several other sectors.

The role of Saskatoon in the work on canola has evolved over the last several decades, and is no longer as central as it once was. Canola was developed from rapeseed to have better nutritional and agronomic properties. The research that led to that development was a broad-based effort mainly in universities, the NRC and the federal Department of Agriculture (now AAFC). That research was intensified after World War II. Canola was given that name in the late 1970s, but the research has continued and now much more of it is done in the private sector around the world. Saskatchewan now contributes about 30 percent of the world's annual research effort in canola, and 60 percent of that is publicly funded.[25] Canada as a whole contributes 48 percent, of which 45 percent is public. Canola is now the generic term for a variety of edible oils derived from rapeseed, and most of canola grown in Canada is a genetically-modified (GM) form.

Based on the data, Phillips has suggested that a good model for the role of this cluster is the trade *entrepot* where goods stop over, receive some added value, and are shipped out for further work and eventually to markets. Two short passages quoted from his paper make the picture very clear: "While one might conclude that Canada is the main Canola innovator, considering its record as the lead innovator and early adopter of all the new traits over the

[25] Peter W.B. Phillips. 2002. "Regional systems of Innovation as Modern R&D Entrepots: The Case of the Saskatoon Biotechnology Cluster," in *Innovation and Entrepreneurship in Western Canada: From family Businesses to Multinationals.* James J. Chrisman, J. Adam D. Holbrook and Jess H. Chua (eds.). Calgary, AB: University of Calgary Press.

past 40 years, in fact, a significant share of applied research used to develop the processes for developing new varieties was done in other countries." So what keeps the Saskatoon cluster there? Phillips' answer: "The net result appears to be that while linkages in the knowledge-creating system are the base for this innovation cluster, the downstream capacity to commercialize the product is quite extensive and is one of the key factors contributing to the location and expansion of this activity in Western Canada."[26]

Phillips makes the point that the cluster is not independent or self-sufficient. Innovation doesn't start and end there. Instead, it flows through the cluster and picks up value along the way. He suggests that the trade *entrepot* might be a better model than a regional innovation system to describe what is happening in Saskatoon.

But some things have changed in Saskatoon since Phillips did his research.[27] In 2002, NRC was given $10 million to support a new cluster called Plants for Health and Wellness Cluster. The idea is to generate new knowledge on plant products that have specific health benefits, including nutraceuticals, functional foods and pharmaceuticals, and to make this new knowledge available to industry. This new and broader cluster's work goes far beyond canola. Its anchor is NRC's Plant Biotechnology Institute which provides companies access to research facilities and technical expertise, and also operates an incubator that provides access to both research and business expertise. This new cluster already seems to have had an impact on the food processing industry in Saskatoon, but only time will tell whether it will lead to a more self-sufficient innovation system or to another *entrepot* in Saskatoon.

## Biotechnology in Vancouver

Biotechnology in Vancouver is a small-to-medium cluster of small companies in a big city. The life sciences companies in BC have a

[26] Peter W.B. Phillips. 2002. "Regional systems of Innovation as Modern R&D Entrepots: The Case of the Saskatoon Biotechnology Cluster," in *Innovation and Entrepreneurship in Western Canada: From family Businesses to Multinationals.* James J. Chrisman, J. Adam D. Holbrook and Jess H. Chua (eds.). Calgary, AB: University of Calgary Press, p. 41 and 52.

[27] "Saskatoon – Plants for Health and Wellness Cluster Fact Sheet," 2010, http://www.nrc-cnrc.gc.ca [accessed on January 9, 2012].

total of some 2,700 employees, 2,200 of them working at the 100 or so biopharmaceutical firms that generate about $800 million in revenues. There are also 60 companies in medical devices, both in manufacturing and distribution, and 30 bio-product companies. Seventy percent of all this activity is in Vancouver.[28] The companies are quite young. Of the top 25 companies engaged in R&D (ranked by the number of R&D staff), the oldest three are 30 years old, nine were founded in the 1990s, and the rest in the 2000s.[29] The highest annual revenue for companies in this list is $65 million, 30 percent higher than the second highest, and almost twice as high as the third. Half of the companies have no revenues, but they all spend on R&D. Their R&D staff numbers range from a high of 224 to a low of six.

The research activities of the Vancouver biotechnology cluster are focused in four areas: oncology, infectious diseases, neurosciences and regenerative medicine. The essential driver of this activity is publicly funded research. The University of British Columbia (UBC) is very strong in biotechnology, with strengths both in its faculty of science and in its school of medicine. It is also very good in dealing with the potential IP suggested by research and taking the first steps toward commercialization. As a result, UBC research has led to more than 100 start-up companies in the life sciences that have created 2,500 jobs and attracted a total of some $2 billion of private investment. Simon Fraser University (SFU) does not have a medical school, but its research is strong and it has contributed about 70 life-science start-ups. Beyond the universities, the BC Cancer Agency is another source of high-quality research ranging from basic to clinical. And the very large BC Institute of Technology (BCIT) provides a broad range of strong practical programs that include training of the technical staff for various functions in the life sciences sector.

Both the federal and BC governments provide strong support for the cluster. The federal role is less visible, because its support occurs mostly behind the scenes, coming through research grants given to individual professors, various Chair and Network programs, support for agencies such as Genome BC, tax credits for

---

[28] Information from the website of the Vancouver Economic Commission [accessed January 25, 2012].

[29] "Life Sciences 2011," *Business in Vancouver* magazine, unsigned, 11 (10), October 2011, http://www.biv.com [accessed January 25, 2012].

companies, initiatives of a regional development agency (Western Diversification), etc. There is an NRC Institute in Vancouver, but it functions in an entirely different subject area, namely fuel cells. In contrast, the Government of BC plays a much more visible role. The universities are provincial institutions, and so is the BC Cancer Agency. In addition, BC provides various additional programs of research support, as well as incentives to business to engage in R&D in the province.

The biotechnology cluster in Vancouver enjoys a conjunction of supportive factors. There is a local venture capital industry. There is a history of entrepreneurship in the mining industry, and wealthy angel investors. An effective industrial association (Life Sciences BC) supports and represents the cluster and assists with partnering and with attracting investment. A supportive municipal government (Vancouver Economic Commission) represents the sector effectively, and together with Life Science BC, provides useful and up-to-date information on the cluster. According to the companies, the competitive advantages of being in the Vancouver biotechnology cluster are: a talented work force, good provincial and federal government support, high quality university research and education, and a proximity to both Washington state and California, where a great deal of related work is done.

So the factors are there, and governments are supportive, but two elements of Porter's Diamond are missing. First, the firms don't really compete among themselves; each is addressing a different health issue, and looking towards a different external market. Secondly, there is no local demanding market that can provide feedback. The demanding customers are all around the world, but the feedback from them comes with a long time lag – the approval processes (by the US FDA, Health Canada, etc.) in a very tightly controlled market. And most of the firms don't actually make a product anyway. They create and sell IP. Holbrook et al. put it this way: the firms "... often do not manufacture and market their own products, but rather sell the intellectual property (including regulatory approval and licences) to larger multinational firms for manufacture elsewhere. The Vancouver entrepreneurial environment seems particularly favourable to the creation of firms, and it is the firms themselves (or their major assets, usually intellectual property) that are the final product of the cluster."[30] And again, Holbrook: "Vancouver's 'niche market' appears to be in the development of IP to the point at which it can be acquired, manufactured and sold by a globally competitive product firm." [31]

If that continued to be the case, it would be another instance of the disconnect between excellent Canadian science and wealth creation in the Canadian economy. However, a recent development may eventually alter the situation. The Centre for Drug Research and Development (CDRD), a not-for-profit organization founded in Vancouver in 2006 and supported by various agencies of both the federal and provincial governments, was set up to make it easier to commercialize new drugs suggested by academic research. The idea is that CDRD with its state-of-the-art early-stage drug development facilities, scientific and business expertise, and the capacity to manage projects will take much of the risk out of investing in commercializing such drugs. That capacity spans part of the gap between invention and wealth creation in drugs. Time will tell if a successful CDRD will lead to more of that wealth creation occurring in Vancouver.

So there are our six sample clusters. Aerospace in Montreal is a manufacturing cluster where two large companies engage in design-based innovation. The other five are engaged in research-based innovation. The Waterloo cluster also manufactures products for sale around the world, and Toronto has some manufacturing too. But Ottawa, Toronto, Waterloo and Vancouver all share one characteristic: some new Canadian ventures sell their IP to multinationals before it has achieved full-scale success in the market. The research is good and the IP attractive, and its sale to a multinational is often presented as a sign of its high quality. But if the research-based IP is sold early to an MNE, then any wealth creation from it is not likely to occur in Canada. The problem may be that we don't have the technical capabilities to develop the required scale of manufacturing

[30] J. Adam Holbrook, M. Salazar, N. Crowden, S. Reibling, K. Warfield and N. Weiner. 2004. "The biotechnology cluster in Vancouver" in *Clusters in a Cold Climate*. David A. Wolfe and Matthew Lucas (eds.). Kingston, ON: School of Policy Studies, Queen's University, McGill-Queen's University Press.

[31] J. Adam Holbrook. 2009. "Monica's Garden: R&D in the Biotech Cluster in Vancouver," http://www.chspr.ubc.ca/files/publications/2009/ [accessed January 23, 2012].

and marketing capacity, or that investors consider it too risky, or both. That's why the new Drug Research and Development Centre in Vancouver is an important experiment. In any case, maybe we need a business model that is designed to capture value for Canada when IP arising from publicly funded research is sold for use abroad. Worth thinking about!

## Innovation intermediaries

We have already pointed out that innovators generally do not have all the capabilities required to complete the commercialization process and bring a product successfully to market. When they encounter a gap in their capabilities, they need someone to help them bridge that gap. Those who do that as a service to the innovators are called innovation intermediaries. The service may be as simple as a community organization hosting events where players in the local innovation system might mingle, meet and make new connections. Or it might be as complicated as a whole sequence of technical services in developing a product and preparing it for manufacture that is offered under contract to the owner of the IP by a not-for-profit institute.

Innovation intermediaries are defined in various ways. Dalziel defines innovation intermediaries very broadly as "organizations or groups within organizations that work to enable innovation, either directly by enabling the innovativeness of one or more firms, or indirectly by enhancing the innovative capacities of regions, nations, or sectors."[32] By contrast, Chesbrough uses the term in a much narrower sense to designate companies active in brokering open innovation (OI). These intermediaries act in the intermediate market for intellectual property, buying and selling patents. "Their function either helps innovators use external ideas more rapidly or helps inventors find more markets where their own ideas can be used by others to mutual benefit."[33] The narrower definition will be referred to again in the next chapter, but the broader definition will be used here.

[32] Margaret Dalziel. 2010. "Why Do Innovation Intermediaries Exist?" paper presented at the Druid Summer Conference on "Opening Up Innovation: Strategy, Organization and Technology," Imperial College Business School, June 16-18.

[33] Henry Chesbrough. 2006. *Open Business Models – how to thrive in the new innovation landscape.* Cambridge, MA: Harvard Business School Press, p. 139.

There are examples of important innovation intermediaries in all six innovation clusters described above. These include: NRC's Aerospace Manufacturing Technology Centre in Montreal; NRC's Canadian Photonics Fabrication Centre and OCRI in Ottawa; MaRS and CCR-OCE in Toronto; Communitech and AC in Waterloo; Innovation Place and NRC's Plant Biotechnology Institute in Saskatoon; Life Sciences BC and CDRD in Vancouver. These and many other similar organizations play important connecting and enabling roles for companies in the local clusters, providing various combinations of business and technical services.

### Three Canadian "fourth-pillar" organizations

Innovation intermediaries of a different kind are the not-for-profit organizations that used to be called "fourth pillar" organizations – the first three pillars being industry, universities and government. The name seems to be going out of fashion, but the role continues to be important. Here are three examples of important and successful Canadian fourth pillars:

### CMC Microsystems

CMC Microsystems (CMCM), the outgrowth of the Canadian Microelectronics Corporation, is a 25-year old, not-for-profit corporation that provides Canada with the capability to stay at the leading edge of a fast-moving and increasingly important technology. Funding comes from the federal government through NSERC (Natural Sciences and Engineering Research Council) and from industry. The technology is microsystems which combines electronic, photonic, mechanical and fluidic technologies on a micro and nano scale with embedded intelligence and wireless network connectivity to produce devices with revolutionary new functionality in fields ranging from ICT to health care. CMC Microsystems has created a national capability for excellent research with an eye to commercialization of inventions. It has developed relationships with suppliers that enable it to provide graduate students and professors across Canada with smooth and uninterrupted access to the latest design, fabrication, and testing tools. In effect, CMC Microsystems enables Canadian researchers to engage in state-of-the-art R&D in microsystems, and then to design, make and test their inventions. It provides Internet-based access to advanced microsystem testing facilities at a fraction of the cost of conventional methods. Through its connections with industry, it can also help in the commercialization of the resulting devices, components and systems. The scale of the operation is very substantial: 46 post-secondary institutions across Canada, more than 700 faculty members and 2,000 graduate students and other researchers use CMCM's services. These graduate students become a source of very highly qualified employees for Canada's successful microsystems industry.

## CANARIE

CANARIE is a not-for-profit corporation supported by membership fees and the federal government.[34] Its goal is to help build the foundations for a digital economy in Canada by providing leading edge digital infrastructure for the country. It does so by providing a high-speed fibre-optic network that connects users, researchers and students across the country. Its motto might well be 'Unconstrained bandwidth for research and innovation.' The CANARIE network is 19,000 km long and acts as a spine connecting the 12 optical regional advanced networks in Canada and 100 peer networks in more than 80 countries. In this way, CANARIE connects a very large population of industrial users, developers of digital products, researchers in many fields where huge volumes of data must be moved, and students. Given that the institutional connections include about 2,000 K-12 schools, the estimate of a total connected population of 1,000,000 scientists, researchers, industrial users, teachers and students at all levels is not unreasonable. In addition to providing the connections, CANARIE also funds programs and software tools for developing both new services for support of research and new products for the market.

## PRECARN

PRECARN created a national research network in artificial intelligence and robotics to work on pre-competitive collaborative projects.[35] The goal of PRECARN was to produce a better match between the technical expertise of Canadian researchers in artificial intelligence and robotics and the 'receptor capacity' of

---

[34] Canada's Advanced Research and Innovation Network (CANARIE).
[35] Initially, the Pre-competitive Applied Research Network (PRECARN).

Canadian industry, i.e., the capacity to understand and exploit the new technology. The two key elements were a pre-commercial collaborative project and the project team. The project team was a partnership that always included a technology developer (e.g., a young high-tech firm), a technology user (a medium to large firm interested in being the first customer), an academic research partner (to advance the state of the art and involve students), a commercialization partner (with business resources and capital) and perhaps another research facilitator such as a government lab. Their goal was to pool expertise, share the risks and costs, accelerate development, and end with a prototype demonstrated at the user site. The IP generated was owned by the project team. The project proposal had to include the market opportunity assessment, and the final deliverable had to be the commercialization strategy. In the process, PRECARN wanted to develop HEQP, that's 'highly *entrepreneurial* qualified people.'

The PRECARN model worked well. In 16 years, over 200 projects were funded, and 38 companies started up. Of these 28 were still in business in 2011. Canadian GDP grew by $4 and tax revenues by $2 for every federal dollar invested. Regrettably, PRECARN ceased to operate in 2011 when its federal funding lapsed.

### Three examples from abroad

To conclude the discussion of innovation intermediaries, we shall look at three organizations that were designed to help people with ideas in various stages of development to bring them to market as manufactured products. This is precisely the area where Canadian new ventures need help. All three examples would be considered very large by Canadian standards, and all three offer a broad array of services to support innovation. One is from the US, one from Taiwan, and one from Germany. The latter two were originally created to meet national strategic needs, and they have succeeded spectacularly. It is interesting to note that the German organization is now setting up an operation in Canada.

The information that follows was obtained from the websites of the three organizations accessed in 2011 and 2012. Direct quotes from the websites are used to show how the organizations represent themselves to their potential clients. In some cases, older quotes have been updated with more recent numbers.

## Battelle Memorial Institute (US)

The Battelle Memorial Institute[36] is a charitable trust, which was set up in Columbus, Ohio in the late 1920s to help the US steel industry. It now calls itself an "international science and technology enterprise that explores emerging areas of science, develops and commercializes technology, and manages laboratories for customers ..." Battelle has a global reach, with three major technology centers in the US (Columbus, Ohio; Richland, Washington; Aberdeen, Maryland); and one in Geneva, Switzerland. It also has specialized facilities, regional centers, and offices located in more than 130 cities worldwide. Battelle's areas of expertise make a long and broad list, but they identify a major focus in five areas:

"**Energy, Environment and Material Sciences** – Battelle is leading the way to an economically competitive and environmentally sustainable future, drawing on science, technology and innovation to translate new discoveries into market-leading innovations.

**Health and Life Sciences** – We're applying a robust science and technology foundation to help solve the most complex challenges in human health through advances in medicine, healthcare, and agriculture.

**National Security and Defense** – Battelle is a valued industry and government collaborator in securing a safer future for all generations.

**Laboratory Management** – We serve as the trustworthy steward of the world's most powerful scientific instruments.

**Community and Education** – Battelle is helping create tomorrow's technology workforce today by leading STEM (science, technology, engineering and math) education initiatives."

The scale of the Battelle operation is large: "Today, we serve more than 800 federal, state, and local government agencies; some of the largest corporations in the world; and private sector customers and partners through offices in more than 130 national and international locations. With the national labs we manage or co-manage for the U.S. Department of Energy and the U.S. Department of Homeland Security, Battelle oversees 22,000 staff members and conducts $6.2 billion in annual research and

---

[36] Battelle Memorial Institute website: http://www.battelle.org/about-us.

development." That makes Battelle's R&D spending per employee a very high number, close to $300,000 p.a.

On the commercialization side of the house, Battelle's best known early achievement was to commercialize the photocopying technology of Xerox®. Their activities in this area are described in these words on their website:

"...Battelle makes commercialization part of the process to bring products to the marketplace. Battelle technology may be embedded in a product; it may be licensed to a manufacturer; or it may be developed and launched through one of our many subsidiaries... As a company, we use every option to bring products to market - from forming an independent venture fund, Battelle Ventures, which invests in technology companies at many early stages of development, to sharing the risk of technical and commercial success with customers. Since playing an instrumental role in developing the technology that led to Xerox®, Battelle has negotiated hundreds of agreements that protect information, expedite collaboration, and speed commercialization of technology. Our know-how and insight has propelled other companies toward commercial solutions... Whether we deliver scientifically defensible analyses to meet your immediate need or design and manage a multi-year program to address your long-range strategies, Battelle custom fits every solution. If we need to, we can tap more scientific disciplines, more specialized equipment, more high tech facilities than most companies have heard of..."

## ITRI (Taiwan)

ITRI is the Industrial Technology Research Institute of Taiwan – "a national research organization that serves to strengthen the technological competitiveness of Taiwan."[37] It was established in 1973 and operates in Hsinchu, Taiwan and also in San José, California.

ITRI has a strategic mission in building up Taiwan's economy and, as a result, it functions quite differently from Battelle. "Since our inception, ITRI has three mission statements: first, to expedite the development of new industrial technology;

[37] ITRI website: http://www.itri.org.tw/eng/.

two, to aid in the process of upgrading industrial technology techniques; and three, to establish future industrial technology. However, in order to face a new economic era and serving as a nation's premier technology research institute, ITRI must transform Taiwan's research capability from a 'follower' to a 'pioneer' in order to provide major advantage and opportunities for domestic industries."

ITRI has focused its activity in "six technical fields: [1] Information and Communications, [2] Electronics and Optoelectronics, [3] Advanced Manufacturing and Systems, [4] Material, Chemical and Nanotechnology, [5] Biomedical Technology, [6] Energy and Environment. In each field, a chairman and a planning commission collaborate with experts of the field to establish long-term development directions and strategies, promote cross-field technical integration, increase exploration of new technological directions, and form large-scale integrative projects (e.g. nanotechnology program)." It is noteworthy that manufacturing is an explicit part of the mandate.

Comparisons between what Canadian institutions do in the economy and what institutions abroad are able to achieve are always useful, but comparisons with Taiwan are particularly instructive. Taiwan's population is two-thirds of Canada's, and that means that if we don't measure up to their performance we can't use the hackneyed excuse that 'We couldn't do the same thing because Canada is a small country.' The National Research Council of Canada, which is our premier national science and technology institution has about 4,000 employees. ITRI is 50 percent larger: "As of today more than 60% of the ITRI's 6,000 employees hold either a Master's degree or PhD in their respective field of studies: Communication and Optoelectronics, Precision Machinery and MEMS, Materials and Chemical Engineering, Biomedical Technology, Sustainable Development, and Nanotechnology." These six fields of study map closely into the six technology domains on which ITRI has focused.

In addition to this technical support for Taiwanese industry, ITRI offers business and management support for innovation through ITRI College. The College offers instruction in 'Five Innovation Competencies' related to the six technology domains. These competencies are innovation leadership and creative thinking, industrial analysis, R&D management, patent analysis and IP management, and business development or a boot camp for technology entrepreneurs.

The results are impressive: "As of 2006, over 160,000 alumni have graduated from ITRI, with more than 140,000 of them currently employed in the business community. Furthermore, more than 5,000 are in Hsinchu Science Park serving in mid to high level management positions, furthermore, more than 60 of our alumni are current domestic corporations CEO. ITRI believes we are not only providing revolutionary technological research, but we are also preparing individual talents for their various future endeavours, preparing them to be Taiwan's next generation of industrial pioneers."

The scale of the operation of ITRI is also illustrated by their outreach activity that seems to combine both incubator and accelerator functions: "In the past few years, ITRI has serviced various technological, research, and consulting services to more than 30,000 domestic companies annually, averaged over two thousand patent applications per year, three research symposiums per day, and four research collaboration opportunities... In 1996, Open Lab was formed to nurture new start-ups and foster their developmental direction to maximize their R&D results. Since Open Lab's inception, there were 255 companies that have utilized the program, with 150 of them being start-ups. In all, ITRI invested more than 47 billion NTD and house more than 7,500 employees under Open Lab."

The ITRI website provides a chronological list of their milestones. The list is not populated with scientific breakthroughs and prize-winning discoveries. Instead, it lists very practical things that ITRI has done that directly affected the capabilities of Taiwan's industry to innovate and grow. The following two examples from a long list illustrate how ITRI fulfills its mission:

- *"1976 Acquisition of Semiconductor Process Technology:* ITRI signed "CMOS IC Technology Transfer Licensing Agreement" with RCA in 1976. RCA transferred CMOS technology which was foundational to semiconductors, to ITRI engineers in the US. ITRI successfully transferred semiconductor process technology to Taiwan and the semiconductor industry has been regarded as the star industry of Taiwan today."
- *"1997 First Ink Jet Printing Head in Taiwan:* ITRI developed the first ink jet printing head in Taiwan, establishing the

development of key parts and components industry and a complete system of up-, mid-, and down-stream industry of ink jet printing head."

These two technological milestones underline the difference between invention and innovation. ITRI did not invent CMOS technology or ink-jet printers, but it made possible the innovations with which Taiwan built a world-leading industry. ITRI is also functioning as a leader in innovation on the business side, specifically in open innovation. The following paragraphs describe ITRI's role as an innovation intermediary in precisely the sense advocated by Chesbrough.

- *"ITRI International Patent Auctions:* Trading and Profiting in Taiwan's IP Market. In today's knowledge-based economy, intellectual property (IP) is the key element for competition in international markets. Many companies have an inventory of patents from shelved projects that no longer fit the company's strategy or core business. However, by expanding their business models and leveraging intangible assets, [i.e., business model innovation] companies can gain liquidity from their IP. In addition, firms can create alliances in new and potentially advantageous business arenas. With its 5,700 employees providing technical assistance to hundreds of companies each year, the Industrial Technology Research Institute (ITRI) has a proven ability to assess a patent's marketability and to assist buyers and sellers in transferring intellectual property. By connecting patent sellers and buyers, ITRI helps to maximize the value of IP for all parties. ITRI's value-added professional services and presences in Taiwan make the ITRI Taiwan International Patent Auction the best choice for getting the most out of your intellectual property."

## Fraunhofer-Gesellschaft (Germany)

The Fraunhofer-Gesellschaft[38] was founded in 1949 to help harness research in the reconstruction of the German economy after World War II. It is now a $2 billion global operation, with 17,000 employees, most of whom are scientists and engineers. It has more than 80 research units, including 60 Fraunhofer

---

[38] Fraunhofer-Gesellschaft website: http://www.fraunhofer.de/en.html.

institutes at different locations in Germany, and also research centres and representative offices in Europe, USA, Asia and in the Middle East. In 2011, Fraunhofer-Gesellschaft arrived in Canada at Western University[39] in London, Ontario, to set up the Fraunhofer Project Centre for Composites Research @ Western.

The Fraunhofer-Gesellschaft receives funding both from the public sector (approximately 40 percent) and through contract research earnings (roughly 60 percent). As a consequence, it operates in the space between applied research and projects to develop innovations. Fraunhofer-Gesellschaft can be invited to set up a branch operation in one's country, presumably at the cost of that 40 percent mentioned above. This is what they do:

"We develop, implement and optimize processes, products and equipment until they are ready for use and for the market ... The Fraunhofer-Gesellschaft carries out research in hundreds of technology fields and makes the results available as patents, licenses, further training opportunities, and particularly in the form of research projects commissioned by industry ... The Fraunhofer-Gesellschaft represents an important source of innovative know-how for small and medium-sized companies that do not maintain their own R&D departments. For our customers in industry we develop and optimize technologies, processes and products right up to the production of prototypes and small batch series. We offer contract research and innovations in all application-relevant fields of expertise."

The Fraunhofer Project Centre in London will concentrate on fibre composite materials. Here is what it plans to do:

"Equipped with ... full industrial scale processing equipment and as a part of The University of Western Ontario, the Fraunhofer Project Centre offers possibilities for collaboration in bilateral projects up to multilateral public funded research projects. The service portfolio of the FPC contains:

- Research in materials, simulation, design
- Optimizing of existing processes and materials
- Development of new processes and materials as well as transition of lab scale basic research results into industrial applications
- Part, process, material and tooling innovations

[39] Previously The University of Western Ontario

- Competence along the whole value chain from product engineering up to manufacturing of demonstrator parts

[Western University] will contribute its scientific excellence in the field of surface technologies and material sciences. The clear strategic orientation of the University towards modern manufacturing systems is also a key aspect within the cooperation. An additional factor is that London is located at the heart of the Canadian automobile industry, and only a short distance away from the major North American automotive construction centres in Detroit. The University has obtained significant funding from the City of London for cooperation within the Fraunhofer Project Centre. The joint Project Centre will run for an initial period of five years."

This initiative has the potential to bridge the gap between research and the manufacturing of a new product in at least one sector of Canada's industry. It needs to be watched carefully by both industry and policy people. If successful, it could become a model that should be emulated in other sectors of Canadian manufacturing.

## Partnerships

We started this chapter with the assertion that innovation is too difficult for any one person to succeed alone, and we conclude it here with a short note on partnerships.

Partnerships emerged as a very popular idea within Canadian governments in the late 1980s. They were touted as the new and better way to get things done, to the extent that 'partnership' became a buzzword in government communications. Organizations and individuals were too often called partners in an activity simply because of a minor involvement in it, and not because they were prepared to share in the risks in return for potential benefits. Nevertheless, many serious endeavours showed that in certain circumstances a partnership could be a better way to get things done than the partners going it alone. Public-private partnerships (PPP or 3P), in particular, seemed so promising that in 2009 the federal government set up a Crown corporation, called PPP Canada, in order to improve the delivery of public infrastructure projects. On their website PPP is called a procurement solution, one that "achieves better value, timeliness and better accountability to taxpayers."[40] PPP was an institutional innovation in procurement.

Public-private partnerships by another name have proved important in Canadian university research in science and engineering. The projects in NSERC's Research Partnership Program are valuable in introducing an element of market pull into university research. Industry and universities share in the work, with industry providing the time of some of their expert staff and their specialized equipment and facilities, and the universities the time of their professors, graduate students and research equipment and facilities as well. The federal government through NSERC provides quality control and part of the cost of the project, and industry matches that amount in cash and may provide additional 'auditable in-kind' support.[41] The Networks of Centres of Excellence (NCE) program extends such partnerships to include multiple universities and companies, often on a national scale. The Canada Foundation for Innovation (CFI) provides research infrastructure to the best university researchers 'in partnership' with the provinces and universities. In practice, that means that CFI puts down 40 cents on the dollar, the provinces match that, and the universities must find the remaining 20 percent, often from private donations. In business, partners share risk and profits; in university research, there is some risk and no profit. The partners share in the costs of the new knowledge produced. The industry partner gets to use it, the university gets the credit for developing it, and the graduate students might get good jobs.

Clearly partnerships can be useful in many aspects of innovation. There is a substantial and varied literature on partnerships for research and for innovation, and the reader will have no difficulty following the reference trail to find out about aspects of partnership that are of particular interest. Here, we will conclude the note on partnerships with four practical observations on making them work that are based on the author's personal experience.

*Setting the agenda properly:* The best way to set the agenda of a partnership is to have the potential partners at the table right

[40] PPP Canada website: http://www.p3canada.ca/home.php.
[41] For which they could get SR&ED tax credits.

from the start. All partners will then own the process. For a lead group to set the agenda and only later invite partners to join in it makes the partnership look like an afterthought, which it probably is in that case.

*Partners' expectations of one another*: Once an agenda has been agreed on, it is important for all the partners to state what they expect of one another. This has to be done explicitly, discussed, agreed and documented.

*Leveraging each other's resources*: A partnership is considered successful by the partners when they each feel that they are achieving more than they could have done alone. That means that all the partners see themselves as leveraging the resources of the other partners. And that makes the partnership a whole that is greater than the sum of the parts.

*Working at it*: Success in a partnership requires more than an agreement that satisfies everybody; the partners have to continue working at it. A large part of that is communications; there should be no surprises between partners. There is also the practical consideration of the partners' representatives. University professors hold stable positions, but civil servants and employees in the private sector are frequently reassigned, change jobs, etc. Part of the work required to make a partnership proceed smoothly is providing continuity of the partners' interest and participation. This may not always be easy, but it's always necessary.

## What this all adds up to

There are many examples of needed interactions that promote innovation in Canada. We have lots of programs, active organizations, clusters, partnerships and innovation intermediaries helping with the details of the innovation process. But there seems to be little capacity for helping innovators to achieve commercial success in world markets on a scale that will result in sustained new wealth creation in Canada. Those few companies that can do this on their own are thriving. But those that need help with it, particularly research-based new ventures, don't have a place where they can get it in integrated fashion. As a result, they may not be able to develop their IP and new technologies to their full commercial value in world markets. When that happens, the company itself and its IP may become the products that are sold. That may make a one-time profit for investors in the new venture, but it fails to set up any sustainable new research-based wealth creation in Canada. This is undoubtedly one of the causes of the weak connection between the research and new wealth creation in the Canadian economy.

There are some very effective innovation intermediaries in Canada, but apparently none with the scope and scale to help develop new Canadian IP into world-scale products, such as illustrated by the three examples from the US, Germany and Taiwan. This defines a need that is just begging to be met by some major institutional innovation in Canada.

# CHAPTER 11

## INNOVATIONS IN INNOVATION

*There are no limits to imagination.*

In this chapter we shall briefly introduce five innovations in innovation – five new ideas in innovation that are receiving much attention. These are: open innovation, innovation in business models, open source, user innovation and social innovation. They might initially seem separate but, in fact, there are important connections among them.

Innovations in innovation are new ways of innovating, or new kinds of innovation that have been implemented. Some of them may have been around for a while, but they seem to attract attention only when they are connected with some spectacular success. Each of the five innovations in innovation discussed here is the subject of an extensive literature of its own; the treatment below is a brief introduction intended to fit them into the big picture being developed in this book.

### Open innovation

The main idea in open innovation is that a company's walls must not be impermeable to ideas. Not all of the company's innovations need to be developed within the company. Technology originating outside the firm may be licensed or purchased, and then incorporated into the company's projects. And conversely, not all of the ideas that an established firm develops need to appear in its own innovations. Projects that have a good chance of technical success but don't fit their originating company's plans are routinely abandoned. However, if the company practices open innovation, such abandoned projects may not be worthless. The intellectual property involved in them might be turned into an asset that is sold or licensed to other companies that will use it in their own innovations. Alternatively, the IP associated with a promising project that doesn't fit with a company's current business might be assigned to a spin-off new venture that is created specifically to take the project forward in a less constrained environment.

At one level, the concept of open innovation is quite obvious. A company that innovates by technology purchase will engage in open innovation that is driven by the capabilities of the technology it buys. In fact, to make the sale the supplier of that technology might provide some assistance in the project that the client company wants to develop with it. In that case, the seller engages in open innovation to some degree as well. The seller's IP that is embodied in the purchased technology and the seller's know-how contribute to innovation by the buyer.

A company that innovates as a craft shop, using the special skills and knowledge of its workers to put new products on the market, engages in open innovation when it hires people with skills new to the firm, specifically to enable innovations that had been out of reach. Acquiring another firm with its specially skilled workers is the same thing on a larger scale.

System integrators engage in nothing but open innovation. Their innovations are new systems that meet the customers' needs. These systems are designed by the integrators and built up from proven ideas and technologies from suppliers.

A tighter definition of open innovation is provided in Wikipedia. Here are the introductory paragraphs of the Wikipedia article:

> Open innovation is a paradigm that assumes that firms can and should use external ideas as well as internal ideas, and internal and external paths to market, as the firms look to advance their technology. The boundaries between a firm and its environment have become more permeable; innovations can be easily transfer[ed] inward and outward. The central idea behind open innovation is that in a world of widely distributed knowledge, companies cannot afford to rely entirely on their own research, but should instead buy or license processes or inventions (e.g. patents) from other companies. In addition, internal inventions not being used in a firm's business should be taken outside the company (e.g., through licensing, joint ventures, spin-offs).[1]

[1] Wikipedia, http://en.wikipedia.org/wiki/Open_innovation, p. 1.

The Wikipedia definition takes open innovation into the realm of research-based innovation and firm intellectual property (IP) strategy. This is the area in which much of the writing has been focused. Two books and numerous articles by Chesbrough have staked out much of that particular field.[2]

Treating its IP as an asset helps open up new possibilities for a company, but determining the value of that IP asset is not always easy. It may be much more than the cost of the R&D that went into it, or it may be much less; it all depends on the current context of the sector. This is why innovation intermediates such as ITRI offer patent assessment as a service to their clients. And even then, the value of IP will not be nailed down until a sale is made.[3] In any case, once the IP has been evaluated, a company may become involved in selling or licensing patents that it does not plan to use, perhaps as a one-time measure or perhaps as part of its new business model. On their part, potential buyers may be able to make a somewhat more certain evaluation of the IP if they have a potential use for it already in mind. Under such circumstances, the sales transaction requires a delicate balance of confidentiality and disclosure on both sides, and the help of brokers is important. Chesbrough calls this kind of market for IP an intermediate innovation market, and the brokers operating in it innovation intermediaries – a narrower definition than the one used in the previous chapter of this book.[4] There, ITRI, Battelle Memorial Institute and the Fraunhofer-Gesellschaft were all labelled innovation intermediaries, but only the website of ITRI showed the explicit role of that organization as a broker in the IP market that would satisfy Chesbrough's definition.

In addition to the above three not-for-profit organizations that act as innovation intermediaries, or open innovation intermediaries, there are other organizations and for-profit companies working in the same space around the world. Their

---

[2] Henry Chesbrough. 2003. *Open Innovation: The New Imperative for Creating and Profiting From Technology.* Cambridge, MA: Harvard Business School Press.

[3] For example, in late 2011, the patent portfolio of Kodak in the field of digital photography was put up for auction to help raise cash for the troubled company. The estimated value was $1 billion. In the end, no bids were received and Kodak filed for bankruptcy protection.

[4] Henry Chesbrough. 2006. *Open Business Models – How to thrive in the new innovation landscape.* Cambridge, MA: Harvard Business School Press.

names include InnoCentive, Hypios, InnovationXchange, Nine Sigma, Tekscout, PRESANS, Innoget and Fellowforce. They contribute to innovation in different and interesting ways that are described on their websites.

But there are more dimensions to open innovation than just the market in patents. Openness can save time and money in research. A major inefficiency in research is that people don't publish reports on the dead ends they have run into. It's not part of the culture of research. One hears lots of success stories, but no failure stories. In basic research, this is not a huge problem. Basic research is open, and research results are presented at international conferences or published openly in the international peer-reviewed literature. That means that other scholars close to the subject will always spot a lack of progress in a particular research direction when the results are reported, even if it is not made explicit. That enables basic researchers to avoid proven dead ends and build on each other's successes, even if the peer-reviewed publication process introduces time lags along the way.

Things are very different in industry when established firms are competing in research-based innovation with a similar goal in mind, for example to develop a drug therapy for a particular condition. It is entirely possible that at any give time several companies might be doing similar research in great secrecy. An enormous amount of time and money could be saved if these competing researchers found a way of informing each other about dead ends and blind alleys at an early stage of that work. Otherwise, a company might be spending money on work that another company has already found to be useless. It would be a big step forward toward open innovation if the interested companies could all agree that certain new knowledge would be pre-competitive, meaning that if they didn't have it they were all dead in the water, and once they did have it they could still compete among themselves. Such an agreement could lead to creating an industrial consortium in which the partners would share both the costs of conducting pre-competitive research and the ownership of the IP that it might lead to.

If such pre-competitive research were performed by (or for) an industry consortium, then expensive duplication would be eliminated, more resources could be assigned to the single project even though the cost to each member would be less, the work might be done more quickly and, perhaps most importantly, the results might be better because of all the communications and learning that would take place within the consortium. Once that new understanding had been gained, and any resulting IP shared, the individual companies could choose for their own reasons whether to pursue competitive product development based on something they all understood equally. Competition would not be eliminated; on the contrary, it would be raised to a higher level. An arrangement much like this operated successfully at PRECARN for sixteen years.

## Innovation in business models

Why is innovation in business models important? Mitchell and Coles put it bluntly: "What matters most in making a company a perennial top performer in its industry, regardless of the current size? ... Our research with top-performing CEOs from 1992 to 2003 has pointed to a new answer, the transforming power of frequent business model innovation."[5]

A business model describes how a company makes money. It is a map of the process by which a company uses its assets to create value and capture some of that value for itself. Business models have not been discussed explicitly so far in the book because there was no need to; they were always working behind the scenes, as it were. The concept of value-added discussed in chapter 4 is, in fact, an output of the company's business model. The business model determines what the company produces, whether it is strictly a good or a service or a blend of the two, where that product fits in a value chain, what its markets are and how its customers are served, what the price point is, what inputs the company makes and what inputs it buys, and other such considerations.

To illustrate the idea, here are two examples of business models that are frequently referred to in the literature. One is called the 'razor' model, also known as the 'printer' model, and the other we shall call the 'platform' model. In the printer model, the manufacturer sells ink-jet printers at a low price, and makes the profit on the sale of papers and inks for several years

---

[5] Donald W. Mitchell and Carol Bruckner Coles. 2004a. "Establishing a continuing business model innovation process," *Journal of Business Strategy*, 25 (3): 39-49

afterwards. In the razor version of that model, the price of the razor itself is kept low, and the profits come from the repeated sale of refill blades. The platform model is possible when the basic product can serve as a platform for products developed by others. So, for example, Apple has invested in the iPhone that now serves as a platform for apps produced by outside developers. The developers invest to create value for themselves by developing new applications for the iPhone platform that they sell to iPhone owners and, in turn, the availability of those apps makes the iPhone more valuable for Apple.

Like innovation of any kind, innovation in business models is not a homogeneous activity. In established firms, it can be quite systematic, but in new ventures it is much more of a hit-and-miss process with intuition and luck playing an important part. It takes an experienced entrepreneur to know that a very big part of the success of a new product is matching it with a business model that is right for it. And it takes an experienced technology developer to know that a given technology can produce very different financial results when it is taken to market by different entrepreneurs using different business models. But it is probably a fair bet that in most new ventures the business model does not get a great deal of initial attention; the founders are likely preoccupied with perfecting the product and finding the first customers. Under these circumstances, a new product that is more of a disruptive innovation than an incremental one may at first be able to compete mainly on the basis of functionality. But once it has been commoditized by similar products from competing firms, it must compete on price and availability. The latter case is what Chesbrough calls an "undifferentiated" business model.[6]

At this point it is useful to distinguish between two kinds of business model innovation (BMI). The first kind of BMI is a company's change from one familiar business model to another. For example, this might include outsourcing some production, or shifting the balance between manufacturing and services, or moving into a new business by an acquisition, or getting out of an existing business through divestment, etc. Guidelines for doing this systematically are starting to appear in the literature.

[6] Henry Chesbrough. 2006. *Open Business Models – How to thrive in the new innovation landscape.* Cambridge, MA: Harvard Business School Press.

The second kind of BMI is very different. It involves creating a business model of a kind that didn't exist before. This might be done in an established firm or in a new venture, but it always requires imagination, intuition, good timing and luck. Here are two examples. The first one has to do with Apple's iPod. Christensen et al. called the iPod/iTunes combination of an MP3 player and a song shop the major innovation in the business model that gave Apple a huge boost.[7] They refer to it as the reverse of the 'razor' model, with the iPod priced high and the songs sold cheap. Isaacson describes how it was Steve Jobs' intuition that made it happen.[8] The iPod was a design-based innovation using established MP3 technology and a proven miniature hard drive, but the concept of iTunes was entirely new. It was based on Jobs' intuition that the selection of songs that people actually owned formed an important part of their self-image. As a result, he negotiated with the music industry to make it possible for consumers to buy high-quality recordings of songs legally through iTunes, and customers by the millions have loved it.

The second example of an entirely new business model came from Research in Motion (RIM), the makers of the BlackBerry smart phone. BlackBerry service is offered through telecommunications carriers around the world, but the high technical demands of network services and security in those services are met by RIM. In effect, RIM is both a manufacturer of handsets and a provider of high-end network services. Another way of looking at it is that the BlackBerry is a product with 'a long service tail'. There are other examples of well-known successes in business model innovations of this second kind, such as Google, Facebook, Amazon, etc..[9] These three companies and RIM were new ventures and new entrants into their markets, each with a way of creating and capturing value that hadn't been seen before.

Business model innovation is growing in importance, and a lot of it has been taking place. A study involving 765 CEO's conducted by IBM in 2006 described the perceived importance

---

[7] Mark W. Johnson, Clayton M. Christensen and Henning Kagermann. 2008. "Reinventing Your Business Model," *Harvard Business Review*, 86 (12): 51-59.

[8] Walter Isaacson. 2011. *Steve Jobs*. New York: Simon & Schuster, p. 403.

[9] ... and there must be failures too, but most of us have never heard about them.

of BMI of the first kind (from one familiar business model to another) along five dimensions.[10] In relative emphasis, process and business model innovation were rated as equal, only slightly behind product and marketing innovation. Based on operating margins over 5 years, companies in the top half of performers emphasized business model innovation twice as much (30 percent vs. 15 percent) as those in the lower half. Among the business model innovators, two-thirds of the companies made organizational and structural changes, half entered into major strategic partnerships, and between 15 and 20 percent started sharing services, moved into alternative financing and investment vehicles, divested or spun off activities, and outsourced operations to third parties. The business model innovators benefited in six major areas, many of them in more than one. These were cost reduction and greater strategic flexibility, each cited by 55 percent; increased focus/specialization and rapid exploitation of new markets/product opportunities, each cited by 43 percent; and sharing/reducing risk and capital investment and moving from fixed to variable costs, both cited by 22 percent. The final benefit is that the business model innovators grew much faster than their competitors. The conclusion of the study is that business model innovation of the first kind has become very important for CEO's because of competitive pressures.

In a useful review paper on business model innovation, Jafarieh concluded that there were three major models and sets of guidelines for business model innovation in the literature.[11] He labelled these Chesbrough, Johnson-Christensen-Kagermann (JCK), and Mitchell-Coles (MC). The authors do not distinguish between the first and second kind of BMI, but the systematic nature of their guidelines is more likely to produce the first kind.

Chesbrough begins with the six functions of a business model: "Articulate the value proposition ... Identify a market segment ... Define the structure of the value chain ... Specify the revenue generation mechanism ... Describe the position of the firm within the value network ... Formulate the competitive strategy ..."

[10] George Pohle and Marc Chapman. 2006. "IBM's global CEO report 2006: business model innovation matters," *Strategy & Leadership*, 34 (5): 34-40.

[11] Omid Jafarieh. 2011. "Business Model Innovation," project for the Masters Degree in Engineering Management. Ottawa: Telfer School of Management, University of Ottawa, April 3.

He then moves on to a six-level "business model framework" in which he labels the business models as "undifferentiated", "differentiated", "segmented", "externally aware", "integrated" and "adaptive."[12] He associates an innovation process and an IP management strategy with each of them. The six levels of the framework are then discussed and illustrated in detail. His chapter 5 ends with a set of diagnostic questions for assessing a company's business model. This material is in a very useful form, and would be good reading for managers, executives and board members. In two additional papers, Chesbrough began to address the barriers to BMI[13] and, more recently, began to discuss business model experimentation.[14]

According to Jafarieh (2011), the JCK approach seems different at first glance, but a careful study shows that most of the elements of the business models are the same as Chesbrough's, even if they are named and assembled differently. Their discussion of the barriers to BMI is also generally similar to Chesbrough's; there is mention of trial and error, but little explicit reference to experimentation.

The Mitchell-Coles approach is presented in a series of three papers.[15] It starts out with quite different language than Chesbrough or JCK, but ultimately conveys similar messages. For Mitchell and Coles, the business model is about "delivering value to customers and getting paid for it," and it deals with the seven questions: "who?," "what?," "when?," "why?," "where?," "how?" and "how much?" Their definition of business model innovation is: "... business model replacements that provide product or service offerings to customers and end users that were not previously

[12] Henry Chesbrough. 2006. *Open Business Models – How to thrive in the new innovation landscape.* Cambridge, MA: Harvard Business School Press.

[13] Henry Chesbrough. 2007. "Business model innovation: it's not just about technology anymore," *Strategy & Leadership*, 35 (6): 12-17.

[14] Henry Chesbrough. 2010. "Business Model innovation: Opportunities and Barriers," *Long Range Planning*, 43: 354-363.

[15] Donald W. Mitchell and Carol Bruckner Coles. 2003. "The ultimate competitive advantage of continuing business model innovation," *Journal of Business Strategy*, 24 (5): 15-21; Donald W. Mitchell and Carol Bruckner Coles. 2004a. "Establishing a continuing business model innovation process," *Journal of Business Strategy*, 25 (3): 39-49; Donald W. Mitchell and Carol Bruckner Coles. 2004b. "Business model innovation breakthrough moves," *Journal of Business Strategy*, 25(1): 16-26.

available", or the process of developing these replacements. Based on their studies, they conclude that the combination of effective strategies and regular (every 2 to 4 years) 'powerful' business model innovation "to create new competitive advantages" works best. And, like Chesbrough, they too advocate inexpensive experimentation in new business models.

Finally, it should be noted that there are guidelines but no recipes for successful business model innovation. Each one of the sources cited acknowledges the sources of resistance and proposes a reasonable way to proceed, based on their analysis of the available cases. One common theme is the need for a thorough understanding of the entire value chain in which the company operates. Another is the need for trial and error and inexpensive experimentation with new business models already referred to.

We will add only two observations to that. First, the understanding of the value chain must include what the customer would value, and the customer's customer would value ... and so on down to the end user at the very end of the value chain. This is more than understanding what the customers need. It moves into understanding their values, preferences, tastes, opportunities, experiences and more. Steve Jobs' successes and many case studies in the literature bear this out. The word 'empathy' does not appear often in the business literature, but something close to that is probably required here.

The second observation has to do with time. A deep understanding of the time dimension all along the value chain is very important. The entrepreneur must understand that time may be very important in satisfying the customers – right down to the end user. Time may be important to the customer in terms of urgency, delay, response, duration, timing, phasing, convenience and probably in other ways as well. Time should also be considered as a dimension of the business model to be managed for profit, as in Just-In-Time manufacturing, and the phasing of cash flows. And time may also be very important far upstream of the end user, in the health of the business itself, where business model innovation can confer a real advantage in terms of time. Mitchell and Coles 2003 quote Robert L. Bailey, the Chairman and CEO of PMC-Sierra, a firm known for its semiconductor innovations, as saying: "Technological innovation gives a company a six-to-12 month advantage at most. A business model advantage can last years, potentially yielding a dominant franchise."

## Open source

The concept of open source is closely related to open innovation, and to user innovation as well. It was originally and still is largely associated with software. Most readers will probably be aware of the Linux operating system, the Mozilla Firefox browser, the Open Office suite of programs, Wikipedia and more.

Since open source software had its origins in the movement for free software, one might think of it as some kind of an unstructured 'free-for-all' jumble. In fact, that is very far from the truth. There is a lot of structure and many rules in open software, but they are open and transparent. Wikipedia and the website of the Open Source Initiative make that very clear.

The Wikipedia statement is sweet irony since Wikipedia itself is a splendid example of an open source development. It is a free encyclopaedia on the Internet that anyone can access and anyone can edit. It creates IP by assembling contributions from a huge number of sources. It is operated by the not-for-profit Wikipedia Foundation. One of its triumphs is the creation of a Wikipedia community that has taken responsibility for the quality control of the articles. As a result, Wikipedia has developed an excellent reputation for being both accurate and up to date.[16] The statistics on the English-language version shown in Table 11.1 below are striking. In particular, the half billion edits of 3.8 million articles are an indicator of its dynamic nature – an impossibility in the world of printed reference books.

---

[16] My own experience with Wikipedia has been very satisfying. In those areas where I have some expert knowledge, I have found that the articles were both accurate and clear.

## TABLE 11.1 Some Wikipedia Statistics

| |
|---|
| It has 3,861,890 content articles, and 26,133,299 pages in total. |
| There have been 514,201,553 edits. |
| There are 794,908 uploaded files. |
| There are 16,185,425 registered users, including 1,507 administrators. |
| This information is correct as of |
| 18:53, 2 February 2012 (UTC) Update |

Source: Wikipedia, http://en.wikipedia.org/wiki/Wikipedia:Statistics [accessed February 2, 2012].

Wikipedia defines open source software in these terms:
*Open source software (OSS) is computer software for which the source code and certain other rights normally reserved for copyright holders are provided under a software license that meets the Open Source Definition or that is in the public domain. This permits users to use, change, and improve the software, and to redistribute it in modified or unmodified forms. It is very often developed in a public, collaborative manner. Open source software is the most prominent example of open source development and often compared to user-generated content. The term open source software originated as part of a marketing campaign for free software. A report by Standish Group states that adoption of open source software models has resulted in savings of about $60 billion per year to consumers.*[17]
And then from the website of the Open Source Initiative:
*The Open Source Initiative (OSI) is a non-profit corporation with global scope formed to educate about and advocate for the benefits of open source and to build bridges among different constituencies in the open source community. Open source is a development method for software that harnesses the power of distributed peer review and transparency of process. The promise of open source is better quality, higher reliability, more flexibility, lower cost, and an end to predatory vendor lock-in. One of our most important activities is as a standards body, maintaining the Open Source Definition for the good of the*

[17] Wikipedia website: http://en.wikipedia.org/wiki/Open-source_software [accessed February 7, 2012].

*community. The Open Source Initiative Approved License trademark and program creates a nexus of trust around which developers, users, corporations and governments can organize open source cooperation.[18]*

In open source software, the source code is available to all users. When bugs are found, the user community sets out to produce a fix which has to be shared. And that process is competitive. Some fixes are better than others and, ultimately, the user community settles on the one that works best. This is very different from proprietary software, where fixes simply come down the line in software updates.

And there is no incompatibility between using open source software and doing business. The use of open software presents different challenges but no special obstacles to creating value, or monetizing the contributions of experts; even some of the biggest industry players in information and communications technology (ICT) have become involved with open source software for straightforward business reasons. Firms using open source software add value by creating proprietary solutions to their clients' problems. This is entirely analogous to a writer being paid for writing a copyrighted article using a dictionary and grammar that are freely available in a public library.

Onetti and Capobianco provide an interesting example of the connections between open source and innovation in business models. They discuss the case of Funambol, a US software company in the open source business. They introduce the case with a useful discussion of the various licensing options and open source business models. Their summary comments about the open source business are very informative: "Open source requires new and different business models ... Open source does not revolutionize how software is manufactured ... The difference emerges after the first releases and resides in the fact that people can review and enhance the original software code ... It is the customer who looks for the product he/she needs and chooses it after reading technical documentation, downloading, looking at the code, testing and so on ... The business flow is 'user pull' and not 'sales push' ... In the open source business 'techies' (users and developers) are the 'king makers' and they base their choices on

[18] Open source website: http://opensource.org/ [accessed February 7, 2012].

technical excellence criteria. There cannot be a successful open source project with a low quality product."[19]

The concept of open source has now spread beyond software. An excellent example exists in the area of genomics. The international Structural Genomics Consortium (SGC), led by Aled Edwards and based at the universities of Oxford and Toronto, is operating under the principles of open access in the area of drug discovery and medicine development. They study the three-dimensional structures of proteins that are linked to various diseases. In the last eight years, SGC has discovered and placed in the public domain the three-dimensional structures of more than 1,300 proteins. This information is basic to the development of new medicines. The worldwide research community will also have open access to the new antibodies and chemical reagents that are developed from the understanding of those structures.

It is significant that the work of SGC is funded by four multinational giants in the pharmaceutical industry, by the federal and Ontario governments in Canada, and by the Wellcome Trust in the UK. The industrial contributions include both cash and the in-kind contributions of various resources in medicinal chemistry. The scale of the operation for the next four years is about $50 million. The SGC is an example of the open access paradigm at work in open innovation. It is also a public-private partnership, and an example of a pre-competitive research consortium. The most recent renewal of its funding for another four years is a clear indication that it is working successfully in all these dimensions.

### User innovation

User innovation is not new, but the attention which it is now getting indicates a growing awareness of the demand side of innovation. In the earlier chapters of this book, the focus has been almost entirely on the supply side. Companies do the innovating and bring new products to market. Their customers buy them and make use of them. In this perspective, the demand side appears as the voice of the customer expressing needs and providing

[19] Alberto Onetti and Fabrizio Capobianco. 2005. "Open Source and Business Model Innovation. The Funambol case," in *Proceedings of the First International Conference on Open Source Systems*. Marco Scotto and Giancarlo Succi (eds.). Genova, July 11-15, p. 224-227.

feedback, such as in the chain-link model of innovation and in the innovation-commerce cycle (chapter 7).

There are two ways of interpreting 'user innovation.' One is the very obvious: it is the work of people who buy tools of various kinds and use them 'as is' to create innovations. A painter using paints and brushes bought at an art supply shop provides one example. Another example discussed in chapter 10 discussed the work of professors and graduate students who used the tools provided by CMC Microsystems to design, build and test their ideas for new microsystem devices.

The other interpretation of user innovation is less obvious but more interesting: it is the work of people who buy and use a product and do something new with it or to it, and thus influence its manufacturer to alter it. This cannot be done easily or quickly with products that are tightly regulated for health and safety, but in other areas it happens frequently. For example, in the case of microsystems, a user innovation would occur if a design tool provided by a supplier to students through CMC Microsystems was modified at the university to design a new class of devices based on a newly discovered effect, and the supplier then incorporated that capability into future versions of the product.

There are very many examples of the second interpretation of user innovation. For a long time, the users of various tools and production machines have been modifying the off-the-shelf equipment to meet their own special needs. This activity has been widespread in Canada.[20] Some manufacturers promote it and make a point of keeping in touch with innovative users. This is an example of von Hippel's concept of "lead users", namely the users who have needs that are not being met by current products and create their own ways of meeting them and, in this way, point industry to the need for new products.[21] Something very similar occurs in the area of scientific instruments. There, some of the most innovative users modifying the instruments are

---

[20] Fred Gault and Eric von Hippel. 2010. "The prevalence of user innovation and free innovation transfers: Implications for statistical indicators and innovation policy," MIT Sloan School of Management Working Paper 4722-09, in *Perspectives on User Innovation*. Stephen Flowers and Flis Henwood (eds.). London, UK: Imperial College Press, chapter 9.

[21] Eric von Hippel. 1988. *The Sources of Innovation*. Oxford, UK: Oxford University Press.

researchers working in the laboratory from which the original concept for the particular instrument had come. New versions of these instruments incorporate many such innovations. Knowledgeable users in many other fields as well have often found ways of adapting existing products to meet their special needs, but there are limits to what users can do if they don't have the required depth in technical capabilities.

And the involvement of manufacturers varies from sector to sector, and among the original equipment manufacturers (OEM) in a sector, and then also according to circumstances. In the 1960s and 1970s, some young men (almost exclusively) would take their cars' engines and suspensions apart, replace some parts, change some others, and produce a 'souped-up' and lowered version. Then commercial garages gradually began to offer such 'customization' as a service. Some ideas from these sources made it into Detroit's 'muscle cars' that used to growl their way around town in the US and Canada. But the reaction to a very different user innovation in the auto sector has been very different. We have all seen TV news images of Toyota pick-up trucks with machine guns bolted to the bed roaring through the scene of some armed clash in a distant land. That certainly is user innovation at work! But you can't go down to the local Toyota dealer and order a pick-up truck with a gun mount as a dealer-installed accessory. There are some user innovations that the OEMs want nothing to do with.

The ICT industry is a particularly interesting case. On the one hand, the computer used as a tool has unleashed a torrent of innovations in software and business tools, as well as in video games. However, the possibility of altering the computer itself varies greatly, depending on the OEM's philosophy. Some make it easy. The personal computer has expansion slots for additional cards that allow its user to customize its capabilities very easily. In contrast, Apple products are sealed and designed to be very hard to open in order to ensure that the user gets the full and undiluted 'Apple experience' that the products are designed to deliver.[22]

For many people, the sports equipment industry has become the icon of user innovation. Surfboards, skateboards, snowboards, sailboats and the gear for some 'extreme' sports are often cited

[22] Walter Isaacson. 2011. *Steve Jobs*. New York: Simon & Schuster, p. 138 and 473.

as examples of today's mainstream products that originated as innovations by expert users.

Given the trend of growing openness, improving communications and increased interaction within the innovation system, user innovation is likely to grow as well. And when that happens, the producers located closest to the lead users may have a particular advantage because of the convenience of face-to-face meetings, demonstrations and tests. This possibility would represent another attraction of clusters.

## Social innovation

We conclude this chapter with a brief discussion of social innovation. At first glance, it seems surprising to call it an innovation in innovation. After all, it's been there all the time as the counterpart of technological innovation. But the appearance of this term here recognizes that it has been appropriated as the label for a very specific innovation of a new kind. It has to do with the use of the branch of ICT that is called social media, namely the capacity for communication by texting, instant messaging, blogging, tweeting and the like.

Social innovation, in this usage, was defined in chapter 4. That definition is repeated here:

**Social innovation:** *the creation of networks of like-minded people committed to achieving a common goal, whose efforts are mobilized and managed with the help of the technology of social media*

This new kind of innovation can be benign, benevolent, or the very opposite, depending on its goal and its leadership. Charitable drives, community projects, fund-raising campaigns, public demonstrations, political campaigns, etc. have produced good examples of social innovation at work. But we must remember that, like any innovation, social innovation can have a dark side too. The assault on Mumbai in 2008[23] was widely reported to have been coordinated by smart-phone messaging among the network of shooters who killed over 170 people.

---

[23] November 26, 2008.

# CHAPTER 12

## WHAT CORPORATE DATA SHOW

*A picture is worth a thousand words.*
*Literally?*
*No, graphically.*

### Introduction

I n the earlier chapters, we discussed many aspects of (mainly) industrial innovation and the factors that affect it. We have seen theory and models, and discussed many aspects of innovation, but we have not dealt with what actually happens on the ground in Canadian industry. To do that, we will now look at the public data on what some of Canada's largest industrial innovators have been doing. We will look at the time series of sales revenues and R&D spending by some large and well-known companies, and we will see two different patterns. These patterns will lead to a model that not only characterizes industrial R&D in Canada, but also suggests what an innovation policy should include and how government support programs could best be offered.

In light of the discussion of innovation to this point in the book, we have to acknowledge that R&D spending is an imperfect indicator of innovation in industry. It sits at the end of the proxy chain of impacts, outcomes and outputs that was described in chapter 3. And it is only one of many inputs to innovation, albeit an important one. It supports quite different activities in research-based innovation by new ventures than in design-based innovation by established firms. In all cases, however, the main goal of industrial R&D spending is to contribute to the firms' commercial success. And the time scales of those contributions are variable, depending on the markets in which the firms operate. In some sectors, R&D spending supports short projects whose results might be used to create wealth almost immediately, while in others it may support strategic long-term developments that are expected to pay off over decades.

We must note also that the goal of industrial R&D spending is different from the goal of R&D spending by government. Government spends on R&D to build up the nation's long-term technical capability, to mitigate the risk in specific industrial projects, and to create public goods, such as the knowledge base for its regulations, the catalogue of natural resources, climate data, etc. Government promotes a high value of GERD/GDP (the ratio of gross expenditure on R&D to gross domestic product) for the nation because that ratio is deemed to be a leading indicator of innovativeness and prosperity, and it urges business to contribute to that increase by raising its share, namely business expenditure on R&D (BERD)/GDP. But things look quite different from the side of business. It is in the best interests of a company to leverage the largest possible revenue flow and value-added with its R&D spending and, the greater that leverage, the better the company's performance. So companies want to maximize their ratio of value-added to R&D spending, and that means minimizing their contribution to BERD/GDP for industry as a whole. There are limits to this, of course, that reflect the intensity of competition in the various sectors. In some sectors, companies have to keep spending on R&D to keep the innovations coming that keep them alive. In others, periodic investments in major innovation projects, such as new processes to reduce cost, are the pattern.

In any case, it is clear that the nation's value of GERD/GDP is framed by the dialectic between government wishing to maximize it and business wishing to minimize it, with some nuance on both sides. It is also clear that the structure of a country's industry is an important factor for where this balance falls. This argument has not been raised before, but it may be one more reason for the so-called shortfall in the innovation performance of Canadian industry that was studied by the Expert Panel of the Council of Canadian Academies. And it may make it less surprising that the Canadian companies were quite profitable during the period covered by the study.

All things considered, the public data on R&D expenditures in Canadian industry that are brought together and analyzed in this chapter are very useful data, and much can be learned from them. It should be noted that parts of this chapter are based on the author's earlier work with the data brought up to date where available.

## The data

The data that follow are the histories of R&D spending, sales revenues and the ratio of the two, called R&D intensity, for named companies spending on R&D in Canada. The time series were constructed by the author from raw data in a commercial database, the Canadian Corporate R&D Database that has been published annually since 2000, and is referred to as CCRD in what follows. The companies listed in it represent about 80 percent of the country's business expenditure on R&D (i.e., BERD). The remaining 20 percent can be attributed to a small number of well-known, large, privately-held companies, who choose not to be included in the CCRD, and a much larger number of small and very small ones about which little is known. The updates came from the annual reports on Canada's top 100 R&D spenders distributed in the *National Post* early in November each year. The companies listed in the CCRD are all named because the data are compiled from annual reports, websites, other sources of public information, as well as a voluntary survey. This feature of the database is very important, since it offers two great advantages. First, it makes it possible to assemble the time series of R&D spending by individual firms. And second, it allows public information about the companies to be used to explain the numbers.

The companies missing from the CCRD are a story in themselves; their numbers lead to a couple of striking conclusions. Table 12.1 sets the scene.

## TABLE 12.1 Who Spends on R&D in Canadian Industry?

| The numbers for 2003 | |
| --- | --- |
| Total number of businesses in Canada in 2003: | 1,018,900 |
| Of those, the total number in sectors where we might expect most R&D (agriculture, forestry, mining, oil and gas extraction, utilities, manufacturing): | 125,600 |
| The number of successful applicants to the SR&ED tax credit program in 2003: | 15,729 |
| The number of companies listed as R&D spenders in the CCRD for the year 2003 – responsible for about 80% of BERD | 663 |

Source: T. A. Brzustowski. 2009b. "Industrial R&D spending in Canada: Model, Policy and Program Delivery," *Optimumonline*, 39 (2): 25-33.

The first conclusion is immediate: industrial R&D is a very thin veneer on the Canadian economic sphere. The successful applicants for the SR&ED tax credit represent 1.5 percent of the total number of businesses. The 663 companies listed in the CCRD for 2003 represent 0.065 percent of the businesses, yet spend 80 percent of BERD, and it also turns out that the top 50 in CCRD account for 78 percent of that amount, or almost two-thirds of the national total. The range of R&D spending by the top 100 companies is from some ten million dollars a year up to a couple of billion. Obviously, Canadian industrial R&D is very top-heavy, but this is not atypical. It seems to be the case in many of the other industrialized countries as well.

The second conclusion follows from the very large difference between the number of successful applicants for the SR&ED tax credit, and the far smaller number of companies listed in CCRD. These numbers have all grown since 2003, but their relative proportions have changed very little. A few of the 15,000 or so SR&ED tax credit recipients missing from the 2003 CCRD are well known and substantial R&D spenders, such as SMART Technologies Inc., a privately held company that didn't report R&D spending in 2003, and the big auto assemblers, some of whom spend millions of dollars on R&D in Canada but don't report it here. Most of the missing companies must be very small. We don't know who they are because of the confidentiality of tax information; we don't know what they do, but we do know something about the average scale of their R&D effort.

Under the program rules, to succeed in applying for the SR&ED tax credit, these companies must have reported spending on R&D that met the definition of the *Frascati Manual* which has been adopted by Statistics Canada and by the Canadian Revenue Agency. Their data are confidential but some simple arithmetic tells us something about their scale. These approximately 15,000 companies are responsible for 20 percent of BERD, or some $3 billion. That means that, on the average, they each spend about $200,000 a year on R&D. Given that the average annual expenditure per full-time equivalent R&D employee was about $100,000, we know that these companies must be very small, with perhaps only two R&D employees, or else they engage in R&D sporadically, using only part of the time of a larger number of employees. But are they new ventures or established SMEs? What businesses are they in? And what do they achieve with their R&D? We don't know, and this is an obvious area for further research.

The discussion here deals only with the companies listed in the Canadian Corporate R&D Directory Data Base. The data important for this work were: revenues, R&D spending, and R&D intensity (called RDI when the R&D spending is expressed as percentage of revenues), from 1999 to 2010 in most cases. The companies listed were grouped in 23 sectors: aerospace, agriculture and food, automotive, chemicals and materials, communications/telecommunications equipment, computer equipment, electrical power and utilities, electronic parts and components, energy/oil and gas, engineering services, environment, financial services, forest and paper products, health services, machinery, medical devices and instrumentation, mining and metals, other manufacturing, pharmaceuticals/biotechnology, rubber and plastics, software and computer services, telecom services, transportation.

The incompleteness of the data, already noted, would make it risky to draw general conclusions about sectors that are represented in the CCRD by only a very small number of companies. However, the time series for the individual companies that are included in the database are not affected by the absence of other companies, and that is the information used in most of what follows.

## The four faces of R&D intensity

The R&D intensity, RDI, is just the ratio of R&D spending to sales revenue expressed as a percentage, but that combination turns out to be useful in several ways.[1] First, it is a useful indicator of the financial commitment to R&D activity because it is normalized by the size of the firm, and it immediately provides a distinction between firms that are being financed to perform R&D and those that pay for their R&D from their own sales revenues. The former will have RDI of 100 percent or more;[2] the latter have RDI of less than 100 percent, and often just a few percent. There seems to be a lot of risk capital to support R&D because the list of Canada's Top 100 R&D spenders includes at least a couple of dozen companies operating at RDI greater than 100 percent, each spending in the tens of millions of dollars a year. Many of them are in the pharmaceuticals/biotechnology sector.

Second, the RDI illustrates the extent to which involvement in R&D can vary across any one sector. It is futile to try and characterize the R&D expenditures in an industrial sector by a single value of RDI, even though this might occasionally seem convenient. Figure 12.1[3] explains why this is so this for four sectors, and the data are similar in others. The pattern in each

[1] There are sound academic reasons for using R&D intensity defined as the ratio of R&D spending to value added instead of RDI, since BERD/GDP is calculated in just that way, but such data are not readily available. Where such a definition of R&D intensity is used, it is denoted by a symbol other than RDI.

[2] In theory, 100% is the upper bound of RDI for companies that can support their R&D out of their sales revenues. In practice, because of overheads, etc. the number would have to be smaller. Barber and Crelinsten have suggested that 50% may be a realistic upper limit of RDI for companies that sustainably fund their own R&D. Details are given by H.D. Barber and J. Crelinsten. 2004. *The Economic Contribution of Canada's R&D Intensive Enterprises 1994-2001.* The Impact Group (www.researchinfosource.com).

[3] T.A. Brzustowski. 2009b. "Industrial R&D spending in Canada: model, policy and program delivery," *Optimumonline,* 39 (2): 25-33.

sector is characterized by what the companies in it actually do. The differences among companies that do different things in one sector can be much greater than the differences between companies that do similar things in different sectors. Note that in Figure 12.1, the RDI is plotted on logarithmic coordinates. That makes it possible for one diagram to show quantities that range over many orders of magnitude, from 0.1 to almost 1000 in chemicals and materials. While each of the four sectors has several companies with RDI values clustered in a little plateau around one percent, one could hardly say that all these sectors have RDI of one percent.

The third advantage of using RDI is that it has an important independent meaning that connects R&D with the dimension of time, or the speed of business. RDI is suggested as an indicator of the market life of a company's products[4] or its reciprocal, the frequency of innovation.[5] The shorter the product market life (PML), the more frequently the company must innovate to avoid commoditization of its products, and the greater the R&D effort required. The Forgacs rule is RDI = 16/PML, where RDI is in percentage, PML is in years, and the coefficient 16 is an empirical value deduced from overall industry trends. This idea immediately connects the low values of RDI with companies that change slowly, and the high values of RDI with companies where change is frequent. Its form can be derived from first principles for an auto-like business model in which products are brought to market in succession, with new products displacing the old ones. In spite of this limitation, Forgacs' rule is so intuitively appealing that it is attractive to use it as a rough first guess for the connection between R&D expenditures, sales revenues and time in other business models as well.

---

[4] Otto Forgacs. 2004. "Who Spends Money on R&D and Why," Paper presented at the Forum, "R&D - The ticket to wealth creation" at La Conférence de Montréal, June 7.

[5] T.A. Brzustowski. 2006. "Innovation in Canada: Learning from the top 100 R&D spenders," *Optimumonline*, 36 (4): 48-56.

### FIGURE 12.1 The R&D Intensity of Companies in the Aerospace, Agriculture and Food, Automotive, and Chemicals and Materials Sectors in Canada

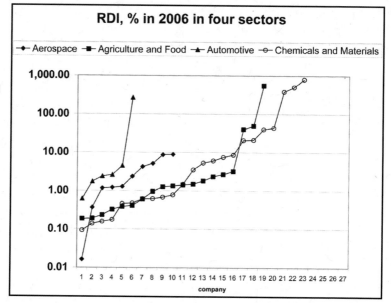

**Source:** T.A. Brzustowski. 2009b. "Industrial R&D spending in Canada: model, policy and program delivery," *Optimumonline*, 39 (2): 25-33.

Note the logarithmic scale of RDI. The data show that it is futile to try and present a single value of RDI for an industrial sector. Differences among companies within a sector can be much greater than differences between sectors. This is particularly clear in the RDI data for the Agriculture and Food and Chemicals and Materials sectors which track each other closely, but span four orders of magnitude within each sector.

The fourth way in which the RDI turns out to be useful is as a leading indicator of success in new ventures engaged in research-based innovation. Such companies are in business to conduct R&D and develop their first products and to find markets for them. They have very little or no sales revenues, and are often called 'pre-revenue' companies. They pay for their R&D from raised capital, they 'burn through' it, and government support programs are very important to them. Such companies start out with very high values of RDI, in the hundreds or even thousands of percent.[6] A few of them will succeed and become established, innovative

[6] That is why it is necessary to plot their numbers on a logarithmic scale.

firms in their sector, with a much lower RDI. Many others will burn through their capital, fail to get more, and disappear. But as a group they are very important, because they are the source of the new established innovative firms for the economy.

During the transition from a new venture burning through capital to a successful innovative firm, the company's RDI will fall. At first glance that might seem to be a bad thing since R&D is their lifeblood at this stage. But what is important is why the RDI falls. When it falls because sales revenue is growing faster than R&D spending, then success is on the way. This means that the R&D spending is leveraging more and more sales revenue, which is what business wants, as indicated at the beginning of this chapter. On the other hand, RDI growing when sales revenue is not increasing can be a sign of moving to a higher level of R&D, but that trend is not sustainable and must reverse eventually. And RDI growing because sales are falling suggests that the end is in sight or, at the very least, that major change is needed. We will have more to say about this later.

## What the data show

We now move on to the data on R&D spending by over forty well-known Canadian companies. These are medium and large enterprises listed among the Top 100 R&D spenders. The time series of their R&D spending, sales revenues and RDI are plotted as line graphs on a time base, with the companies named in the figures. Many of the time series span 12 years, but some are interrupted or cut short for reasons that are themselves interesting. Most of the figures span many orders of magnitude in the data, and are easier to understand when plotted on a logarithmic scale. In some other cases, however, the patterns are more clearly shown on a linear scale. In either case, the figure caption alerts the reader to the scale used. A quick flip through the following pages will show the reader that the figures are of two kinds: those in which the data lie in more or less horizontal lines, showing steady behaviour, and those that show big swings from year to year, showing deep and rapid change.

### Information and communications technology

Let's begin at the top of the Top 100. Figure 12.2 shows the data for Research in Motion Limited (RIM) for 1999-2010, and Figure 12.3

the data for Nortel Networks Corporation (Nortel) over the same period. Both were established firms over that time, and both were undergoing change, but their histories couldn't be more different.

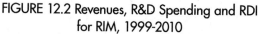

### FIGURE 12.2 Revenues, R&D Spending and RDI for RIM, 1999-2010

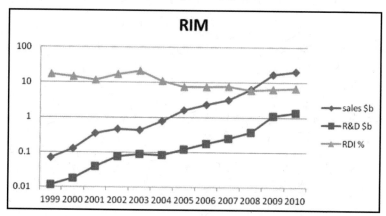

The company enjoyed several periods where RDI declined because revenues grew faster than R&D spending – always a good sign. Note the log scale for RDI.

RIM was the top R&D spender in Canada in 2010. The company's sales have grown from $70 million in 1999 to $20.5 billion in 2010. Over the same period, their R&D spending has grown almost without interruption from $12 million in 1999 to almost $1.4 billion. However, their RDI has declined almost steadily during that time from 16 percent in 1999 to 6.8 percent in 2010. That decline can clearly be seen by eye in Figure 12.2 in the period 2003-2005, where both sales and R&D spending are growing, but the growth of revenues is clearly much greater than the growth of R&D spending. In fact, sales have grown faster than R&D spending, and RDI has declined over the whole 12-year period. This, of course, is an example of the leading indicator of success introduced above.

The data in Figure 12.3 show that Nortel was spending more than $1 billion annually on R&D for ten years. In fact, Nortel was Canada's leading R&D spender for that time, with no other company coming close. At its peak in 2000, Nortel had revenues of $45 billion, R&D spending of almost $6 billion (close to 40 percent of the national total BERD), and RDI of 13 percent. Things went downhill very fast starting in 2008, and now Nortel no longer exists. In hindsight (and that's what this is), the signals were all there in Nortel's history of RDI. The left part of Figure 12.3 (the years 2000-2002) shows RDI growing, but for the worst possible reason. Sales revenue and R&D spending were both declining, but sales revenue was declining faster. That should have been seen as a warning, but if it was, nobody acted on it at the time. The same thing happened again in 2008-2009 and for the same reason, but by then it was too late for any warning.

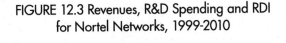

FIGURE 12.3 Revenues, R&D Spending and RDI
for Nortel Networks, 1999-2010

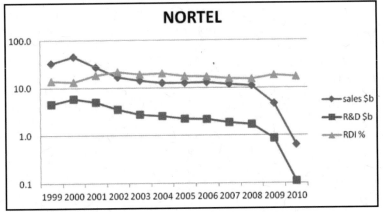

In hindsight, the rise of RDI in 2001-02 when sales declined faster than R&D spending was a sign of trouble to come. Note the log scale for RDI. It makes the huge sales decline seem smaller.

We will now move on to six other technology companies among Canada's top R&D spenders. Most of their histories are much more nearly steady than those of RIM and Nortel. The companies are ATI Technologies Inc., Cognos Inc., Open Text, Celestica Inc., DALSA Corporation and Xerox Canada Inc. Three of them were recently bought by multinational firms.

## FIGURE 12.4 Revenues, R&D Spending and RDI
## for ATI, 1999-2006

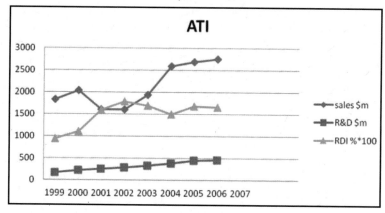

The scale is linear. To show the data most clearly, the numbers shown for the RDI are 100 times its value in %, e.g.: the highest value of RDI is 17.5% in 2002. ATI was bought by AMD in 2007.

ATI in Markham, Ontario was a maker of chips and chip sets for computer graphics. In 2006, the company reported revenues of about $2.75 billion and R&D spending of almost $460 million, which put it in fifth place among R&D spenders in Canada. During 2002-2004, its RDI declined from 17.5 percent to 14 percent for the right reason. Sales had grown during that time, and R&D spending had grown as well, but sales had grown more quickly. In 2007, ATI was bought by Advanced Micro Devices Inc. (AMD), a US chip maker, and it disappeared from the CCRD. For three years, ATI continued as a brand under the AMD umbrella, but the ATI name was removed in 2010. The ATI activity in Markham continues under the AMD name, and its website advertises vacancies, but its scale and scope are no longer reported. A great deal of one-time wealth creation occurred when ATI was bought by AMD, but the company's continuing wealth creation is under AMD's control.

## FIGURE 12.5 Revenues, R&D Spending and RDI
## for Cognos, 1999-2007

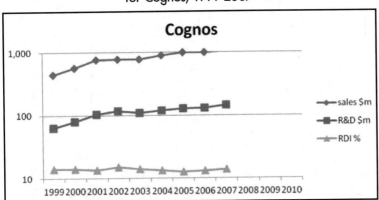

Cognos was bought by IBM in 2007. Note the log scale.

Cognos was a business software company whose sales grew steadily and passed the $1 billion level in 2007. Its R&D spending grew in proportion, to $145 million in 2007, and its RDI held remarkably constant, near 14 percent over the years 1999-2007. In 2007, Cognos was bought by IBM Canada Ltd. and became 'Cognos, an IBM Company'. The R&D activity remained in Ottawa, and there are signs that it is continuing at the previous level. IBM Canada increased its R&D spending from $397 million in 2008 to $557 million in 2009 and kept it at almost the same level in 2010. Cognos had spent $145.8 million on R&D in 2007, so the numbers suggest that the scale of Cognos R&D effort has remained the same. But the remarks made about wealth creation by ATI would hold here as well.

Figure 12.6 shows the R&D history of another large software company. Open Text is a billion-dollar Canadian software company, specializing in content management. It grew from a start-up that emerged from research at the University of Waterloo. It is remarkable how similar its R&D history is to that of Cognos. Both the numbers and the trends resemble each other closely. Open Text is one of the '5/95' companies, such that only 5 percent of its business is in Canada, and 95 percent is abroad.

### FIGURE 12.6 Revenues, R&D Spending and RDI
### for Open Text, 1999-2010

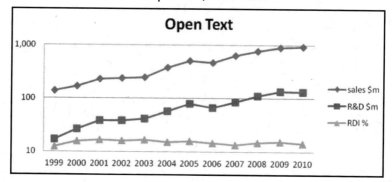

Open Text grew out of a research-based university start-up in Waterloo. It is now Canada's largest software company. Note the log scale.

But software companies don't all grow as smoothly. Figure 12.7 shows the R&D history of Corel Corporation, a company whose name at one time was synonymous with computer graphics in Canada and abroad. The company started off with a bang, and the signals were very positive in 1999-2000, but business problems arose and a restructuring took place between 2002 and 2004. The company is still active in Ottawa, but dropped out of the CCRD Top 100 in 2009.

### FIGURE 12.7 Revenues, R&D Spending and RDI
### for Corel Corporation, 1999-2008

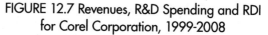
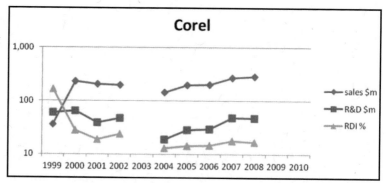

Once a leader in computer graphics, Corel had business problems and underwent restructuring in 2002-04. Note the log scale.

The next company to look at is another start-up that emerged from university research. Figure 12.8 shows the R&D history of DALSA Corporation, a medium-size Canadian company with world reach that was founded as a start-up based on research in electrical engineering at the University of Waterloo. DALSA makes high-end digital image sensors that are used in commercial photography, industrial vision, astronomy and other custom applications. One of those applications landed DALSA sensors on Mars in 2004 and brought much public attention to the company's technology.[7] In terms of its R&D history, DALSA has enjoyed steady progress, with revenues growing from $38 million to $180 million over eight years, R&D spending growing from $8.7 million to $42 million, and a high RDI ranging between 14 and 23 percent. It might be noted here again that the RDI declined in 2001-2003 as revenues grew faster than R&D spending. DALSA illustrates a blend of high R&D spending, leading-edge, high-technology products, and commercial success in an international business where innovation is constant and not far removed from research advances in science and engineering.

### FIGURE 12.8 Revenues, R&D Spending and RDI for DALSA Corporation, 1999-2009

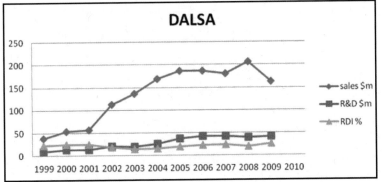

The scale is linear. RDI is high for the sector. DALSA makes high-end digital image sensors, some of which travelled to Mars. In 2010, DALSA was acquired by Teledyne Technologies.

---

[7] DALSA manufactured the image sensors (CCDs) for all nine cameras on the Mars rover "Spirit" and also for the cameras on the rover "Opportunity."

In 2010, DALSA was acquired by Teledyne Technologies Inc., and is now Teledyne DALSA. Company headquarters continue to be in Waterloo. No R&D spending data for 2010 were available for the CCRD update.

For comparison, consider the Gennum Corporation, a company originally spun off from the industrial giant Westinghouse Canada. Gennum is comparable in size to DALSA and, like DALSA, it also develops hardware, in particular chips designed to process data at very high rates. Both companies have operated at relatively very high values of RDI.

At one time, the company had also been a leader in electronics for the hearing-aid industry, but got out of that business. The R&D history of Gennum is shown in Figure 12.9. The sales decline from 2006 to 2009 may have had to do with the change of the business, but the signal in 2009-2010 is entirely positive. As this is being written, Gennum Corporation is in the process of being acquired by Semtech Corporation of California.

### FIGURE 12.9 Revenues, R&D Spending and RDI for Gennum Corp., 1999-2010

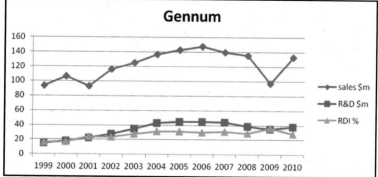

The scale is linear. The value of RDI is high for an established firm in the tech sector. Gennum is currently in the process of being acquired.

## FIGURE 12.10 Revenues, R&D Spending and RDI
for Sierra Wireless, 1999-2010

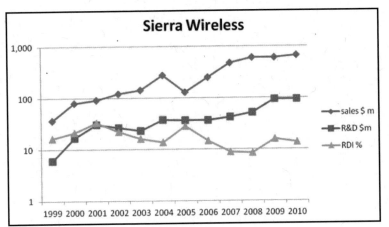

Note the log scale.

Sierra Wireless Inc. is a hardware company specializing in wireless data communications and computing. It was founded in 1993 and its headquarters are in Richmond, BC. Its R&D history is shown in Figure 12.10. The company has been growing almost without interruption since 1999, and it is interesting to note that it has gone through three episodes of RDI decline when sales revenues grew faster than R&D spending.

The next two figures show the R&D histories of two companies that were big players in R&D, and vanished from the Canadian scene. This happened in different ways and for very different reasons.

## FIGURE 12.11 Revenues, R&D Spending and RDI
for JDS Uniphase, 1999-2002

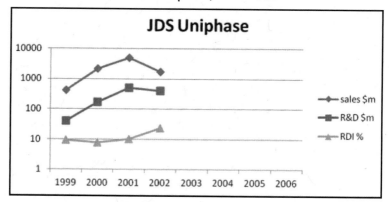

JDS Uniphase was a multi-billion dollar giant that essentially disappeared from the photonics business. Note the log scale.

Figure 12.11 shows what happened to JDS Uniphase, once a giant in photonics and fibre optics. Revenues peaked at $5 billion in 2001, and dropped by 65 percent to just above $1.7 billion in 2002 when the dot-com bubble burst. R&D spending also peaked in 2001, at $505 million, and dropped by about 20 percent to $400 million in 2002, so that RDI more than doubled to 23 percent. That increase in RDI with sales going down signalled trouble ahead. And, indeed, in 2003 the company was essentially gone from the Canadian R&D scene. It is now known as JDSU, a California company active in photonics in a broader range of applications, with revenues in the range of $1.5 billion. Its Canadian R&D activities are minor.

The story of Creo Inc. is very different even though its R&D history (Figure 12.12) looks similar at first glance. A company from BC, Creo had built up world leadership in 'pre-press' digital technology for commercial printing. Its revenues peaked at $1 billion in 2001, and it was spending close to $150 million on R&D. Creo was acquired by Eastman Kodak Company for its technology and its market niche in 2004-2005. The company no longer reports publicly on R&D spending in Canada, even though its R&D activities in Canada appear to be maintained. This is an example of a situation in which the continuing activity in Canada of what was once a very successful Canadian

R&D performer has become very difficult to assess. A recent complication is that Kodak applied for bankruptcy protection in late 2011. It remains to be seen what will happen to the R&D effort under these new circumstances.

### FIGURE 12.12 Revenues, R&D Spending and RDI for CREO Inc., 1999-2003

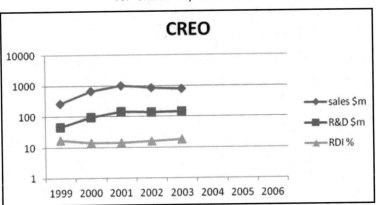

CREO grew to a successful billion dollar company and was bought by Kodak in 2004-05. Note the log scale.

Celestica Inc., whose R&D history is shown in Figure 12.13, is a contract manufacturer of information and communications technology equipment that had been spun off from IBM Canada. Its revenue has been steady at $10 billion since 2003, but its R&D spending has been declining steadily from some $35 million in 2003 to about $5 million in 2006. The RDI, already very low at 0.3 percent in 2003 declined to 0.05 percent in 2006.[8] These are surprisingly low numbers for the ICT sector. Even though Celestica is associated with the production of many high-tech products, the assembly of other companies' technology seems to require relatively little R&D on Celestica's part.

---

[8] If the trend in Figure 12.13 continued, the R&D spending by Celestica in 2007 would have put it out of the top 100 R&D spenders, and therefore outside of the data set available to the author at the time of writing.

## FIGURE 12.13 Revenues, R&D Spending and RDI
### for Celestica, 1999-2006

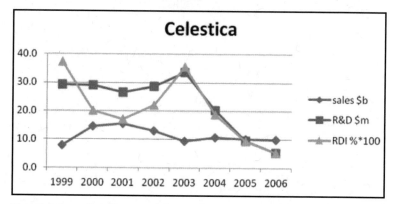

Note that the scale is linear and the numbers shown for the RDI are 100 times its value in %, e.g., the highest value of RDI is 0.37% in 1999.

The next company in this group is Xerox Canada whose R&D history is shown in Figure 12.14.

## FIGURE 12.14 Revenues, R&D Spending and RDI
### for Xerox Canada, 1999-2010

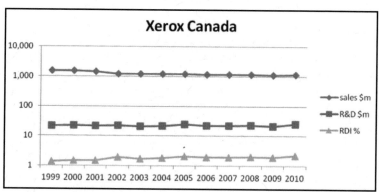

The RDI is very low for the sector because the revenues were produced by sales of products developed by Xerox around the world, but the R&D spending is for the Canadian labs only. Note the log scale.

The R&D history of Xerox Canada Inc. shown in Figure 12.14 is an example of the very steady behaviour of an established firm. The surprise in the data is the low value of RDI that suggests less frequent innovation than is common in this sector.

Revenues have held just above $1 billion for nine years, R&D spending has been steady at close to $22 million, and the RDI at almost 2 percent. But Xerox is a brand known worldwide for advanced technology and leading-edge innovation in document processing, and one would expect a much higher RDI. The explanation lies in the business model of Xerox Canada. The company operates an advanced research centre in Canada, but it is also the local marketing arm of a multinational corporation. The research centre develops inks and toners, but Xerox Canada markets a much wider range of products. The low RDI here is the ratio of the R&D spending in one lab to revenues from the sale of a broad range of products developed in the company's many labs. When the sales revenues are uncoupled from the R&D in this way, the low value of RDI for Xerox Canada Inc. cannot be taken as an indicator of a low frequency of innovation at the Xerox Canada research lab.

### Aerospace

Next we shall look at three companies in the aerospace cluster in Montreal: CAE Inc., Pratt & Whitney Canada and Bombardier Inc. Their data are shown in Figures 12.15, 12.16 and 12.17 respectively.

### FIGURE 12.15 Revenues, R&D Spending and RDI for CAE, 1999-2010

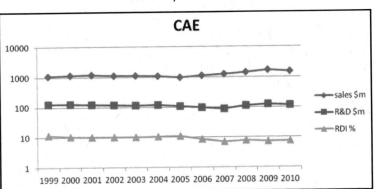

The company makes simulators for flight training on a great range of commercial and military aircraft. Note the log scale.

The data for CAE are perfectly straightforward and, by now, much as expected. CAE is a world leader in building flight simulators used to train pilots to fly a variety of modern aircraft. It's a billion dollar company that spends $100 million on R&D and operates at an RDI of 10 percent. The slight decline in RDI in recent years is explained by sales growing somewhat faster than R&D spending, a good sign.

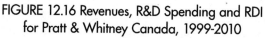

### FIGURE 12.16 Revenues, R&D Spending and RDI for Pratt & Whitney Canada, 1999-2010

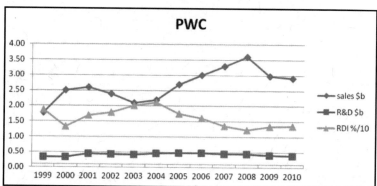

The scale is linear. To show the data most clearly, the values of RDI are reduced by a factor of 10. That means that the highest value of RDI was about 21% in 2004.

Pratt & Whitney Canada (PWC), the Canadian branch of United Technologies Corporation, has the world mandate for the development and manufacture of small and medium aircraft engines. It is now a $3 billion company that spends $400 million on R&D, with RDI of 14 percent. It is notable that during the period from 2004 to 2008, RDI decreased very markedly because sales almost doubled while R&D spending stayed constant. This was a very healthy sign. Note that PWC operates at a very high RDI because in their business model PWC pays for all the R&D for new engine projects, and sometimes even develops new technologies for their suppliers.

## FIGURE 12.17 Revenues, R&D Spending and RDI for Bombardier, 1999-2010

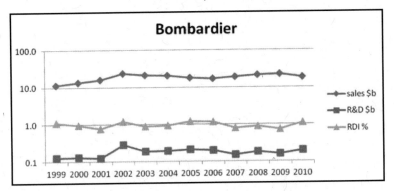

Bombardier is in the same sector and the same city as both CAE and PWC, but its RDI is lower by an order of magnitude. The reason for this is a different business model in which R&D is shared with suppliers. Note the log scale.

The R&D history of Bombardier, a manufacturer of trains and aircraft, is somewhat less steady than that of CAE, but the biggest difference is that its RDI is ten times lower, and almost twenty times lower than for PWC. Bombardier is a $20 billion company that spends $200 million on R&D. Its lower RDI could be interpreted to mean that innovations in planes and trains cost less than innovations in simulators, or are relatively less frequent. That may or may not be the case, but another big factor is probably more important. As pointed out in the discussion of the Montreal aerospace cluster in chapter 10, Bombardier functions as a systems integrator, at least in aerospace. Both the costs and the risks of the R&D are shared by its suppliers. And that means that Bombardier's own share of R&D spending is only a fraction of the total associated with its projects, leading to the RDI being much lower than that of CAE or PWC.

### Automotive

It is instructive to compare Bombardier with Magna International Inc., another manufacturing company whose revenues are in the same ballpark. Magna is a giant in the auto parts sector, with revenues of $24 billion and R&D spending of $460 million in 2010. Its R&D history is shown in Figure 12.18. This is another reasonably steady picture, with the RDI rising from 1 percent to a peak of 3 percent and then falling back to 2 percent. Magna spends twice as much on R&D as Bombardier, but that may reflect Bombardier's shared-R&D business model as much as it does the level of innovation at Magna.

### FIGURE 12.18 Revenues, R&D Spending and RDI for Magna International Inc., 1999-2010

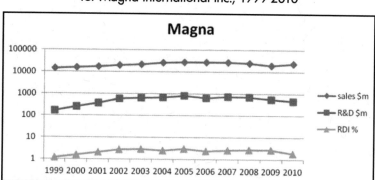

Magna is by far the biggest R&D spender in the automotive sector in Canada. Note the log scale.

## Space technology

The next two companies are both involved in space, and particularly satellite communications and remote sensing. COM DEV International Limited is a $200 million company that builds satellite communications hardware and has its systems currently flying in several hundred satellites. Its R&D history is shown in Figure 12.19. Its sales have grown steadily, doubling since 2003. The company went through a rough patch in 2001-2003, and that shows up as the period when RDI was going down because R&D spending was decreasing faster than sales were. Things have turned around, and in 2007-2009, RDI was declining for the right reason.

## FIGURE 12.19 Revenues, R&D Spending and RDI for COM DEV International Limited, 1999-2010

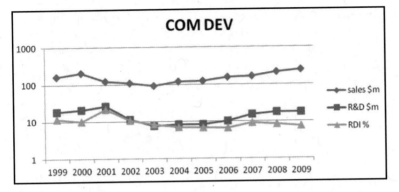

The company builds satellites and communications systems. Its systems are flying in hundreds of satellites. Note the log scale.

The R&D history of MacDonald, Dettwiler & Assoc. (MDA) is shown in Figure 12.20. MDA is a $1 billion company best known to the public for its association with the Canadarm robotic manipulator on the Space Shuttle. MDA has recently seen some decline of sales and its RDI has recently reached close to 10 percent. After some substantial adjustments in the business in 1999-2002, the company had experienced steady growth until 2007, with R&D spending constant and RDI declining. In 2009-2010, R&D spending increased and sales dropped, a possible signal of weakness ahead.

## FIGURE 12.20 Revenues, R&D Spending and RDI for MacDonald, Dettwiler & Assoc., 1999-2010

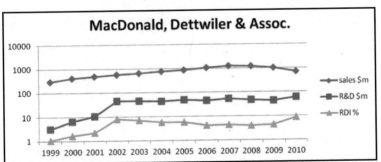

The company is best known for developing the Canadarm robotic arm for the space shuttle and International Space Station. Note the log scale.

### Engineering services

For comparison, consider the R&D history of SNC-Lavalin Group Inc., a giant in engineering services. The data are shown in Figure 12.21. The revenues are about ten times greater than for MDA, but the R&D spending is less than half as much. As a result RDI is well below 1 percent. This result may be typical for engineering services firms, but there are no other data to verify that.

### FIGURE 12.21 Revenues, R&D Spending and RDI for SNC-Lavalin, 1999-2010

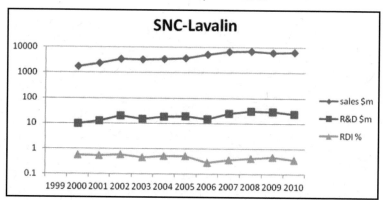

The firm is Canada's largest engineering services company. Note the log scale.

### Natural resources

We now move on to a group of companies in the natural resource and commodity sectors. These are huge companies with annual sales revenues in the billions of dollars. They operate at a very low RDI in the range of 1 percent or less, but because their revenues are so large that still represents tens of millions of dollars of annual spending on R&D, reaching $100 million in some cases. This money is generally spent on large multi-year projects such as the development of new exploration and extraction techniques in the field. Among these companies, the steadiest R&D history belongs to Imperial Oil Limited. It is shown in Figure 12.22.

## FIGURE 12.22 Revenues, R&D Spending and RDI for Imperial Oil Limited, 1999-2010

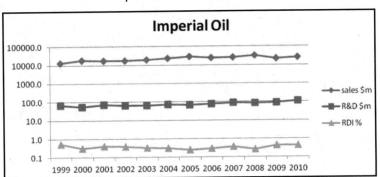

Note the log scale. The steady behaviour, huge revenues, and low RDI are typical of the large companies in the resource sectors.

## FIGURE 12.23 Revenues, R&D Spending and RDI for EnCana Corporation,1999-2010

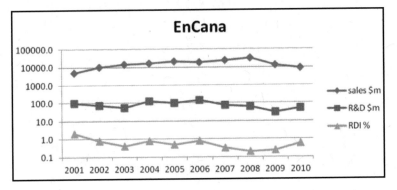

Note the log scale.

The R&D history of EnCana Corporation (Figure 12.23) shows more time variation than that of Imperial Oil, but the numbers are all in the same range. The variations may reflect differences between the oil and natural gas markets during the time period covered.

Petro-Canada/Suncor has a somewhat different R&D history. Petro-Canada revenues grew consistently from 1999 to 2008, but the company operated at a fraction of the RDI of Imperial Oil or EnCana. This changed in 2008-2009 as RDI shot up to 1 percent.

It has since declined at a time when sales rose more sharply. It is likely that the changes in 2008-2010 were the result of adjustments made when Petro-Canada was acquired by Suncor Energy Inc.

FIGURE 12.24 Revenues, R&D Spending and RDI
for Petro-Canada, 1999-2008 and Suncor Energy Inc., 2009-2010

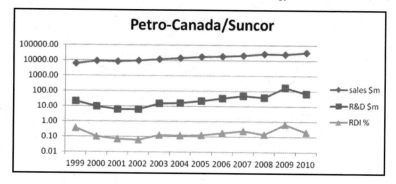

Suncor had acquired Petro-Canada in 2008. Note the log scale.

The data for NOVA Chemicals Corporation are shown in Figure 12.24. This company operated in fairly steady fashion until 2009 when the sales dipped significantly. Its RDI is greater than that of the three oil and gas companies since it produces value-added products and must engage in process innovations to keep its costs down.

FIGURE 12.25 Revenues, R&D Spending and RDI
for NOVA Chemicals Corporation, 1999-2010

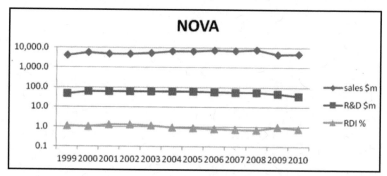

The value of RDI is higher than for the preceding three oil and gas companies because of the greater value-added nature of NOVA's chemicals business. Note the log scale.

The R&D history of the mining company Vale Canada Limited is shown in Figure 12.26. This includes the R&D history of Inco Limited through 2005. In 2006, Inco was bought by the Companhia Vale do Rio Doce (CVRD) of Brazil and renamed Vale Inco Limited, and more recently Vale Limited. The data for 2007-2010 suggest that the R&D of Inco Limited is being maintained by Vale. The pattern is typical of the natural resource and commodity sectors: a fairly steady operation with multi-billion dollar revenues, a low RDI around 1 percent or less, and R&D spending of tens of millions annually.

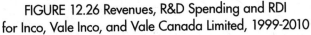

FIGURE 12.26 Revenues, R&D Spending and RDI for Inco, Vale Inco, and Vale Canada Limited, 1999-2010

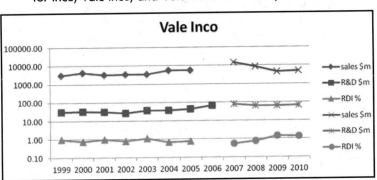

Inco was acquired by Vale in 2006. Note the log scale.

Tembec Inc. has long enjoyed the reputation as Canada's leading value-added integrated forest products company. Its R&D history is shown in Figure 12.27. The relatively high RDI for a natural resource company was consistent with the reputation, but the decline in sales and R&D spending since 2006 raises questions about the sustainability of its business model.[9]

[9] Much of Tembec's capacity in BC was acquired by Canfor in 2012. The impact of this transaction on Tembec's sales and R&D remains to be seen.

## FIGURE 12.27 Revenues, R&D Spending and RDI
### for Tembec Inc., 1999-2010

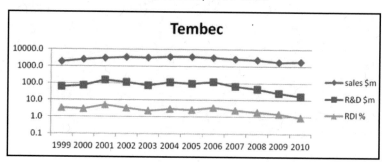

Tembec has long enjoyed the reputation of being the most innovative company in the forest products sector. Note the log scale (no pun intended).

### Utilities

The next five companies are in the energy area. Two are very large utilities; the other three are among Canada's innovation icons. The model of steady performance in the utility sector is Hydro-Québec, whose R&D history is shown in Figure 12.28. Revenues have been running at $10 billion, R&D spending at $100 million and RDI at 1 percent for over a decade.

### FIGURE 12.28 Revenues, R&D Spending and RDI
### for Hydro-Québec, 1999-2010

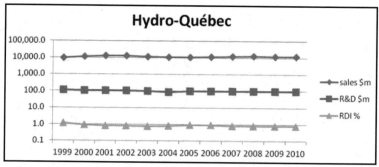

These data make Hydro-Québec the poster child for steady operation of an established firm that engages in R&D. Note the log scale.

Ontario Power Generation (OPG) is a utility of comparable scale, but its numbers are somewhat different. Its R&D history is shown in Figure 12.29.

### FIGURE 12.29 Revenues, R&D Spending and RDI
### for Ontario Power Generation, 1999-2010

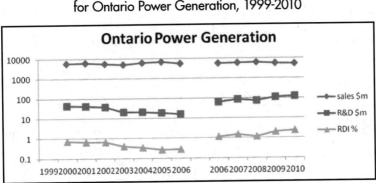

Note the log scale.

The current numbers are close to those of Hydro-Québec, with the revenues somewhat lower and the RDI slightly higher. Obviously some administrative adjustment occurred in 2006 and additional R&D activity was transferred to OPG.

### Nuclear energy

Atomic Energy of Canada Limited, a crown corporation until very recently, has a complicated R&D history. This company has essentially been funded to perform R&D. Its sales come mainly from the maintenance and refurbishment of the existing fleet of CANDU reactors in Canada and elsewhere. The RDI has been at 50 percent or more since 2005, and there have been periods (2003-2005 and 2008-2009) when R&D spending was going up as sales were falling. This was not a sustainable business model. After the sale of most of AECL to SNC-Lavalin in 2011 it is being changed.

### FIGURE 12.30 Revenues, R&D Spending and RDI for Atomic Energy of Canada Limited, 1999-2010

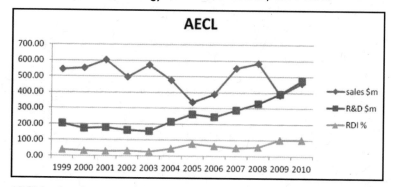

AECL has long been one of Canada's innovation icons, but the data show that its business model was not sustainable. Most of AECL was bought by SNC-Lavalin in 2011.

## Clean-tech

Perhaps Canada's best known 'clean-tech' icon is Ballard Power Systems, a BC company famous for its R&D work on the hydrogen fuel-cell. Their entirely unsteady R&D history shown in Figure 12.31 demonstrates that revenues peaked at about $170 million in 2003 and have been declining since, as have the R&D spending and RDI (dropping steadily from 225 percent except for the rise in 2003-2005). There was an uptick in revenues in 2010 that may signal the beginning of a new trend.

### FIGURE 12.31 Revenues, R&D Spending and RDI for Ballard Power Systems, 1999-2010

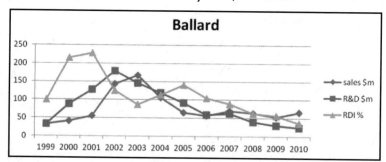

Ballard has long been another of Canada's innovation icons. It has been developing fuel cells to provide electric power from hydrogen, but the "hydrogen economy" has been slow in coming.

Clearly, Ballard is a company whose business is to do R&D on fuel cells. Ballard fuel cells are running in numerous prototype cars and buses in North America and Europe. Ballard Power Systems had often been referred to as the company that would lead road transport into the 'hydrogen economy'. However that is now not likely to happen, at least not quickly, because of challenges with the supporting infrastructure.

Hydrogen is not found in nature; it must be manufactured, and that takes energy. So hydrogen is not an energy source; it's more of an energy 'currency'. It is a very light and flammable gas that must be safely distributed and transferred, and finally stored in the vehicle at a very high pressure so that a tank of reasonable size might provide fuel for a practical range. Many companies are working on aspects of the hydrogen infrastructure, but progress is slow. In the meantime, the hybrid car is already here, the development of the plug-in hybrid is coming along, and both offer great improvements in fuel economy within the existing energy infrastructure. As a result, Ballard Power Systems is now changing its focus to providing fuel cells for materials handling applications (e.g., forklift trucks operating in closed spaces, where its total absence of air-polluting emissions is a huge advantage) and for stationary back-up power generation. This is a technology company that has achieved technical success with its R&D, but now has to refocus its business because of changing market conditions.

Another research-based new venture in BC dealing with clean(er) energy for transportation is Westport Innovations Inc. Its R&D history is shown in Figure 12.32. After a period of rapid change in the early years with big spending on R&D, almost no revenues, and huge values of RDI, it saw a quick rise in revenues and then a period of steady sales growth and declining RDI.

### FIGURE 12.32 Revenues, R&D Spending and RDI for Westport Innovations Inc., 1999-2010

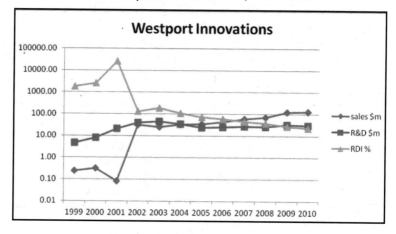

Westport Innovations makes systems for replacing liquid fuel with natural gas in diesel engines. They went through some huge swings in revenues a decade ago, but the recent growth in the supplies of natural gas from shale might mean that this company is now catching the wave. Note the log scale.

Westport Innovations Inc. is commercializing inventions coming out of engineering research done at University of British Columbia (UBC). The company works on converting diesel engines to use natural gas, a fuel that is much cheaper and burns much more cleanly than diesel oil. Its fortunes changed in 2001 when it entered into an agreement with Cummins Inc., the world's largest independent maker of diesel engines. Since then sales have been rising, R&D spending has been maintained, and RDI has been falling in a healthy fashion. The recent discovery of huge reserves of natural gas in shale will undoubtedly improve the prospects for much wider use of Westport's technology.[10]

### Pharmaceuticals/biotechnology

The last group of eight companies to be discussed here are in the pharmaceuticals/biotechnology sector. They include four established billion-dollar firms: three makers of patented

[10] As this was being written, the business press reported that Westport had signed a deal with Caterpillar Inc., one of the world's largest manufacturers of diesel engines for mobile and stationary applications. This could lead to another surge in Westport's income.

drugs, and one maker of generic drugs, as well as four new or relatively new ventures. The data for the four established firms look generally similar, with close to $1 billion in sales and $100 million in R&D spending. But they differ in some important details.

The R&D history of GlaxoSmithKline Canada (GSK) is shown in Figure 12.33. GSK has been a billion-dollar company since 2001, spending more than $100 million on R&D, with RDI running above 10 percent as a result. This is important, since the patented drug industry made a commitment to spend 10 percent of Canadian sales on R&D in Canada when Bill C-22 was passed in 1987.

### FIGURE 12.33 Revenues, R&D Spending and RD for GlaxoSmithKline Canada, 1999-2010

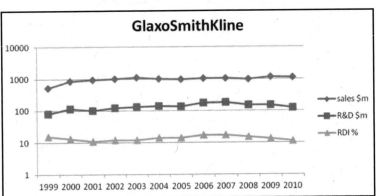

Note also that GSK has been meeting the industry's commitment to operate at an RDI of 10% or more in Canada. Note the log scale.

The picture looks different for Merck, whose data are shown in Figure 12.34. As a result of increasing sales since 2008, Merck is now also a $1 billion company. Its R&D spending has declined during that time, and the RDI has fallen well below 10 percent. According to the logic we have used many times in discussing these data, the decline in RDI since 2008 is a healthy sign of future success, but in this case that trend runs up against the commitment made to keep RDI above 10 percent.

## FIGURE 12.34 Revenues, R&D Spending and RDI
### for Merck, 1999-2010

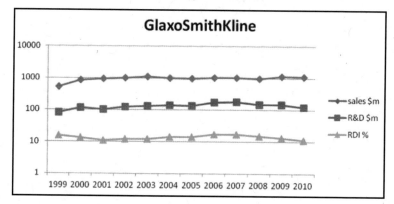

The recent decline of RDI has occurred in a way that we have identified as an indicator of success – revenues growing faster than R&D spending. But it's not clear what will happen to the 10% commitment. Note the log scale.

As shown in Figure 12.35, AstraZeneca Canada Inc. has shown a steady growth in revenues since 2000. Its R&D spending has been constant for about half that time and declining since. Its RDI has been well below 10 percent for most of the period, and has recently fallen to 4.3 percent.

## FIGURE 12.35 Revenues, R&D Spending and RDI
### for AstraZeneca Canada Inc., 1999-2010

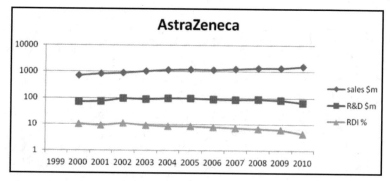

The data show almost a decade of gradual decline of RDI as sales revenues grew faster than R&D spending. The 10% commitment is a question mark. Note the log scale.

Pfizer Canada is almost a $2 billion company, and their R&D spending has been between $100 and $200 million for most of the last decade. Pfizer's RDI, however, has been well below 10 percent for most of that time, with a substantial increase to 7.4 percent only in 2010. Pfizer's data are shown in Figure 12.36.

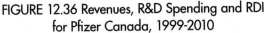

### FIGURE 12.36 Revenues, R&D Spending and RDI for Pfizer Canada, 1999-2010

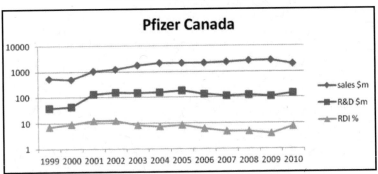

The recent uptick in RDI brings it closer to the 10% commitment, but in the wrong way, as sales dipped and R&D spending grew. Note the log scale.

The last in our sample of large established pharmaceutical companies is Apotex Inc., a Canadian manufacturer of generic drugs. The R&D history of Apotex is shown in Figure 12.37. This is another billion-dollar firm that spends close to $200 million on R&D. Apotex was not party to the 10 percent commitment, but its RDI has been well above 10 percent for the whole period, and close to 20 percent for much of the time. It is important to remember, however, that the R&D done by generic drug firms is very different from what the patented drug firms do. The latter are engaged in drug discovery, process research and clinical trials. The generic manufacturers emphasize process research and proving the equivalence of their drug to the patented original.

## FIGURE 12.37 Revenues, R&D Spending and RDI for Apotex Inc., 1999-2010

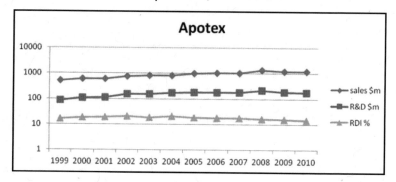

Apotex is Canada's largest generic drug manufacturer. Their RDI has been well over 10%, reflecting their business model. Recall that R&D done by generic drug firms is very different from what the patented drug firms do. Note the log scale.

We now move on to discuss three newer and smaller firms that are commercializing drugs discovered in recent university and hospital research. The best known of these is undoubtedly QLT Inc. which emerged from research at UBC into light-sensitive drugs. The R&D history of QLT is shown in Figure 12.38. It is obvious at first glance that these data look nothing at all like the data for the first four firms. QLT's sales peaked at $300 million in 2005, and have been declining since. In 1999-2001, QLT was a textbook case of the healthy decline in RDI from 200 percent as sales grew and R&D spending stayed fixed. The signs were all good, even if RDI continued at a high level of 30 to 40 percent. However, since 2005 the sales have been declining steadily and, most recently, RDI rose to 75 percent. What that means for the future is not at all clear.

## FIGURE 12.38 Revenues, R&D Spending and RDI for QLT Inc., 1999-2010

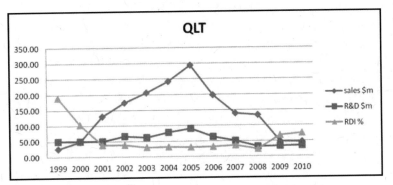

QLT has been another of Canada's innovation icons, a start-up emerging from university research on light-activated drugs. The early years have shown very positive signs, but the trends since 2005 are not encouraging.

## FIGURE 12.39 Revenues, R&D Spending and RDI for Cardiome Pharma, 1999-2010

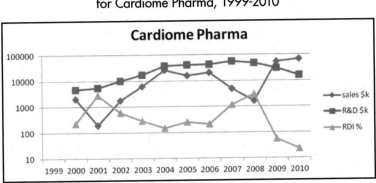

The swings have been huge. The company has seen almost a thousand-fold variation in revenues but has sustained a large R&D effort. Note the log scale.

Cardiome Pharma Corp. is a BC company specializing in developing drugs for cardiovascular conditions. Its R&D history is shown in Figure 12.39. Once again, we see big swings in sales revenue, but the dominant trend is upward. RDI has been very high, with two peaks of several thousand percent when sales collapsed, and the low value of 23 percent reached only in 2010. The recent fall in RDI because of a rise in sales is encouraging.

We conclude our sample of the pharmaceutical/biotechnology sector by looking at Bellus Health Inc. that was earlier known as Neurochem. The R&D history is shown in Figure 12.40. Here the swings are wild. Sales rise to a few million dollars, and then drop to almost zero. RDI is all over the place, from a hundred percent to a million. There is no stability there and, in 2006-2008, we see the danger sign of RDI rising because sales are falling faster than R&D spending. And there's no sign of the company in the Top 100 after 2008.

### FIGURE 12.40 Revenues, R&D Spending and RDI for Neurochem/BELLUS, 1999-2008

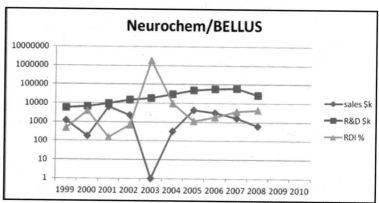

The data show an unstable situation: an R&D effort in the tens of millions of dollars per year, and revenue swings from several million dollars to virtually nil. Note the log scale.

When we consider the last three new pharmaceutical ventures we see wild swings in revenues and RDI. The remarkable thing is that the R&D spending was continuous in all three cases. This reinforces the impression that their strength lies in research – investors recognize that and are prepared to support it. Their performance in commercialization is much less predictable.

## Telecommunications

We will conclude this part of the chapter with one more comparison between two giants, the telecom providers BCE and TELUS Corporation. Their R&D histories are shown in Figures 12.41 and 12.42. Their sales are in the $10 billion range, with BCE larger by a factor of two. But the big difference between them is in the R&D. Through various reorganizations of predecessor firms, BCE got to $1 billion in R&D by 2002. TELUS climbed much more slowly, probably by developing new R&D activities, hung around $100 million for three years, and got to two-thirds of $1 billion in 2009, only to drop by 81 percent in the next year. It will be interesting to watch what impact these different approaches to R&D have on these firms' future success.

### FIGURE 12.41 Revenues, R&D Spending and RDI for BCE, 1999-2010

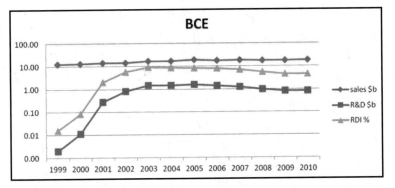

After a period of enormous growth in R&D spending early in the last decade, much of it through reorganization of related firms, this telecom giant has operated quite steadily at an RDI level comparable to much of the tech industry. Note that the log scale starts at 0.001, but the last digit has been truncated in the plot.

FIGURE 12.42 Revenues, R&D Spending and RDI
for TELUS Corporation, 1999-2010

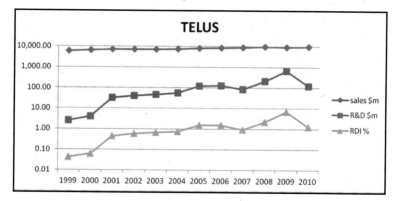

Telus has revenues comparable with BCE's, and reached comparable R&D
spending and RDI, but much more slowly. The recent big downturn in R&D
spending occurred while revenues held steady. Note the log scale.

## A model of industrial R&D in Canada

Much more could be learned from the R&D histories of Canadian
R&D spenders if the sample was enlarged and the data studied in
greater detail. But an important general conclusion that needs no
more detail is staring us in the face. As suggested earlier, it can be
seen by flipping the pages and glancing at the R&D histories of
the firms. It is obvious that there are two kinds of R&D histories:
those that seem more or less steady or growing steadily (e.g.,
Figures 12.28, 12.5, 12.22, 12.25), and others that are far from
steady and show big annual swings in the data (e.g., Figures 12.31,
12.39, 12.40). The first group operates at mean RDI of a few percent,
and the second at much higher values, with RDI sometimes far
exceeding 100 percent. This visual impression is substantiated by
a recent statistical analysis of the data.[11]

[11] T.A. Brzustowski. 2012. "The Connections Between R&D Intensity and Time in
Industrial Innovation," Working paper. Ottawa: Telfer School of Management,
WP.2012.01, p. 1-19. The mean values and standard deviations of RDI were
calculated from the time series of RDI for 100 companies. At low mean values
of RDI of a few percent or less, the standard deviation of annual fluctuations in
RDI is smaller than the mean value by as much as an order of magnitude. At
mean RDI of about 50% to 100% the mean and the standard deviation become
equal. And at higher values of mean RDI, the standard deviation exceeds the
mean value.

It's a safe conclusion, then, that Canadian R&D spending firms fall into two groups: those whose operations are more or less steady, and those who must deal with rapid and deep change in their financial conditions. This distinction becomes particularly interesting when we go back and gather the attributes of these two kinds of firms. It turns out that they differ in many other ways as well. This leads to a model of industrial R&D spending in Canada that divides the firms into two categories and makes it very clear that they operate under different financial conditions and on different time scales. Its important implication for policy is that any government assistance for their R&D must take that into account.

When I first published this model, I had called the two groups of firms "steady" and "changing".[12] Those labels were not very satisfying, but they seemed the best I could do at the time. Some colleagues suggested that the "changing" firms should be called 'dynamic' instead, but that did not seem to be a very good fit since many of the "steady" firms were obviously dynamic in the popular sense of the word. My thinking since has also been helped by the publication of the report "Innovation and Business Strategy: Why Canada Falls Short" by the Council of Canadian Academies also in 2009.[13] Their Table 7 on p. 120 "Innovation Strategies – Incumbents versus New Ventures" was similar in format but entirely qualitative in content, and very informative. It both supported and complemented my model very well. Adding one more ingredient into the mix, namely the quad taxonomy of innovation introduced in chapter 5, leads me to propose a model of industrial R&D spending in Canada that now divides the companies into "established firms" and "research-based new ventures". The model is shown below in the form of a table.

[12] T. A. Brzustowski. 2009. "Industrial R&D Spending in Canada: Model, Policy and Program Delivery," *Optimumonline*, 39 (2): 25-33.

[13] Expert Panel on Business Innovation. 2009. *Innovation and Business Strategy: Why Canada Falls Short*. Ottawa: Council of Canadian Academies, June.

## TABLE 12.2 A Model of Industrial R&D Spending in Canada

| Group label | Established firms | Research-based new ventures |
|---|---|---|
| Business model | do R&D to stay in business | are in business to do R&D |
| Size | many large and medium, with annual R&D spending of the order of $30 to100 million, or more | many small, with annual R&D spending of a few $ million or less |
| Examples | manufacturers with established product lines in many sectors, natural resource companies | research-based start-ups emerging from universities, government labs; technology spin-offs from large companies |
| R&D intensity | a few up to 20%, most below 10%, some far below | most near 100% or above, many much higher |
| R&D funding source | sales revenues and some tax credits | raised capital, tax credits and some sales revenues |
| Goal of R&D | improved or new products and processes; more sustaining innovation than disruptive | new products, with regulatory approval if necessary; new markets; more disruptive innovation than sustaining |
| Rhythm of business as indicated by RDI | steady or quasi-steady | fluctuating: involved in frequent and rapid change; big swings in RDI often driven by swings in revenues |
| Leading indicator of commercial success | RDI decreasing moderately with time when revenues grow faster than R&D spending | RDI greatly decreasing with time — from >100% down to mainstream value for the sector when revenues grow much faster than R&D spending |
| Implications for support policies and programs | policies must recognize long time scales and the need for big investments, steady model of program delivery suitable | policies must recognize that these companies are short of both cash and time; programs must be responsive with quick decisions — need the attention of an "account executive" |

Source: Modified slightly from T. A. Brzustowski. 2009. "Industrial R&D Spending in Canada: Model, Policy and Program Delivery," *Optimumonline,* 39 (2): 28.

A more detailed understanding of how the established innovative firms spend money on R&D is emerging from the massive data-rich study of Miller et al. discussed at the end of chapter 7.[14] Their data came from an exhaustive survey of 1,000

[14] Roger Miller, Xavier Olleros and Luis Molinié. 2008. "Innovation Games: A New Approach to the Competitive Challenge," *Long Range Planning,* 41 (4): 378-394.

established firms around the world. It turns out that it is useful to represent what these firms do by seven innovation 'games', each with its own competitive context, innovation effort, strategy and performance in terms of profit from innovation and sales growth. These games would provide a 'fine structure' to the left-hand column of Table 12.2 and explain the range of values of RDI encountered among the established firms that spend on R&D. This is useful new understanding, and one hopes that research of comparable sophistication will be done on the research-based new ventures as well, but for the moment they seem to be largely under the radar.

## Some loose ends

The R&D histories of the three dozen (out of 41) established companies described in this chapter have provided some useful information, but also raised an important question. The companies are all among Canada's Top 100 R&D spenders. They are all large established companies that have been in business for many years, and are probably much more involved in sustaining than in disruptive innovation.[15] Yet some of them have been spending much more on R&D than others. That observation becomes more emphatic when their R&D spending is normalized by company size and expressed in the form of RDI. All have been spending less than 20 percent of sales revenues on R&D, and some as little as 0.1 percent. Why?

This question is made more pointed by a widely touted study of the world's top 1,000 R&D spenders, whose average RDI was 4.2 percent. That study showed no correlation between RDI in 1999 on the one hand, and several indicators of business success in 1999-2004 on the other. The authors labelled their surprising conclusion "The Performance Disconnect" and stated: "There is no discernible relationship between spending levels [on R&D] and most measures of business success."[16] This was picked up by The Economist and trumpeted as a challenge to conventional wisdom.[17]

---

[15] Clayton M. Christensen. 1997. *The Innovator's Dilemma*. Cambridge, MA: Harvard Business Press.

[16] B. Jaruzelski, K. Dehoff and R. Bordia. 2005. "The Booz Allen Hamilton Global Innovation 1000: Money Isn't Everything," *Strategy+Business*, (41): 1-14.

[17] *The Economist*. 2006. "A survey of the company," January 21, p. 9.

While the quick answer 'Companies spend on R&D what they need to spend' may sound smart-alecky, a few obvious observations lend it some substance. First, companies don't spend on R&D by accident. They don't spend tens or even hundreds of millions of dollars per year on activities involving hundreds of people and specialized facilities if they don't have to. Second, sustained R&D spending by companies is driven by need, the need to succeed in their business in the face of competition. The needs are different in different sectors. Companies in the commodities sectors must take the market price for their products. They do R&D to improve their processes and reduce their costs to remain profitable. Companies in value-added manufacturing must do R&D to keep a full pipeline of improved or new products for which they can set the price as their older products become commoditized. As suggested by the Forgacs rule, RDI is an indicator of how frequently these producers need to innovate. If they stopped spending on R&D, they would fairly quickly find themselves being commodity producers, and if they then didn't start spending on process R&D to reduce their costs, they would eventually go out of business. And third, and perhaps most obvious, if the established companies have been doing this for years and enjoying business success, then they were spending enough on R&D to meet their business needs but probably not more.

These simple considerations combine to explain the surprising findings of Jaruzelski, Dehoff and Bordia. It turns out that all the values of RDI considered in their study were below 7 percent. That means that the companies studied were all established firms doing R&D to compete and stay in business – not a surprise for the world's top 1,000 R&D spenders. These companies spend on R&D just the amount they need to keep their business model working in steady fashion, no more and no less. However, all the new ventures that spend more than their revenues on R&D in order to grow and change their businesses, to develop their products and establish their markets were excluded from the study, because their RDI exceeds 100 percent, let alone 7 percent. So the conclusion of Jaruzelski et al. seems to say only that the established companies that were the world's top 1,000 R&D spenders were doing what they had to do to stay in a steady state during the study period. At that level, they were spending on R&D mainly to maintain their businesses. And that seems perfectly reasonable, and not at all surprising. But it doesn't justify the sweeping statement made about R&D spending in general. The study looked at only one corner of industrial innovation space where changes are limited, and then applied the conclusion to the whole thing, including a region where changes abound.

And there's something else. Numerous examples, involving both established firms and new ventures, have suggested a useful leading indicator of commercial success for companies spending on R&D, namely a period of decline of RDI, driven by sales revenues rising more quickly than R&D spending. This is most visible in the case of the research-based new ventures that start off spending much more on R&D than they earn in sales. The successful ones eventually settle into the group of established firms in their sector, enjoying much greater revenues but spending a much smaller fraction of them on R&D. In such cases, the drop in RDI from values often much above 100 percent to just a few percent is very obvious and rapid, as is the revenue growth. In theory, such a drop in RDI requires only that revenues grow faster (or decline more slowly) than R&D spending and, within that, the R&D spending could grow fast, or slowly, or even decline, as determined by business considerations.

The decline of RDI when sales revenue grows faster than R&D spending also occurs among established companies. It is usually less pronounced, since the revenue growth and decline in RDI are both relatively much smaller, but it is still a leading indicator of commercial success. (One striking example appears in Figure 12.16 which shows the R&D history of Pratt & Whitney Canada on a linear scale). It is interesting that Jaruzelski and Dehoff noticed precisely this in looking at the performance of the world's top 1,000 R&D spenders in 2002-2007, but made no comment on that observation. Their Exhibit 5 shows aggregate revenue for the world's top 1,000 R&D spenders growing more quickly than their aggregate R&D spending, which was also growing.[18] While the conclusion would be more certain if their data used R&D intensity based on value-added rather than sales revenues, this is likely to be an illustration of established

---

[18] B. Jaruzelski and K. Dehoff. 2008. "Beyond Borders: the Global Innovation 1000," *Strategy+Business*, (53): 4.

companies contributing to reducing GERD/GDP, as described at the beginning of this chapter.

The important lesson in this chapter is the possibility of very deep and rapid change in the fiscal situation of research-based new ventures. These companies have not been getting much attention either in the literature or in policy. They may face severe year-over-year fluctuations in their financial circumstances, generally driven more by the fluctuations in their revenues than in their R&D spending. These are important companies because a few of them are stars being born. These few will become Canada's new, large innovative companies, and there is no other source of such companies. The rest will burn through their cash and disappear. If the research-based new ventures are to receive any assistance from the government, they must get it promptly when they demonstrate that they need it and are qualified to get it, because otherwise it may be too late. For these new ventures, assistance delayed may be success denied.

# PART III

## WHAT NEEDS TO BE DONE

# CHAPTER 13

## AN INNOVATION POLICY FOR CANADA

*Innovation policy doesn't produce innovations. Entrepreneurs do that.*

### Innovation Action Plan

The thesis of this book is that Canada needs to build and sustain a surge of innovation to deal with our prosperity problem, and that we can do it if we manage to put the pieces together and act in concert.

This won't happen spontaneously. It will take wise and strong leadership, hard work and persistence.

The action must be strategic, concerted and sustained – a national innovation project, let's call it the 'Innovation Action Plan' – led jointly from the very top of government and the private sector, with buy-in from all orders of government in all regions, and from all sectors of the economy and of society.

To begin the process, a small group of the top leaders of government and equal numbers of the acknowledged leading figures from business and from post-secondary education must jointly develop a strategy for meeting the goal. The strategy must specify who will do what and when. It must also create a transparent mechanism for receiving regular feedback on progress and making changes in response to it.

The goal of the Innovation Action Plan should be threefold. The wealth-creating private sector should step up its innovation to raise the Canadian gross domestic product (GDP) per capita significantly above the 'business as usual' trend, and keep it there. In quantitative terms, an increase of annual GDP growth by 2 percent per year above 'business as usual', and sustaining that increase for a decade, would be a very ambitious but justified target.

The wealth-consuming public sector should innovate to update its institutions, systems and practices to meet the needs of Canadians as they actually are today, achieving increasing effectiveness and, at the same time, improving efficiency in the use of resources.

All sectors should work together in innovating to improve the protection and preservation of Canada's environment, treating it as a national asset whose benefits must continue to be available to future generations.

The buy-in of the private sector should be driven by new business opportunities; the buy-in of the public sector by obligation.

To help these things happen, a supportive policy climate is needed to encourage innovation in all sectors, but this must be approached with a dose of humility. Innovation policy doesn't produce innovations; entrepreneurs do that. As pointed out in chapter 3, the innovation policy is only one of the many influences on the decisions that business makes. And in the public sector, the lack of competition and an ambiguous culture of innovation are obstacles that have to be overcome. A good innovation policy will not be sufficient, but we must certainly have one.

## Ten principles of an innovation policy

A policy is a framework of general principles that guide actions taken in particular circumstances so that they might contribute to achieving an identified goal. It is evidence-based if there is evidence that these principles actually help in achieving the desired goal.

In this final chapter, we distill the lessons learned about innovation in Canada into ten principles that should be the basis of a Canadian innovation policy. The same principles should apply to federal and provincial policies. The policy principles are followed by nine program principles to guide the implementation of any government assistance.

The proposed principles of an innovation policy for Canada are listed below. They are framed as recommendations for action.

    1.  Do no harm.

2. Recognize that the cultures in the private and public sectors are very different, that innovation takes place differently, and that it must be supported, managed and evaluated differently in the two sectors.

3. Support both the supply and the demand sides of innovation in the private sector.

4. For innovation in the public sector, recalibrate the balance among innovation, speed, risk and accountability, involving the media in the process.

5. Develop Canada's cultural diversity as an advantage in marketing Canadian value-added products in world markets.

6. Promote the export of value-added Canadian products, not raw materials. Export Canadian innovations, not the Canadian capacity to innovate.

7. Encourage the development of a national capacity for modern value-added manufacturing so that Canadians might be able to make and sell what we invent.

8. Pay attention to new ventures that have found the financing to spend substantially more on R&D than they collect in sales revenues, and have sustained that effort for a long enough period of time to achieve important milestones for their new products. They need help with commercialization, not with R&D. They are very important because they are the only source of Canada's future large, innovative companies.

9. Provide incentives for patient long-term investment in successful new ventures, so that they might grow to a large enough scale to compete in world markets. Encourage investors not to cash in and walk away from them too soon, leaving acquisition by a multinational enterprise as their only path to world markets.

10. Ensure that government programs of support for innovation are entirely consistent with the goals of the Innovation Action Plan and are organized and delivered as a system, taking the needs of the demand side into account.

These ten principles of an innovation policy for Canada are expanded and discussed below.

## PRINCIPLE 1: Do no harm.

This very simple-sounding statement has far-reaching implications. Innovation is such a complex interplay of many factors that government actions in seemingly unrelated areas could unexpectedly affect it. To implement the principle, it is necessary to test proposed government measures to ensure that, at the very least, they do not inhibit innovation or undermine other measures that promote it, either directly or through unintended consequences.[1] The object is to avoid surprises, so the test would have to be applied across government, and not just in departments whose mandate involved innovation explicitly. In practice, much of the desired effect could probably be achieved by requiring those responsible for introducing bills, amendments, policies, regulations, etc. to consider any impacts on innovation in the drafting stages. This principle applies equally to all levels of government.

## PRINCIPLE 2:
### Recognize that the cultures in the private and public sectors are very different, that innovation takes place differently, and that it must be supported, managed and evaluated in the two sectors.

In the short to medium term, Canada needs more innovation in the private sector to increase wealth creation in the economy and accelerate GDP growth. At the same time, there is a need for innovation in the public and not-for-profit sectors to deal better with our long-term demographic challenges, and in all sectors to address the environmental challenges.

Meeting Canada's current prosperity challenge requires moving the economy up the value chain. To do that, Canadian business has to innovate more, find new opportunities to add value, and create more private and public wealth. Competition is a strong driver of innovation in the private sector. There is also a need for innovation in how things are done in the public and not-for-profit sectors, and many of those needs are urgent, particularly in health care. However, these latter innovations will

---

[1] The author first heard this idea in a speech in Ottawa in 1996 by Lewis M. Branscomb, then Vice President and Chief Scientist of IBM, who mused that such a test might be all the innovation policy that a nation needs.

have no potential for increasing wealth creation in Canada. Their goal is to create more public good for the public resources being spent, and to prepare for dealing with the challenges of the future. There is no competition driving such innovations; in fact there exists a weak or ambiguous culture of innovation within which they must occur. Governments must encourage and support innovation of both these kinds, but in different ways. And they must be prepared for the fact that they will not be neatly grouped by technologies or disciplines.

## PRINCIPLE 3:
### Support both the supply and the demand sides of innovation in the private sector.

The discussion of support for innovation almost always deals with the supply side, with the producers of innovations and their needs. Relatively little attention is given to the demand side – to those who buy the innovations and put them to use. This is an important oversight because the economic impact of using innovations may be much greater than the impact of producing them. Think, for example of the huge impact of computers across the entire economy in contrast to the much more limited impact of computer manufacturers. Government can play a useful role in promoting the use of innovations. One thing they can do is become the lead customer when an innovation meets the government's own needs. Another is to institute measures to reduce the risk for third-party first users of innovative technologies.

## PRINCIPLE 4:
### For innovation in the public sector, recalibrate the balance among innovation, speed, risk and accountability, involving the media in the process.

The culture in the public sector, and particularly in government, is risk averse. Very strict accountability within government and the great attention paid by media to unsuccessful government initiatives put a damper on innovation. This is at a time when there is a growing need for innovation to change the systems and practices to respond to the evolving demand for public services in a changing environment. Speed and promptness are very important in business, but much of the public sector that deals with business continues to operate according to its own internal rhythms. Speed seems to get confused with haste that raises risk and breeds carelessness. Innovation is needed in many things, but innovation is inherently risky, and taking risks could be hazardous to one's career in the public service. Strict accountability is essential because public funds are at stake, but it must be in a proper balance with the need for trying new things, and with the risk that they might not succeed. The way out of this situation is itself a risky innovation. It calls for high-level leadership in recalibrating the balance among innovation, speed, risk and accountability. The media would have to be involved in this process somehow so that they might come to understand that it is a strategic initiative rather than invitation to carelessness. To help make this process credible, it would be useful to start estimating and communicating explicitly the risk of continuing with the status quo or with business as usual.

## PRINCIPLE 5:
### Develop Canada's cultural diversity as an advantage in marketing Canadian value-added products in world markets.

Canada's post-secondary classrooms are filled with students who have family or community connections with just about every country with which we might want to trade. This is a unique opportunity to develop candidates for a global marketing force for Canadian industry that must export, but we are not seizing that opportunity on an adequate scale. Some Canadian post-secondary students have gone abroad on individual exchanges and co-op work terms, and they have probably numbered in the hundreds at any one time, but not in the tens of thousands (out of a million and half or so post-secondary students enrolled across Canada), year after year that would be needed to have the desired impact. Some promising new programs have been launched recently, such as through Mitacs,[2] but these generally have more to do with bringing outstanding foreign students to Canada than with sending Canadian students abroad for a structured, in depth exposure to another culture, perhaps

[2] For details on the The Mitacs Globalink program, go to www.mitacs.ca.

that of their own ancestors. This is an area where some major institutional innovation is needed on the part of the post-secondary educational system and the federal government acting as partners.

## PRINCIPLE 6:
### Promote the export of value-added Canadian products, not raw materials. Export Canadian innovations, not the Canadian capacity to innovate.

When we export raw materials based on our natural resources, we leave it up to our customers to add value to them. We do the extraction and the bulk shipping, and they get the value-added jobs. We may export materials worth several dollars a ton, and we import products worth several dollars a kilogram, or perhaps even several dollars a gram. The call to move the economy up the value chain in all sectors is intended to deal with just this situation.

In certain areas of research-based innovation in goods, producing the new value-added products may not be feasible because of a lack of technical capability to manufacture them and market them on a sufficient scale. This is not an issue of outsourcing established production to a lower-cost area. It's an issue of inventing the manufacturing process for the new product and finding the channels to market on the scale required to be profitable. The BC Biotechnology cluster has faced this situation and is trying to deal with it through the Centre for Drug Research and Development (CDRD). All too often good research is done, intellectual property (IP) is created, and then sold for commercialization abroad. Sometimes the new venture is sold as well. When that happens, we sell our capacity to innovate to meet our own goals. This is a concern because it prevents the connection between our excellence in science and engineering research and sustained wealth creation in the Canadian economy. But when that outcome turns out to be unavoidable, as may sometimes happen, then we need a business model to ensure that enough value for Canada is captured in this truncated process.

## PRINCIPLE 7:
### Encourage the development of a national capacity for modern value-added manufacturing so that Canadians might be able to make and sell what we invent.

One way of dealing with this situation described under Principle 6 is to support modern manufacturing. Target existing Canadian manufacturing as a priority area for government policy attention and make manufacturing a target area for research support in the four priority areas that the government has identified,[3] namely: environmental science and technologies, natural resources and energy, health and related life sciences and technologies, information and communication technologies.

Canadian industry has a history of being very good in manufacturing. The high quality of the workforce leads to a high quality of products, and this has led to the success of Canadian manufacturers as well as attracting the branch plant operations of many multinational enterprises (e.g., Toyota, Honda and IBM) that do very well in international markets. But we have also seen some manufacturing plants shut down, usually more for business reasons than for technical ones. The responses to that situation must be for the government to support the continuing development of modern manufacturing capacity in Canada. It would be folly to turn away from manufacturing on the grounds that 'it's all services now.' Somebody has to make the things we need to buy. It is good to remember that China did not become an industrial power by selling services. A country cannot leave itself without the capacity to make at least some of the things it can invent; if it did, then the goal of its innovation policy could *de facto* become job creation in the rest of the world. But this is not a uniquely Canadian issue; concerns have been raised about something very similar in the US.[4]

---

[3] Industry Canada. 2007. *Mobilizing Science and Technology to Canada's Advantage – Summary*. Ottawa: Industry Canada, ISBN 978-0-662-69228-7.
[4] David Rotman. 2012. "Can We Build Tomorrow's Breakthroughs?" *Technology Review*, 15 (1): 36-45.

## PRINCIPLE 8:

Pay attention to new ventures that have found the financing to spend substantially more on R&D than they collect in sales revenues, and have sustained that effort for a long enough period of time to achieve important milestones for their new products.
They need help with commercialization, not with R&D.
They are very important because Canada's new large, innovative companies will emerge from among them.

Tomorrow's established firms engaged in research-based innovation will come out of today's new ventures that are spending on R&D. Since most of these new ventures do not yet have established markets and significant sales revenues, they are being financed to do research, and they operate with RDI above 100 percent, sometimes very much above. There are about two dozen such firms in Canada's top 100 R&D spenders at any given time, and they each spend $10 million or more per year on R&D. And there are many more such firms below the top 100 that spend less, but still in the millions of dollars annually. Many of these companies have maintained their R&D spending for several years and their products have passed important milestones. Since they were able to get funding for R&D, it is safe to say that their product ideas have been validated. At this stage, they still need help, not in R&D but in commercialization, in getting their products to market quickly and in finding their lead customers. They may get that help from innovation intermediaries funded by government or, more directly, through government procurement. Or they might seek financial assistance through government programs of support, such as SR&ED, for the R&D they are already doing, These companies deserve close and prompt attention from an 'account executive', based on the model of the IRAP program, so that their chances of success might be increased. And, as already noted several times, the RDI of the successful ones will start to decrease as they become established and their sales revenues begin to grow faster than their R&D spending. The others will vanish when their financing runs out.

## PRINCIPLE 9:
Provide incentives for patient, long-term investment in successful new ventures, so that they might grow to a large enough scale to compete in world markets. Encourage investors not to cash in and walk away from them too soon, leaving acquisition by a multinational as their only path to world markets.

This is another aspect of the issue raised under Principle 6. It's all about helping successful new companies to grow through patient investment. Consider the case of a new venture with an important invention that embodies good IP and achieves initial success in the market, but does not have the funding to take the commercialization as far as it should. This means not being able to get capital to grow the firm big enough to serve the potential market. In such cases, the firm and its IP may be sold to a much larger, established firm in the sector, most likely not a Canadian one. When that happens, the private investors in the new venture may make a good, one-time profit, but the sustainable wealth creation that provides a return on the Canadian public investment through new economic activity and the tax system will not be established. The IP will be sold for much less than it might eventually have been worth, and the benefits of value-added activity based on the invention will increase some other country's prosperity.

The government has a role to play in heading off such an unproductive outcome. At the front end, government might devise incentives for investors to leave their money in the company while it grows to the necessary scale in its market. The capital gains tax might be a useful instrument in this regard, with the tax rate decreasing the longer the investment stays in. Alternatively, government might have to take measures to reduce the risk for private investors and attract growth capital. The main point is that it is important for Canada that our successful, new innovative ventures should not be truncated in their growth before they reach their commercial potential.

## PRINCIPLE 10:

**Ensure that government programs that supply support for innovation are entirely consistent with the principles of the Innovation Action Plan and are organized and delivered as a system, taking the needs of the demand side into account.**

When government assistance for innovation is supplied, it is delivered through programs operated by agencies. Programs have rules: criteria for awarding support, rules for the use of money, requirements for reporting, etc. as they must, since full accountability in the use of public funds is essential. However, there are aspects of the program delivery that should pay more attention to the pressures faced by the recipients on the demand side. This is particularly true of the new ventures discussed under Principles 8 and 9. They are always short of time and money. If they need support and qualify for it under program criteria, they should get it promptly. Filing an application and waiting most of a year for the outcome may work for established firms, but it could be fatally slow for new ventures for whom support delayed may be support denied and an opportunity lost.

Programs to support innovation in industry should be organized as a continuous system. There should be a steady progression of potential support from research through commercialization, with no gaps in programs and the program goals entirely aligned with the Innovation Action Plan. Companies that succeed in one stage of the innovation process should be eligible to apply for support for the next stage by means of an incremental application that requires information only about what has changed from the previous one. Those companies that meet the criteria for that next stage should again be eligible for support as they continue into the following stage. The criteria might become tougher and the number of companies supported in succeeding stages of innovation might decrease sharply, as happens in industry, but the potential support should be available and not unnecessarily difficult to apply for.

## Nine program principles

To round out the picture, we propose nine additional principles that focus on the programs that deliver government support for innovation.

### PROGRAM PRINCIPLE 1:
Design program delivery to meet the needs of the demand side. Recognize that time matters in business, and that urgency is on the demand side. In the effective delivery of government programs to help innovative companies, the time scales that matter most are those of the companies that need prompt assistance, and not those of the agencies delivering the programs.

This point has been made indirectly in several of the policy principles above, but it is so important that it needs to be made again in the narrower context of programs that support innovation. It affects the new ventures most.

### PROGRAM PRINCIPLE 2:
Government doesn't pick winners; competition in the market does that. Since it spends public money, government should invest only in strong competitors who have a good chance to succeed. That worked in the Olympics. If government doesn't do that, it will pick losers.

Governments are sometimes accused of trying to pick winners in awarding support to business. That's just rhetoric, of course, because governments couldn't pick winners even if they tried. Winners in business are picked by their customers. They emerge as winners by competing successfully in the market. However, governments spend public funds when they invest in helping companies, and they owe it to the taxpayers to do all they can to ensure that the investments have the potential to pay off. And that means that they should award support only to those firms that appear to have a very good chance to succeed. That's not picking winners; that's picking good competitors. But the way that picking is done is fundamental. If companies are being supported to help achieve commercial success, then the criteria by which they are picked must be business criteria. There is no room in this process of government's due diligence for any other considerations, not historical, not regional, not political, not sentimental. It is well known that Canadian governments have picked some famous losers when they forgot this principle.[5]

## PROGRAM PRINCIPLE 3:

Mobilize government's purchasing power in support
of innovation to achieve two simultaneous goals:
first, deliver value to Canadian taxpayers by purchasing new
Canadian goods and services that satisfy a new need or one that
could not be met before; and, second, provide innovative Canadian
companies with lead customers who can provide useful feedback
for improving the products and references for use by the
companies in developing other markets.

New ventures engaged in innovation must learn commerce in the process. Finding the first customer for a new product is very important, and a record of selling to one's own government provides an important reference in global markets. Governments in many countries use strategic procurement as an instrument to develop the innovation capacity of their nation's industry, and the Government of Canada has recently made a good start in that direction with a program in its Budget 2012. In terms of innovation, government purchasing can be a win-win process if it is done the right way. Government can exert a market pull on innovation by defining the functional requirements – but not the detailed specifications – of a product it needs that is not available in the market. Or it can respond to an unsolicited proposal from a company that is familiar with government needs. A contract to supply some quantity of product version 1.0 to government as the lead customer provides important validation of the company's ideas, and a revenue stream to support its development of later versions with improved price/performance characteristics for high-volume sales to government and beyond. If things work out, government wins because its needs are met, and the money it spends stays in the Canadian economy. The company wins because they have sales revenues, a lead customer to work with to improve the product, and prospects for more sales. If the Canadian government needs something that is not available in

---

[5] Some [in]famous examples that readily come to mind are the Bricklin car in New Brunswick, Ontario's "Bionic Beaver" computer for schools, and greenhouse cucumbers in Newfoundland.

the market, then other governments might need it too. And if the product can be offered in civilian markets, the improvements in price/performance under the government contract will help make it competitive.

## PROGRAM PRINCIPLE 4:
### Deliver support programs through people with subject expertise and experience, and give them the authority to make spending decisions in the field, in a way that balances strict accountability with judgment.

The report of the Jenkins Panel pointed out that there were so many government support programs for R&D (60!) that companies often failed to take advantage of them because they didn't understand them, or didn't even know about them.[6] The panel called for a "concierge service" to connect firms with programs that might meet their needs. Fortunately, there is a good model to build on for dealing with both this issue and the issue of timing raised under Principle 1. The Industrial Technology Advisors (ITA) of the National Research Council's Industrial Research Assistance Program (IRAP) visit their client companies regularly, know what they do and understand their problems. Based on that knowledge, they can pre-qualify their clients with a minimum of paperwork and then judge whether a particular request meets the program rules and, if so, they can authorize funding support from the IRAP program quickly. The need for a "concierge service" identified by the Jenkins Panel would be met if the role of the ITAs was expanded to represent not just IRAP but a whole slate of programs relevant to the needs of their clients that were offered across government. They would help their clients by selecting the most appropriate program for their current needs, checking if they met its criteria, and authorizing support within days if they did. They might then be seen as government's agents, helping their client firms succeed, rather than as gatekeepers to a single support program. If they combined business experience with expertise in the areas in which they work, they would be an important source of advice to help their clients. The companies would benefit even

---

[6] Industry Canada. 2011. "Innovation Canada: A Call to Action – Review of Federal Support to R&D," Expert Panel Report, Tom Jenkins, Chairman. Ottawa: Industry Canada, October 17, ISBN 978-1-100-19384-7.

if they failed to qualify for support; they would not have spent the time filling out a complex application and then waiting with uncertainty for its outcome, and they would have received good advice along the way.

## PROGRAM PRINCIPLE 5:
### The subject of IP rights is dynamic around the world. Don't get left behind because innovators will not stay where they will be disadvantaged.

The protection of the IP of inventors, authors, composers, and other creative people is an increasingly important matter in knowledge-intensive businesses that needs to be taken into account in programs of government support. The intellectual property rights (IPR) established in a nation's laws are becoming an important consideration in the decisions of companies on where to invest in R&D. Whether the instrument of protection is a patent, copyright, trade mark or trade secret, it must offer effective protection of the IP owner's rights and clear penalties for their infringement. The issues involved are many and varied. In the pharmaceutical industry, for instance, the length of patent protection is the main issue, because branded drugs are quickly commoditized by generic versions when the original patents expire, and numerous approval processes delay the time when market exclusivity can begin. In ICT, the issue often is the validity of the patent issued in the first place. We are in a period of change in how IPR are used in business. In open innovation, research-intensive firms have recently started using patents as marketable assets, and many companies are now realizing significant income from the sale or licensing of patents that they themselves were not using. Moreover, certain features of patent law have made it possible for companies to make money from the ownership of patent portfolios without actually producing anything. The field of IPR is in a state of flux, and events such as the recent auction of Nortel's patents and the blackout of Wikipedia to protest a proposed US law on copyright infringement just underline its importance. IPR reform is under way in the EU and the US. There is probably no clear opportunity in this for Canada to gain any advantage, but there is a very clear opportunity for self-inflicted damage if we fall behind and our IPR are no longer competitive with those of our trading partners. This could lead to an exodus of industrial innovation from Canada.

## PROGRAM PRINCIPLE 6:

Avoid a hardening of the categories. Recognize that private-sector innovation is not a homogeneous process that is always done the same way, but a great diversity of processes that may require new rules and new accountability mechanisms. Be ready to support an activity that is demonstrably needed to promote innovation even if it is not yet included in any formal definition.

Innovation in the private sector is not a homogeneous process. The issues are different in established firms than in new ventures; different when innovation is research-based than when it is design-based.

This principle calls for the innovation support programs for business and industry to be tailored to the particular challenges and issues at play in the various forms of innovation. 'One size fits all' does not work; it doesn't fit any very well. Even though it might be desirable from the point of view of simplifying government programs to treat innovation in the same way wherever and however it occurs, the evidence is that the issues are so different that a single policy or program design will not address them all adequately. For example, tax credits may be the best form of support for established firms in some sectors, but upfront risk-sharing in big projects may be essential for others. And a tight definition of eligible activities might be necessary in some cases to ensure good use of funds but, in other cases, it might shortchange an essential activity. The program staff delivering any government support for innovation must be both expert enough and experienced enough that they can be trusted to make good judgments.

## PROGRAM PRINCIPLE 7:

Recognize that research is not innovation, that generally in the private sector Innovation = Invention + Commercialization, and also that successful commercialization requires a business model that is appropriate to the invention.

This principle means that government support for innovation must offer support for commercialization as well as invention. Since commercialization is predominantly an activity of the private sector, most government support for commercialization will have to be directed to companies. Government subsidies for business are nothing new in Canada, but this form may be. However, there is no shortage of international examples to learn from. The one that may fit best is the Small Business Innovation Research (SBIR) program of the US. This program has been an acknowledged success for several decades. It is known by many Canadians, and has often been recommended for implementation here. Since it operates within a funding system not too unlike our own, it should be easy to adapt to Canadian conditions.

Inventions are either design-based or research-based, and all involve design. So also do the innovations developed from them. It follows therefore, that support for invention must include support for both research and design. The two best established forms of government support for innovation in Canada are the funding of university research and the SR&ED tax credit. In the universities, support for design is very limited, mainly through the program of NSERC (Natural Sciences and Engineering Research Council) Chairs in Design Engineering. For industry, the definition of R&D used in the SR&ED program is based on the *Frascati Manual* of the OECD. It is considered to ignore design and be heavily slanted to technical details rather than business activity. Some critics of the present system have said that Canada does not have an innovation policy; we have an invention policy. That statement is only half right. We certainly don't have an innovation policy, but we really don't have an invention policy either. We have a research policy. Invention is a challenging process on its own; it involves design, and it goes far beyond just using research results. A complete innovation policy must support all three key activities: research, design and commercialization wherever they are done, provided always that they meet high standards of quality as determined by appropriate measures. And people moving through these three activities and applying for government support should be able to find it in the programs of one agency.

## PROGRAM PRINCIPLE 8:
Recognize that innovations have both technical and social dimensions and that in the private sector the balance of innovations will lean to the technical, and in the public sector innovations it will lean to the social.

Innovation in either sector should be supported with appropriate policies and with any required public funding provided in an accountable way. In the private sector, most innovations in the goods-producing industries will be technical, and most in the service industries are likely to be social.[7] In either case, the goal of the policy is to help innovative Canadian companies succeed in their markets and to leverage any government funding assistance into greater national prosperity. When this virtual cycle succeeds, government investments are repaid many times over through the tax system, and its capacity to support even more innovation increases.

In the public sector, both within government itself and in external organizations, innovation in what these organizations do and how they function[8] should be encouraged across the board, and supported by government practices that promote a culture of innovation. Since organizations in the public sector offer mainly services to their clients, most of the innovations there will be social. However, technical innovations might arise as well, particularly in health care. The costs of commercialization are not likely to arise often, but there may be a need to provide additional government support to help successful innovations diffuse through their areas of practice.

## PROGRAM PRINCIPLE 9:
Focus on quality. Support only excellent innovation, wherever it occurs.

The quality of a proposed innovation can be assessed. It depends on the entrepreneurial quality of the team involved, on their perception of the driving need or opportunity, on the clarity of

---

[7] Here we revert to the common meaning of social innovation, as distinct from the narrow meaning in chapter 11.

[8] This is distinct from innovations that might arise out of research done in government labs, universities and hospitals that have already been discussed separately.

their vision of the innovation, on their ability to work as a team, and on their track record. It also depends on the personal attributes of the individuals, such as imagination, depth and breadth of knowledge, energy, determination, persistence, versatility, good business sense, demonstrated skills, and awareness of their own limitations. And, of course, it depends on the importance of the problem being solved, the nature and quality of the proposed solution, and the business case made for it. If Canada is to meet its prosperity challenge and recover its productivity deficit, then we must focus our support on the best people with the best ideas, giving them what they need to do the job. Giving enough to the best people to do an excellent job is much better than giving inadequate amounts to many more. This has to be about preparing gold-medalists for the podium, not distributing badges for participating.

## Final words

At this time in Canadian history innovation is much more than a research challenge, much more than a business issue, much more than a question of creating new ventures. I believe it is a major economic and societal issue for the future of the country. The policy and program principles discussed above are intended to promote innovation to deal with Canada's current prosperity challenge, and to help us innovate to deal with the long-term challenges of world demographics and climate change. We already believe that both societal and technical innovations will be required, and that flexibility and a broad reach will be essential. Learning how to innovate will be a must, an essential part of the ingenuity that we need in order to prosper in that fast-changing new world. But it isn't clear that today we are as good as we need to be at learning to innovate. Perhaps we need to start innovating in learning how to innovate.

# INDEX

# Other titles published by INVENIRE

# Titles in the Collaborative Decentred Metagovernance Series